The SCIENTIFIC AMERICAN BOOK OF LOVE, SEX, AND THE BRAIN

Previous Books in the Scientific American Brain Series

The Scientific American *Brave New Brain*

The Scientific American *Day in the Life of Your Brain*

SCIENTIFIC
AMERICAN™

The SCIENTIFIC AMERICAN BOOK OF LOVE, SEX, AND THE BRAIN

The Neuroscience of How, When, Why, and Who We Love

Judith Horstman

JOSSEY-BASS
A Wiley Imprint
www.josseybass.com

Published by Jossey-Bass
A Wiley Imprint
989 Market Street, San Francisco, CA 94103-1741—www.josseybass.com

Jossey-Bass books and products are available through most bookstores. To contact Jossey-Bass directly call our Customer Care Department within the U.S. at 800-956-7739, outside the U.S. at 317-572-3986, or fax 317-572-4002.

Wiley also publishes its books in a variety of electronic formats and by print-on-demand. Not all content that is available in standard print versions of this book may appear or be packaged in all book formats. If you have purchased a version of this book that did not include media that is referenced by or accompanies a standard print version, you may request this media by visiting http://booksupport.wiley.com. For more information about Wiley products, visit us www.wiley.com.

Library of Congress Cataloging-in-Publication Data
Horstman, Judith.
  The Scientific American book of love, sex, and the brain : the neuroscience of how, when, why, and who we love / Judith Horstman. – 1st ed.
      p. cm. – (Scientific American ; 3)
  Includes bibliographical references and index.
  ISBN 978-0-470-64778-3 (cloth); ISBN 978-1-118-10951-9 (ebk.); ISBN 978-1-118-10952-6 (ebk.); ISBN 978-1-118-10953-3 (ebk.)
  1. Love. 2. Sex (Psychology) 3. Sex (Biology) 4. Neurosciences. I. Scientific American, inc. II. Title. III. Title: Book of love, sex, and the brain.
  BF575.L8H663 2012
  155.3–dc23

                                        2011029321

Printed in the United States of America
FIRST EDITION
HB Printing   10 9 8 7 6 5 4 3 2 1

CONTENTS

To my family, my friends, and my Tribe,
who taught me the meaning of love

ACKNOWLEDGMENTS

My thanks to the wonderful writers and editors of *Scientific American* and *Scientific American Mind* for the excellent articles on which so much of this book is based (they and their work are acknowledged in detail in the Sources) and to scientists everywhere for their deep and keen interest in sex and, more important, in how and why we love.

The creative and hard-working team at Jossey-Bass, who has worked on three brain books with me, are much appreciated. Special thanks to executive editor emeritus Alan Rinzler, who contributed much to the shaping and creation of this book; to senior editorial assistant extraordinaire Nana Twumasi, who ushered it through its final edits and revisions; my new editor, Margie McAneny; Carol Hartland, production genius; Bev Miller, much more than a copyeditor; Paula Goldstein, who designed the book's interior; and all the marketing people who put my book in your hands, including Jennifer Wenzel, P. J. Campbell, Karen Warner. Ace freelance researcher Brianna Smith and Harvard University neuroscientist Kelly Dakin were invaluable. At *Scientific American,* Diane McGarvey and Karin Tucker were responsible for finding and approving years of archived material. Thank you.

Writing is a lonely activity. My family, good friends, and fellow writers supported me with company and cheer and had much to say on the subject of love. Many thanks to you all, in particular to first readers Judith Auberjonois, Ann Crew, Ferris Buck Kelley, J. T. Long, and the wonderfully productive and generous writing community of Sacramento, especially the Writers Who Wine.

Who do we love? Who loves us? And why? Why does some love die while other love lasts? Is it really a mystery—or can science (specifically neuroscience) shed some light on how, why, and who our brains love? Probably it can.

We've been learning more about sex every day, especially since Alfred Kinsey began asking Americans exactly what we were doing sexually, where, and with whom, and since William H. Masters and Virginia E. Johnson began scrutinizing and categorizing what our genitals were doing while our brains were having sex.

Recently researchers have been studying what in our brains makes our hearts go pitter-patter with lust and with lasting love—with the whole smorgasbord of emotions, including the love of parent and child, the affectionate love of companionship, the role that the love of animals can play in our lives, and the love of God.

Scientists have learned that the brain in love and sex uses an entire pharmacy of chemicals and chemical actions and reactions, calling forth a tsunami of neurotransmitters and hormones. And now we are able to actually look at a brain that's in love, lust, or both. New imaging technology allows scientists to peer inside our brains, our primary sex and love organ, to see what's happening in there. Brain scans, especially the functional magnetic resonance imaging scans, allow scientists to see brain activity in real time in a live, thinking, feeling, loving (or sexually excited) brain. They allow scientists to watch as our brain experiences romance, sex, love, and loss, and several emotions in between.

This book is structured around the way your brain encounters and experiences various kinds of love, beginning with prenatal influences and continuing through parental love, friendship, sex, romance, marriage, religious love, and beyond. It is based on the indisputable evidence that we are hardwired to connect to one another. Love is who we are.

Introduction: What Is This Thing Called Love?

Much is written of the mysteries of love, but there is no mystery about our need for it. We crave the comfort of others, especially those who have become special to us. People will kill, die, starve, and commit crimes for love. They have faced torture and prison, defending their rights to love the god or person of their choice. Children and spouses cling to abusers out of the need for their love. People go mad in solitary confinement, or even, studies show, die of loneliness or the emotional blow of a "broken heart."

Love is so vital to the human condition that it is beyond mere emotion. Indeed, many researchers have described love as a drive, an urge, and even a hunger. A multistudy analysis confirms that the powerful rush we feel when we are madly, deeply, passionately in love is not really an emotion. It's a reward produced by ancient brain pathways that similarly motivate our most basic needs such as those for food or sleep.

And that's not just sexual love. Consider the results of a 2010 meta analysis of 148 studies of how and why people die and the causes. Loneliness ranks right up there on the top. The study found that a lack of relationships can be as deadly as well-established risk factors for death such as smoking and alcohol, and it is even greater than other risk factors such as obesity. Shunning, abandonment, and forced solitary confinement are among the worst punishments, considered to be cruel and excessive, or even torture, and the rejected brain is a very wretched brain.

So What Is Love?

Everyone in every culture knows what love is, in all its many guises, as both a noun and a verb. It is tender, sweet, protective, passionate, lustful, jealous, trustful, and sometimes mad. But just try to get a good, clear, take-to-the-bank definition, and you will be stymied. Google alone yields 6,730,000,000 hits for the simple word *love*.

The poets say it in verse, as Shakespeare did in his Sonnet 116:

> Love is not love
> Which alters when it alteration finds,
> Or Bends with the remover to remove.
> O, no! It is an ever-fixed mark,
> That looks on tempests and is never shaken.
> —WILLIAM SHAKESPEARE

Kahlil Gibran in *The Prophet* describes love thus:

> Love has no desire but to fulfill itself. To melt and be like a
> running brook that sings its melody to the night. . . . To
> wake at dawn with a winged heart and give thanks for
> another day of loving.

The New Testament offers the well-quoted passage from 1 Corinthians 13:47:

> Love is patient, love is kind. It does not envy, it does not
> boast, it is not proud. It is not rude, it is not self-seeking, it
> is not easily angered, it keeps no record of wrongs. Love
> does not delight in evil but rejoices with the truth. It always
> protects, always trusts, always hopes, always perseveres.

And, of course (and anonymously), "God is love."

Philosophers don't sound very philosophical when it comes to love. Sophocles wrote, "One word frees us of all the weight and pain of life: That word is love." Plato wrote, "At the touch of love everyone becomes a poet," and later added, "Love is a serious mental disease."

Scientists reduce love to its basics, exemplified by these definitions from Stephanie Ortigue and associates:

> Love is the existence of a complex rewarding emotional state
> involving chemical, cognitive, and goal-directed behavioral
> components.

> Romantic love is a mammalian brain system for mate choice.

And this basic truth is from the twentieth-century psychoanalyst Eric Fromm:

> Love is the only sane and satisfactory answer to the problem
> of human existence.

Even fictional characters have an opinion. The character Hawkeye from the TV show *M*A*S*H* said on one episode in 1973, "Without love, what are we worth? Eighty-nine cents! Eighty-nine cents worth of chemicals walking around lonely."

We all have our own definitions when it comes to being in love, but most of us would agree, "I know it when I see it" (which just happens to also be the way Supreme Court Justice Potter Stewart famously defined pornography).

Love Is a Many Splendored Thing—and the Greeks Had a Word for All of the Types

There are as many types of love and ways to express love as there are cultures, languages, and perhaps even people: puppy love, friendship love, affectionate love, courtly love, parental love, passionate love, sexual love, baby love, unconditional love, possessive love, and love for a pastime, a pet, a purchase, an object, or a pleasure. *Love,* as used in the English language (and a few others), can range from a mild liking to a passionate obsession. It has also been described, and not humorously, as a form of obsessive compulsive disorder.

But when we talk about love, we can generally describe it in five ways, based on words from the ancient Greeks. While the meanings of the Greek words have shifted and changed over millennia and been adopted and adapted by newcomer cultures, the basic concepts remain pretty accurate.

So how do I love thee? Let us count the ways:

Agape. In ancient Greece, it meant loving in general. It then became used widely in Christianity to describe what is considered the highest form of love: unconditional love, divine love, or even sacrificial love. In Greece today, it's often used to say, "I love you," but it implies a deeper, truer love—more than just eros.

Philia (or *Phileo*). Brotherly love, generous love, affection. Philadelphia is the city of brotherly love, and *philanthropy* refers to the unselfish concern and efforts of goodwill to better or benefit others.

Storge. Affection and family love, especially the love of parents for children and children for parents, but also love for other family members.

Platonic. From the dialogues of the philosopher Plato and his descriptions of a chaste, nonsexual, but passionate love between two people, usually of the same sex (Plato liked young men). The term actually came about in the Renaissance and continues to mean a

WHAT NEUROSCIENCE KNOWS ABOUT
YOUR BRAIN IN LOVE

Much fascinating information about our brains and the many kinds of human love is coming from curious scientists and new imaging technologies that allow a look inside our living, loving brain—our primary sex and love organ—to see what's happening in there.

Among some of the findings are:

- Our brains are hardwired to seek the love and the companionship of others. In fact, social isolation is so bad for your brain that solitary confinement could be considered torture.
- Sex, love, and orgasm are good for your brain, contribute to your health, and may even help lower your risk of developing dementia—and loss of a mate may increase your risk of death.
- Your genes contribute to your love life, from your gender choice in sex partners, to how easily your brain reaches orgasm, to how likely you are to dabble in one-night stands—but your life experiences may trump those tendencies.
- Love lives in your brain, and many of the same parts involved in sexual and romantic love are activated by drugs, music, and even religious ecstasy.
- Parenthood actually causes the brain to grow in both moms and dads and your friendships may be (next to your mother) the most important loving relationships in your life.
- As the body ages, the brain is still more than willing to engage in sex. Studies show some of us are having sex and desiring sex well into very old age, health permitting (and with or without partners).

strong (or even passionate) but nonsexual relationship between persons of any gender or sexual preference.

Eros. Passionate love, sensual desire, romantic love, and usually (but not always) sexual love. In ancient Greece, the god Eros was the spirit of love that arose from chaos. Later, Eros was depicted as a mischievous little god of love, and in Roman mythology, he became Cupid or Amor.

The Basics of Your Brain in Love and Sex

The chapters that follow detail which parts of your brain are doing what while your body is having sex, thinking about having sex, thinking about being in love, being in love, loving children, loving parents, losing love, and more. The inescapable observation is that a very large proportion of our brain's real estate is dedicated to love and sex. And the question is: Why?

Social scientists and evolutionary psychologists have plenty of theories about why social behaviors (or what we call love) are so important. They say our need for other people goes back to primitive cultures of the past (and remote cultures today) when isolation and exile often meant death. Being banished from friends and family and the community campfire meant literally being thrown to the wolves or other predators of the night—a fate as bad as (or in fact resulting in) death. They speculate that social behaviors, including sex, not only help humans survive as individuals, they ensure cooperation, reproduction, and care for offspring and thus the survival of the species.

Psychologists, philosophers, poets, and neuroscientists have also given this a lot of thought. Among their conclusions are these:

- The brain evolved to protect the body (and mind, presumably). Therefore, the brain tells us what to do that will improve our chances of surviving and passing on our genes so that our species survives.
- Choice of sexual partners is driven in men by the evolutionary-fueled drive to spread their sperm, and love by a man's urge to know any offspring are his own.

- A female's sex urge is also spurred by reproductive desire, and her love by a need to keep a male partner to help improve survival of the offspring.
- Parental love for a child is essential for survival of the species. Unlike most other mammals, humans are not only born helpless but remain in need of intensive adult attention and care for years.

Based on these theories, it's no surprise that sex and love are highly pleasurable—so much so that many neuroscientists posit they are basic needs. That may be so, because we crave the company of each other: it just makes us feel good. The experience of loving is intimately connected to a biochemical reward circuit in our brains not very different from, and as powerful as, any addiction, including heroin.

I've Got You Under My Skull: Love in Your Brain

It's still not possible to say exactly how love works in your brain, but we are beginning to get a good idea of the brain activities and anatomy involved.

Those three pounds of flesh, nerves, and fluid that make up your brain contain 1 billion or so specialized cells called neurons that communicate and form and dissolve networks through chemicals (especially those called neurotransmitters) and minuscule electrical charges that pass over the tiny gaps, or synapses, between them. Each neuron can communicate with hundreds of thousands of other neurons and can (and does) change its connections and networks all the time, a process called neuroplasticity. Some of these will be temporary and fleeting, rather like a one-night stand, while others will become more established with repeated use, into a lasting marriage of sorts.

The brain and its functions can be described in three parts, from bottom to top, in the order in which it evolved: the primitive brain, the emotional brain, and the thinking brain.

The primitive brain—the brain stem or hindbrain—sits at the top of the spine and takes care of the automated basics, such as breathing, heartbeat, digestion, reflexive actions, sleeping, and arousal. It includes the spinal cord, which sends messages to and from the brain to the rest of the body, including to and from your sex organs, and the cerebellum, which coordinates balance and rote motions, such as dancing and making love.

Above this is your emotional brain, tucked deep inside the bulk of the midbrain. It acts as the gatekeeper between the spinal cord below and the thinking brain in the cerebrum above. The major players for love, both sexual attraction and deep bonding, most likely originate here in what's also called the limbic system. This regulates survival mechanisms such as sex hormones, sleep cycles, hunger, emotions, and, most important, fear, sensory input, and pleasure.

The ever-alert amygdala resides here, ready to sound the fight-or-flight alarm. It helps decide whether an experience is pleasurable or bad, and whether it should be repeated or avoided. It sends that message along to the hypothalamus, which produces and releases chemicals that spur your body to action, and to the hippocampus, your gateway to short-term memory that helps record memories of the event, including where and when and with whom it happened so you can do that good thing again and reject the bad thing (or person) next time around.

You Make Me Feel So Good: The Pleasure Center

Now this is important for understanding love: the so-called pleasure center, or reward circuit, is also based in the limbic system, involving the nucleus accumbens, ventral tegmental area (VTA), and the caudate nucleus—midbrain reward/motivation systems that are connected with pleasure and addiction. So while you are experiencing something you like very much, such as sex or cuddling with your newborn, a pathway (called the VTA-accumbens pathway) evaluates how good the experience is and sends that rating along to other parts of your reward circuit, including your amygdala and prefrontal cortex. There they file it away: the more rewarding the experience, the more likely your brain is to want to repeat it.

And flooding your system with the neurohormone dopamine is what makes sex feel so good and keeps us coming back for more: it's no figure of speech to say love is addictive. Just as all drugs of potential abuse prompt a veritable tsunami of dopamine, so love and lust can also overwhelm, capture, and change the pleasure circuit, leaving us craving more and more. Oxytocin, the neurohormone of trust and attachment, also gets involved, contributing to bonding and lasting love. It can help convert and dampen that insane lust reflex into lasting affection.

The Very Thought of You

More than attraction and addiction are involved in love. Studies show that your thinking brain also chimes in for lasting love (even sexual love). The thinking brain—the wrinkly and crevassed cerebrum, the part we usually see when we picture a brain—sits like a crown on the very top of your brain, covered with the nickel-thin layer of the cerebral cortex (or neocortex).

This is the most recently evolved part of the brain—the part, some say, that makes us human. Its four major sections, or lobes, control thoughts, language, planning, and imagination and process all of the sensations of being in love. The frontal lobes take care of emotions and reasoning, the occipital lobes in the back process what you see, and the temporal lobes (above your ears) are responsible for what you hear and for understanding speech, appreciating music (and perhaps thinking of a supreme being). The parietal lobes running across the top and sides of the brain are the primary sensory areas, taking in information about taste, touch, and movement.

Eventually your thinking brain will coordinate and process all the important information it is receiving from your limbic and reward systems. Over time, it will decide how you actually feel about love and your love objects and experiences. But at first, your emotional brain is in charge—and it wants what it wants, and it's going to get it. There are many more connections running from the amygdala to the cerebral cortex than the other way around, so your emotional brain will rule in any tug of war between feeling and thinking—something that all of us already know.

New advances in technology are showing us more and more about what happens inside our skulls and are beginning to connect actions, feelings, and even thoughts to activity in specific parts of our brains. The functional magnetic resonance imaging (fMRI) technique, which can show activity inside a living, thinking, and even fornicating brain, has contributed much to our understanding of love and other emotions.

A word of caution: The technology of brain imaging is amazing; however, announcements about how the sources of some emotions and functions have been "mapped" in the brain need to be taken with care. Brain-imaging technology is remarkable and has revolutionized surgery but it is still very new and relatively crude, and it can't prove cause and effect. Although brain scans can indeed show what parts of your brain become active at certain times, scientists say they don't yet know exactly what that activity means or even if they are seeing all the action going on. Brain researchers are still trying to figure out much of what goes on between your ears.

How Scientists Research Love and Sex in Your Brain

You may be wondering how scientists get all this information about what's going on in your brain. They use several research tools to put together theories about what your brain is thinking (and doing) about love. Sometimes several or all of these investigative techniques are used in one research project. Throughout this book, you'll read about examples of these techniques:

1. *They ask you (interviews).* Surveys and questionnaires tell us what people say they think about sex and love, including choice of partners, frequency of sex, and satisfaction with sex and relationships. Since the information is self-reported, it may not be completely objective but is still useful. For example, recent studies where some elderly men said they have intercourse every week may not be true—but it shows these men are still thinking about sex in old age.

2. *They watch you (observation).* Observing animals and people as they perform or react to situations and stimuli, including sexy images and even sex acts, hints at what is going on in the body and brain and helps to connect the actions with the amount and location of brain activity.

3. *They sample your tissue and fluids (laboratory tests).* Humans and other mammals produce specific neurochemicals and hormones related to fear, stress, pleasure, sexual activity, orgasm, and even love. Measuring these chemicals gives insights into what people are thinking and feeling, as well as what their brains are doing. For example, they found that many who are unable to bond with others have lower levels of oxytocin, the hormone produced along with feelings of love and connection.

4. *They wire you up (electroencephalography).* An older technique, it is still useful to record your brain's electrical activity from outside your skull.

5. *They look inside your brain (brain scans).* A host of imaging techniques and tools show which parts of your brain are active when you are feeling or even experiencing sex or love.

TOOLS FOR LOOKING INSIDE YOUR BRAIN

Today's array of sophisticated imaging technologies has come a long way since the X-ray was discovered in 1895.

Here's what that alphabet soup of acronyms means:

EEG (electroencephalograph). A direct reading of the brain's electrical activity taken from multiple electrodes placed on the scalp is displayed as squiggly lines on a chart. It has been in use since the 1920s and is relatively inexpensive and effective. But it can't detect activity deep inside the brain very well or produce an image.

CAT (computed axial tomography); also CT (computed tomography). Uses special X-ray equipment and computers to create cross-sectional pictures of the body at different angles (*tomography* means imaging by sections). It has been used since the 1970s and has the advantage over X-rays of being able to show body sections behind other parts and in much more detail.

PET (positron emission tomography). A small amount of radioactive material is given and then detected by special cameras in images that allow researchers to observe and measure activity in different parts of the brain by monitoring blood flow and other substances such as oxygen and glucose.

SPECT (single photon emission computed tomography). Uses a small amount of radioactive tracer in a way similar to PET to measure and monitor blood flow in the brain and produce a three-dimensional image.

MRI (magnetic resonance imaging). Uses magnetic fields to generate a computer image of internal structures in the body; particularly good for imaging the brain and soft tissues.

fMRI (functional magnetic resonance imaging). Today's favorite imaging tool: Can measure blood flow and other activity in a living brain in action and in real time, showing abnormalities, mapping functions and anatomy, and showing activity in the brain as it is happening.

MEG (magnetoencephalography). Measures the magnetic fields created by the electric current flowing within the neurons, and detects brain activity associated with various functions in real time.

DTI (diffusion tensor imaging). Measures the flow of water molecules along the white matter, or myelin, which makes up 50 percent of the brain and connects many regions. We're just learning the importance of myelin, and this very new technology is not yet easily interpreted.

A caveat: While it is tantalizing to draw conclusions from brain images, we need to be careful about deducing cause and effect from what is now still mostly correlating observations. In other words, when there is brain activity in particular regions at the same time someone is thinking about something or performing an action, it may not be that one is producing the other. It could be only that both are occurring at the same time and may or may not be related.

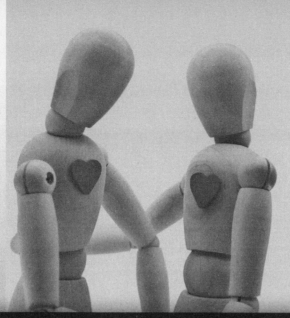

CHAPTER ONE

Born to Love

Why People Need People

Love makes the world go round, no doubt about it.

We're created in love, or some approximation thereof, when egg meets sperm. Then we're carried and cradled under our mother's heart from conception to birth, dependent on love for our very survival for the next several years—and when we're grown and independent, the dance starts all over again, with us meeting, mating, making love and, sometimes, new lives.

Along the way, all of us seek to get and give love: erotic love, romantic love, brotherly love, platonic love, the love of animals, parents, children, and God. It's about when mum meets babe, boy meets girl, girl meets girl, boy meets other boy, man meets dog—the whole mess of attachment and relating that our brains crave to develop and stay healthy and happy.

Scientists can see it in our brains and in our biochemistry, but we know it's so even without the evidence: we're hardwired to love. We crave sex, connection, and companionship so much that we will do almost anything and put up with almost anything to have love and loving relationships.

When we don't have loving connections, we don't do very well. Research proves it over and over again: lonely and disconnected people are sicker, more prone to depression, die younger, and are at greater risk of losing their memories and their minds as they age. An equally impressive group of recent studies shows the inverse is true: people who are married, mated, or have a circle of friends have longer, healthier, and happier lives and a lower risk of developing dementia in old age.

In a series of fascinating experiments from the 1950s, psychology professor Harry Harlow at the University of Wisconsin at Madison demonstrated vividly and heartbreakingly what we primates will do for love.

Harlow was raising rhesus macaque monkeys from birth for his research, using the most accepted scientific methods for human child care. At that time, experts believed that nourishment—food—was the most important need of a newborn primate and the reason babies clung to their mothers. In fact, child-rearing theories of the time discouraged "spoiling" babies, even newborns, with too much attention. The best scientific institutions and hospitals isolated infants to lower risks of infection and provided good physical care and food but little, if any, attention or touching.

Harlow applied these accepted principles from human child care in raising the infant monkeys. But he noticed that while they thrived physically, they were mentally distraught, some to the point of self-mutilation. He wondered whether what the newborns were missing was a mother. So in an odd and brilliant experiment, he gave them a choice of two artificial ones.

One mother was a wire form with a warming device covered with soft cloth but with no food; the other was a bare wire frame that offered a nipple and bottle. The baby monkeys, Harlow discovered, became deeply attached to the cloth mother and approached the wire mother only for food. They claimed and clung to the soft warm form, rejecting any replacements. Even when sharp spikes or cold jets of air were thrust randomly out of the mother's body, the rhesus babies still clung to it. Comfort, not food, was what the babies craved.

Videos of the babies suffering in these experiments are painful to watch. Yet the prevailing child-rearing theories of that time considered this deprivation the best, most scientific way to care for human babies as well. Harlow's experiments were controversial and contributed to stricter regulation of animal experiments. His work also contributed, perhaps inadvertently, to the revolution about the best care for human newborns.

Do You See What I See? How Mirror Neurons Connect Us

Where and how does this near-desperate need for love—so basic that we're born craving it—live in the brain?

Neuroscientists know that love and sex activate our powerful dopamine-driven reward and pleasure system. Neurohormones such as oxytocin, the hormone of attachment that is released in both mother and child and in lovers after orgasm, play a crucial role in our ability to love and be loved. (For more on oxytocin, see "The Chemistry of Love" later in this chapter.)

Thanks to new imaging technology such as functional magnetic resonance imaging (fMRI), researchers are discovering what parts of the brain surge with activity when we feel love and lust in many different guises. And they are discovering that our yearning for connection may be based at least in part in our very neural physiology—on the activity of subsets of brain cells called *mirror neurons,* which are specialized to respond to others. These specific neurons may be responsible for empathy, altruism, our ability to understand others, and possibly synchronized swimming, line dancing, and the appeal of pornography.

Mirror neurons are exactly what they sound like: they are neurons in several parts of the brain that mirror and mimic the activities we see, hear, deduce, and perhaps feel from others. They are a sort of mind-reading fail-safe for connection and communication. And they are bred into our brain.

The presence of mirror neurons, which were discovered less than two decades ago, is often linked with what's called "theory of mind": the ability we develop naturally by the age of four or so that allows us to interpret the thoughts and feelings of others and to understand that others have beliefs, desires, and intentions that are different from our own.

This goes a long way toward explaining how and why we can act in unison and partnership, how we can understand each other—and why and how long-term partners, spouses, and friends appear to read each other's minds, anticipate each other's actions and reactions, and even start to look alike.

These specialized neurons are busy both when we act and when we observe the same action performed by another. That means that parts of our brain become active when we witness other people's actions in the same way that our brain does when we perform those same actions ourselves. The actions we mirror include not just what we do but the way emotions are displayed, cuing us to the emotional content of statements and actions.

Mirror neurons may teach us both how to connect and keep us connected. They help give us a direct internal experience and understanding of another person's action, intention, or emotion, and they underlie our ability to imitate another's action and thereby learn. That imitation means, neuroscientists say, that we can literally experience what others do and feel. It explains why we wince when we see others hurt and the truth in the statement, "I feel your pain."

Scientists discovered mirror neurons in the 1990s by happenstance while researching brain activity in monkeys. Neuroscientists Giacomo Rizzolatti, Leonardo Fogassi, and Vittorio Gallese of the University of Parma in Italy had run electrodes to individual neurons in a monkey's premotor cortex to study brain activity as the monkey reached for different objects.

Then these scientists began to notice something strange: when one of them happened to be reaching for something within the monkey's line of vision, the monkey's premotor neurons fired just as they had when the monkey grasped something itself. The researchers could hardly believe what they had witnessed. But after replicating that experiment and similar ones many times, they realized they had discovered something new. They at first called it "monkey see, monkey do," a good description, but hardly scientific: it was replaced with the more academic and equally descriptive term, *mirror neurons*, when they published their findings.

Since then, the findings have been greatly expanded by the team in Parma, working often with Marco Iacoboni, Michael A. Arbib of the University of Southern California, and Christian Keysers of the University of Groningen in the Netherlands. The researchers have learned, for instance, that mirror neurons do not only fire when an animal is watching someone else perform an action. Mirror neurons also fire if a monkey hears the sound of someone doing something it has experienced—say, tearing a piece of paper.

And as the scientists began studying humans, using brain imaging rather than electrodes, they found that humans have mirror neurons in higher numbers and in more places than did the monkeys. Mirror neurons revealed themselves not only in the premotor cortex and the inferior parietal areas—areas associated with movement and perception—but also in the medial temporal cortex and the insula: regions that correspond to our abilities to comprehend someone else's feelings and use language.

Further experiments showed that mirror neurons help us share other people's experiences as reflected in their expressions, providing a biological basis for the well-known contagiousness of yawns, laughter, and good or bad moods. Newborns search the faces of their mothers or other caregivers and imitate the expressions they see almost from the moment of birth.

Studies also have shown that our mirror neurons can be choosy: they respond to the context of a situation and what we perceive to be its purpose, not only to specific muscle movements of others. Neurons that discharge when a monkey watches a human reach for an object, for example, will continue to respond to the logical progression of the movement even if much of it is hidden by a screen. Recently researchers have discovered that human infants less than a year old respond the same way in similar tests.

Another study showed that mirror neurons play a key role in perceiving intentions—the first step in understanding others and also in building social relations and feeling empathy. Iacoboni had volunteers watch films of people reaching for various objects within a teatime setting—a teapot, a mug, a pitcher of milk, a plate of pastries, napkins—in different contexts. In every instance, a basic collection of "grasping" mirror neurons fired. But different additional mirror neurons would also fire depending on what action was suggested by various details in the scene. If the viewer saw a neatly set table and expected the hand to pick up a teacup to drink, one array fired; if the viewer saw a messy table and expected the hand to pick up a cup to clear it away, another group of neurons fired.

Malfunctioning or absent mirror neurons have been considered one of the possible contributors to the poor social skills of those with autism, Asperger's syndrome, and other mental disorders.

If mirror neurons allow us to feel what others are feeling (at least in part), they explain the power of imitation and may explain some of the "how" of human loving and connection.

ALL THE WORLD LOVES A LOVER:
WHY HAPPY PEOPLE HAVE HAPPY FRIENDS

Sociologists have long noted that human behavior appears to be contagious, but they had no scientific basis for how or why. Social scientists Nicholas Christakis and James Fowler have come up with some interesting theories, based on studying mirror neurons and analyzing data from the Framingham Heart Study, a mother lode of information. Begun in 1948 by the National Heart Institute, the study has followed more than fifteen thousand Framingham, Massachusetts, residents and their descendants over decades, bringing them to a doctor's office every four years, on average, for a comprehensive physical examination and quizzing them multiple times about their lives.

Sifting through the data and connecting what they found to behavior and mirror neuron research, the scientists speculate that mirror neurons may explain why fat people have fat friends, happy people have happy friends, and long-time spouses often die soon after the death of a loved one—the so-called widowhood effect. (See Chapter Seven, "You've Lost That Lovin' Feelin.'")

They speculate that we pick up unconscious signals from those nearest and dearest to us about what is considered normal and even desirable. So if our friends are overweight or alcoholic, we adjust our subconscious image of what is a desirable weight or alcohol intake and pack on the pounds and the booze. The closer the relationship is with this person, the more we are affected by the other's activities. Happiness is the same: a smiling face coaxes us to smile in response, and the giddy happiness of the newly in love is known to be infectious.

You've probably also noted that your own expressions have an effect on how you feel, another reason to put on a happy face. Psychologist Paul Ekman, who confirmed that the facial expression of emotions is the same the world over, inadvertently discovered the effect that making faces has on our emotions. While simulating and recording a wide range of facial expressions in front of a mirror, he discovered that some days he would just be bummed out: he realized that these turned out to be the days he was experimenting with making sad, angry, or distressed expressions.

The Dangers of Involuntary Mind Merging

Of course, you need to take care what you hold up to those mirrors: mirror neurons do not always reflect well on us, Marco Iacoboni notes.

Take the example of violent video games (and possibly violent pornography). Iacoboni's initial studies suggest that such games reinforce, at a basic neuronal level, an association of pleasure and accomplishment with inflicting harm—even if it's virtual harm—an impetus that we would not ordinarily want to encourage. He has speculated that imitative violence may so powerfully affect mirror neurons that if it is reinforced by other input, we may not be able to control acting it out.

Iacoboni has also said that mirror neurons work best in real life when people are face-to-face, and he concedes that virtual reality, films, and videos of anything are but shadowy substitutes. Still, violent videos and games stimulate mirror neurons. And since the neurons mirror the action, it is not so virtual, but as if one was experiencing the activity firsthand. Mirror neurons then might explain the power of pornographic films. And wouldn't you know it, the French have done a study to try to prove it.

Men get sexually aroused by looking at pornography, but it hasn't been known exactly how that worked in the brain. A group of French scientists devised an experiment to study it. They hooked a group of men up to a volumetric penile plethysmograph (an instrument that measures blood volume in the penis) and an fMRI brain scanner and then showed them sexy videos. When the men (and their penises) responded sexually, researchers could see activity in brain areas that contain mirror neurons (the left frontal operculum and the inferior parietal lobules). And when correlated to the measurements taken from the penile plethysmograph, the level of activity in those brain areas predicted the magnitude of the measured erection. Several other brain areas were also activated. More research is needed to understand the role of mirror neurons in pornography.

The Chemistry of Love

Your brain is more than its neurons. When people smitten with love or lust say there is chemistry or electricity between them, they speak the truth: the brain (and your love life) is powerfully affected by honest-to-goodness electrical sparks—tiny amounts of electricity created by chemical reactions that transmit information among your neurons. Specialized chemicals called neurotransmitters and hormones fan the flames.

Love in your brain, then, is indeed a potent brew. It involves the blending and balance of more than one hundred of those hormones and neurochemical messengers. Lust is driven by testosterone (in men and in women), norepinephrine gives that excitatory rush, and dopamine provides the over-the-moon high that rivals heroin in its orgasmic and addictive kick. These chemicals can so heighten the passion of sex and sexual craving that it becomes a basic need, such as hunger or thirst—so powerful it can feel like an obsessive compulsive disorder.

Lasting love and devotion can be credited to the kinder, gentler neurohormone oxytocin, also known as the "cuddle hormone," which is produced in the brains of newborns, nursing mothers, and at orgasm. It's the hormone of love, trust, and attachment and is involved in every kind of human and mammal bonding. Unlike the hot spurs of testosterone and dopamine, oxytocin contributes to feelings of comfort and security.

Commitment is fueled by oxytocin and its companion neurohormone vasopressin. In women, oxytocin stimulates birth contractions, the letting down of breast milk, mother love, and bonding with both a nursing infant and a postcoital lover. In both men and women (but more in women), it increases during sex and surges at orgasm, playing a role in pair bonding (and possibly an evolutionary adaptation for long-term care of helpless infants). It's the hormone that attaches newborns to their moms and also, it turns out, to the dads

Love Potions: **The Love Stars of Brain Chemistry**

These are the chemicals most involved in sex, love, and bonding:

- *Testosterone.* This is the steroid hormone that makes men male and drives their aggression and sexual urges, but it's also key for desire in women, where it's produced in much smaller amounts.

- *Estrogen.* This steroid hormone makes women female, regulates reproductive cycles and menstruation, and is important for mental health. Men need some estrogen for sperm production and possibly desire.

- *Progesterone.* It balances estrogen and has such major effects on fertilization and reproduction that it's known as the hormone of pregnancy.

- *Dopamine.* Lust is enhanced by dopamine, a neurohormone of many roles produced by the hypothalamus, which triggers the release of testosterone, the hormone that drives sexual desire in women as well as men. Dopamine is vital for voluntary movement, attentiveness, motivation, and pleasure, and it's the key player in addiction, ecstasy, and love. It's the fire in your fireworks.

- *Oxytocin.* Love is supported by oxytocin, a hormone secreted by the pituitary. Oxytocin reinforces attachment and trust and is vital for childbirth and breastfeeding. In both men and women (but more in women), it increases during sex and surges at orgasm, playing a role in pair bonding (and possibly an evolutionary adaptation for long-term care of helpless infants).

- *Vasopressin.* Also know as arginine vasopressin, it regulates the body's retention of water, but more important to us in this context, it resembles and acts much like oxytocin, facilitating and coordinating reward circuits crucial for bonding.

- *Norepinephrine.* Also known as adrenaline, it keeps us alert and jumps in when we need a sudden burst of energy. It's produced and released by the adrenal glands in times of stress and excitement. A little bit hypes desire; too much can increase anxiety or tension.

- *Serotonin.* This mood leveler helps regulate memory, emotion, sleep, appetite, and mood, among other functions. Too little serotonin is connected with depression, and too much serotonin withers sexual desire, as those on serotonin-enhancing antidepressants know all too well.

- *Endorphins:* These act as hormones and neurotransmitters to reduce pain sensations and increase pleasure. No wonder: these are your body's natural narcotics. The word is a combination of end(ogenous) and (m)orphine. They surge with exercise, orgasm, and love.

who participate actively in child care. Researchers are finding that those powerful neurochemicals, when released in the presence of a loved one, can basically train us to become addicted to the object of our affection.

There seems to be a balancing act going on among all these love-related hormones that may help explain some of the progression of love from hot, mad lust and sex to comfortable, loving companionship. High levels of testosterone that fuel desire actually suppress the release of the attachment hormones oxytocin and vasopressin—and high levels of oxytocin and vasopressin offset the crazy passion effects of testosterone, dopamine, and norepinephrine, leading to calmer feelings of attachment. Research shows that a man's levels of testosterone actually go down when he holds a baby.

Love Is Everywhere: Where Love Grows in the Brain

The number and types of brain scans that show activity in a living, loving brain in real time are increasing and increasingly popular (Don't we all want to know the secrets of love in our brain?), and some of the findings show that love involves a network of areas in the brain, regardless of the object of your affections.

It's also true that different sections of the brain become involved in specific and different types of love, from wild erotic passion to the unshakable devotion of maternal or unconditional love. But many areas overlap: Stephanie Ortigue at the University of Syracuse, who is researching the relationship of different kinds of love to specific brain areas, finds that a dozen sections of the brain often work in tandem with the release of those powerful love chemicals of dopamine, oxytocin, and vasopressin.

Ortigue, Francesco Bianchi-Demicheli, and colleagues reviewed a sampling of a half-dozen fMRI brain studies, looking for some common ground about where love resides. In examining the fMRI studies of the brains of those deeply, truly, and madly in love—those in the thralls of romantic passionate love—they confirmed what earlier studies show: such passion recruits brain areas involving emotion, motivation, reward, social cognition, attention, and self-representation. In other words, they found activity in the same brain regions that are buzzing when they are under the influence of cocaine, especially the dopaminergic subcortical system (including the ventral tegmental area and caudate nucleus).

Interestingly, activity wasn't limited to the brain areas related to cocaine. Rather, love activates part of the cognitive system, confirming that love is not only an addiction or a basic emotion. Love is also cognition. Love acts, feels, and thinks. Meanwhile, areas in the loving brain concerned with fear, grieving, and self-protection, such as the amygdala, were snoozing. (Read more about this in Chapter Four, "That Old Black Magic.")

In the imaging studies of the maternal brain, they found overlap with the areas activated by passionate love such as those rich in the dopamine-reward cycle. But they also found activity in areas associated with higher thinking and processing, and with the periaqueductal (central) gray matter (PAG). This would make sense, the researchers wrote, since the PAG receives direct connections from the emotional brain and contains a high density of vasopressin receptors, which are related to oxytocin (both neurohormones important in maternal bonding as well as pair bonding) and help suppress pain during extreme emotional experiences such as childbirth.

To examine unconditional love, they reviewed studies of brains of people expressing love for those with diminished intellectual abilities. Once again, the reward system was activated (that seems to be constant for many kinds of love), but so were the PAG and the thinking brain, similar to the maternal brain.

Together, researchers conclude, the results show that different types of love call for different brain networks and that love is more than a basic emotion. Even passionate love, it turns out, involves the thinking brain. Love, they wrote, is a complex function including appraisals, goal-directed motivation, reward, self-representation, and body image. Just about any of us could have told them that, but it's good to have it scientifically verified.

A Brain Unable to Love: Inside the Brain of a Psychopath

Sometimes love messages get tangled in the brain. There are many reasons: it can be connected to genetics, prenatal conditions or birth injuries, childhood trauma, abandonment, neglect, abuse, illness, or brain damage.

Those with such problems can find it hard to form strong attachments. Others might be drawn to obsessions not condoned by most cultures, such as a sexual attraction to children, animals, or objects. Or in a really, really bad case of miswiring or injury, the result could be a brain unable to feel emotion, empathy, or love at all: the brain of a psychopath.

These brains are not like those of the rest of us. Aided by EEGs and brain scans, scientists have discovered that psychopaths have significant and serious brain defects in areas that affect their ability to relate to others. Their brains process information differently from most other people's. It's as if they have a learning disability that impairs emotional development.

And yet one of the most striking peculiarities of psychopaths is how normal they appear at first, unlike the monsters depicted in horror and thriller films. You may not know when you are face-to-face with a psychopath since most psychopaths act just like the rest of us. They are killers making nice. Ted Bundy, for example, an attractive law student and aide to the governor of the state of Washington, was a mass rapist and murderer of thirty women. John Wayne Gacy was a Junior Chamber of Commerce's Man of the Year who murdered thirty-three teenage boys and young men. Other sociopaths are polished career criminals or con men (sociopaths are usually men).

Psychopaths are likable guys when they want to be, but they lack empathy and the most universal and basic social obligations and emotions. They are unable to read other people's cues and learn from their mistakes. They lie and manipulate, commit crimes, and might maim and murder and feel no compunction or regret. In fact, they don't feel particularly deeply about anything at all.

So much of the way regular people make sense of the world is through emotion. It informs our gut decisions, our connections to people and places, our sense of belonging and purpose. It's almost impossible to imagine life without feelings—until you meet a psychopath. They often cover up their deficiencies with a ready and engaging

DO YOU KNOW A PSYCHOPATH?

Chances are you've met a psychopath. People with the disorder make up 0.5 to 1 percent of the general population. When you discount children, women (since few women, for unknown reasons, are psychopaths), and the estimated 500,000 who are already imprisoned, that translates to approximately 250,000 psychopaths living freely among us in the United States.

You probably have not fallen in love with one, but it's possible. Psychopaths can appear not only normal but charming: mass murderer and rapist Ted Bundy was attractive to many women.

Without a brain scan, how can you recognize a psychopath? The test that experts use, known as the Hare Psychopathy Checklist–Revised, consists of twenty criteria. Among the items on the list are behaviors and traits such as pathological lying, poor impulse control, proneness to boredom and sexual promiscuity, and having many short-term marital relationships. Other traits are a parasitic lifestyle; irresponsibility; a record of crime and conning; lack of empathy, remorse, or guilt; and a failure to accept responsibility for actions.

charm, so it can take time to realize what you are dealing with, if you ever do. Although guilty of the most erratic, irresponsible, and sometimes destructive and violent behavior, they show none of the classic signs of mental illness. They don't have hallucinations or hear voices. They aren't confused, or anxious, or driven by overwhelming compulsions. Nor do they tend to be socially awkward. They are often of better-than-average intelligence.

They just don't care, and they don't express true remorse or a desire to change. Are they mad or simply bad? Nearly every culture on earth has recorded the existence of individuals whose antisocial behavior threatens community peace.

Thanks to technology that captures brain activity in real time, experts are able to investigate what is happening inside a psychopathic brain as they think, make decisions, and react to the world around them. And what they find is that psychopaths suffer from a serious biological defect. It's as if they have a learning disability that impairs emotional development, and this disconnect is sometimes seen as early as age five.

Psychopaths are curiously oblivious to emotional cues, and they also have trouble identifying fearful facial expressions. Once fixed on a goal, psychopaths proceed as if they can't get off the train until it reaches the station. This narrowly focused, full-speed-ahead tendency, paired with the psychopath's impulsivity, produced the kind of horror described in Truman Capote's *In Cold Blood,* an all-night torture fest that appears almost aimless, the work of criminals who, having begun the violence, are blind and deaf to a victim's pleas, unable to stop until it has been completed.

Some of the early information about brain areas involved in psychopathic behavior comes from the famous and curious case of Phineas Gage, a handsome, dark-haired young man working as a construction foreman on the Rutland & Burlington Railroad in Vermont in 1848. An accidental explosion blew a tamping iron—a heavy metal rod more than three feet long—through the left side of Gage's face and out the top of his head. Such an injury seemed sure to kill or at the very least cripple, but Gage never lost consciousness and apparently recovered. However, his compatriots noticed the formerly savvy, even-tempered, and responsible Gage was now churlish and unpredictable, driven by his immediate passions. Gage had lost the use of a part of the brain called the ventromedial prefrontal cortex, an area structurally similar to its neighbor, the orbitofrontal cortex, which many scientists believe malfunctions in psychopaths.

The orbitofrontal cortex is involved in sophisticated decision-making tasks that involve sensitivity to risk, reward, and punishment. People whose brains are damaged in this area develop problems with impulsivity and insight and lash out in response to perceived affronts—much as Gage did. In fact, such patients are often said to suffer from acquired psychopathy. But even transformed as Gage was by his accident, he did not show all the characteristics of psychopathy, such as lack of empathy.

Evidence today suggests that psychopathy is due to errors in several interconnected brain structures that are involved in emotion processing, goal seeking, motivation, and self-control, including part of the thinking brain, the orbitofrontal cortex; the fight-or-flight controlling amygdala; and the paralimbic system.

A group of fMRI images of psychopaths' brains show a pronounced thinning of the paralimbic tissue. The paralimbic system includes the anterior cingulate cortex and the insula. The anterior cingulate regulates emotional states and helps people control their impulses and monitor their behavior for mistakes. The amygdala generates emotions such as fear, and the insula plays a key role in recognizing violations of social norms, as well as in experiencing anger, fear, empathy, disgust, and pain perception. Psychopaths are unfazed by pain and notable for their fearlessness: when confronted with images such as a looming attacker or a weapon aimed their way, they literally don't blink.

One study that looked at the brains of nine men who were diagnosed as psychopaths used a new scanning technique called DTI-MRI. The team at the Institute of Psychiatry at King's College, London, found that a white matter tract called the uncinate fasciculus, which connects the amygdala and the orbitofrontal cortex (the emotional and the thinking brains, respectively), was significantly different between the psychopaths and the control group and that the more extreme the psychopathy, the greater the abnormality was. Some of the psychopaths they imaged had committed multiple rapes, manslaughter, and attempted murder. (Incidentally, none of the men were incarcerated at the time of the study, which gives one pause.)

Psychopaths are not the only ones with aberrant brains. The brains of some hard-core pedophiles also have something wrong in the frontal lobe, a region of the brain critical for impulse control among its higher-level reasoning functions. Research suggests that pedophiles might have faulty wiring and connections in the brain. A study using MRIs and computer analysis techniques found that brains of some pedophiles had significantly less white matter in brain regions involved in sexual arousal, suggesting poorer connections, among other things.

Researchers are looking for effective treatments—and you don't have to feel sympathy to want to help psychopaths. Consider it preventive and protective treatment for the rest of us. Psychopaths offend earlier, more frequently, and more violently than other criminals. If for no other reasons than to ease the prison burden, psychopaths deserve and need treatment just as anyone else with a severe mental illness: Between 15 and 35 percent of U.S. prisoners are psychopaths, and they are four to eight times more likely to commit new crimes on release. In fact, there is a direct correlation between how high people score on a screening test for psychopathy and how likely they are to violate parole.

Recent estimates put the expense of prosecuting and incarcerating psychopaths, combined with the costs of the havoc they wreak in others' lives, at $250 billion to $400 billion a year. An ambitious multimillion-dollar project, funded by the National Institutes of Mental Health and Drug Abuse and the John D. and Catherine T. MacArthur Foundation, is gathering genetic information, brain images, and case histories from one thousand psychopaths (using portable functional MRI scanners that can be brought inside prison walls and used on-site to scan dangerous prisoners) and compiling it all into a searchable database. The research may identify psychopaths earlier and help devise effective treatments to help them, and protect the rest of us.

THE POWER OF LOVE—AND ITS ABSENCE

Still doubting the power of human relationships? Consider the results of this 2010 meta analysis of 148 studies of how and why people die. Guess what ranks right up there on the top of influences on mortality? Yep. Loneliness.

Noting that the quantity and quality of social interaction are drastically declining in industrialized countries as loneliness continues to rise, the study found that the lack of relationships is comparable to well-established risk factors for death such as smoking and alcohol consumption, and is even greater than other risk factors such as physical inactivity and obesity. (See Chapter Five, "Friendship, Such a Perfect Blendship.")

Shunning, abandonment, and forced solitary confinement are among the worst punishments, considered to be cruel and excessive or even akin to torture. They can cause physical brain damage—electroencephalograph (EEG) studies going back over decades show changes in the brain waves of prisoners after only a week or so of solitary confinement—and the rejected brain is a wretched brain. (See Chapter Seven, "You've Lost That Lovin' Feelin'.")

When the rejection or abuse is extreme, the very young brain can have its capacity for love broken, perhaps permanently. Children neglected or abandoned in orphanages from birth, where they receive adequate physical care but little human contact, often have lifelong problems relating to others and an inability to bond lovingly. Reactive attachment disorder is an issue among children who have been adopted in recent years from orphanages in eastern Europe and Russia, where they received physical care but little affection.

Baby Face, You've Got the Cutest Little Baby Face

If there is one type of love wired into our basic brain, that's baby love. For example: let's say you found a wallet on the street. What would you do? Take it to the nearest police station? Mail it back to the owner?

Keep it? The answer, it emerges, depends less on a question of individual morality and a great deal more on how the brain is wired to our collective evolutionary heritage.

In 2009 psychologist Richard Wiseman of the University of Hertfordshire in England left a bunch of wallets on the streets of Edinburgh, Scotland, each containing one of four photographs: a happy family, a cute puppy, an elderly couple, and a smiling baby. Which wallets, he wondered, would be most likely to find their way home?

There was no doubting the outcome: 88 percent of the wallets with the picture of the smiling baby were returned, beating all the others out of sight. Wiseman says that was not surprising: "The baby kicks off a caring feeling in people," a nurturing instinct toward vulnerable infants that has evolved to safeguard the survival of our future generations.

You don't even have to be a mother to have your brain respond to images of infants. In another 2009 study, Melanie Glocker of the Institute of Neural and Behavioral Biology at the University of Muenster in Germany flashed pictures of newborns to a group of childless women while their brains were scanned by a fMRI. Using a special image-editing program, Glocker manipulated the pictures so some of the infant faces were even more baby-like (large, round eyes; round, chubby faces) and some were less babyish (smaller eyes, narrower faces). The more babyish faces prompted an increase in activity in not just the amygdala (the brain's emotional control tower) but also the nucleus accumbens, a key structure of the mesocorticolimbic system connected with reward.

Studies that compared adult responses to the sounds of babies and adults crying found a 900 percent increase in amygdala responses to the babies. Additional research showed that sudden and unexpected changes in the babies' crying pitch got the most emotional brain response from adults.

Adults have many of the same protective instincts to the babies of other mammalians species, which is no doubt why they are all engineered to be so cute. Other loves may come any go, but baby love, it seems, just lasts and lasts.

CHAPTER TWO

Learning to Love

Our very first lovers give us our most important lessons in loving. These first and greatest affairs have an enormous impact on how well we will love later, whether (or how much) we enjoy sex, and even who we will choose for our most passionate partners. No, we don't mean schoolyard crushes or teenage sex explorations or even your mate. We're talking about your parents.

Developmental scientists believe the places and ways we will seek love and our very ability to give and receive it are profoundly influenced in the first few years of our existence, beginning at conception when that specific egg and sperm combine genetic material. The wash of maternal hormones in utero further influences our developing brain.

Our conscious experiences of loving begin as soon as we emerge into the world and connect with others—or not. Mom (or our primary

Five Ways Your Brain Is Primed for Love

1. *Your dad's sperm.* We have known that older eggs increase the risks for Down's and other syndromes. Now we also know that sperm from dads over age forty also carries risks of mental disorders, including autism, which affect your ability to connect to others.

2. *Your genes.* These contribute to your gender, your gender preference in sexual partners, your predilection for one-night stands, and how easily you have orgasms (among other things).

3. *Your gestation.* Hormones in utero affect your development and fine-tune your gender preferences and sexual characteristics.

4. *Your early bonding.* Consistent and caring attention in infancy (usually from Mom) prompts oxytocin release and contributes to making attachments with others later in life.

5. *Your dad's presence or absence.* It's not just your mom. Research also shows that a loving, nurturing dad in the nest helps babies bond, and an absent dad can mean an absent ability to relate.

caretaker) is our first lover, and researchers have long said that much in our brain depends on how well that love affair goes. Now they are finding that dads who stick around and get involved in child care also have a profound effect on the brain.

The circle of love lessons are completed when those who decide to become parents have children and find their own brains are changed—literally. Love spurs the very growth of the parental brain and even causes new brain cells to develop.

How Your Parents Affect Your Love Life

Those parental impacts on your brain begin long before birth, setting into motion major factors for your future relationships. Your gender, for openers, is determined by the specific sperm that wins the race to mate with your mom's egg.

The combined genes from that egg and sperm contribute to your everything, and that includes some basics about how you will love. For example, having a dopamine-related gene known as DRD4 seems to be connected to a predilection for risky business, including one-night stands, and researchers have found that anxiety and depression, downers in forming relationships, are connected to genes. Even the very age that your parents were when they blended that genetic material affects whether you will be mentally well enough to have satisfying relationships.

Then there are the prenatal influences—and not just good nutrition, regular medical care, and whether Mom smokes, drinks, or is exposed to toxic substances. The hormonal brew in utero prompts the development of female or male characteristics, calibrates sexuality, and adds to the outcome of gender preference in sexual partners.

After birth, the consistency and quality of parental attention have a major impact on oxytocin production, how well you bond with your first primary caregiver (and first lover), and how you will relate to others during your lifetime. Even whether you are breast-fed can have an effect: breast-fed babies reportedly have higher IQs, and functional magnetic resonance imaging (fMRI) of breast-feeding moms showed activity in the limbic (or emotional) parts of her brain that respond to signals from their babies.

But don't despair if some (or all) of these potential influences were problematic. Genes and prenatal influences are not destiny: For one thing, not all the genes you inherit are active (or expressed). The brain has proven to be remarkably plastic, able to be changed by life experiences that can offset genetic material and the effects of many prenatal influences, for good and for ill. Good mothering can trump many bad genes and prenatal influences. Fussy babies who were born anxious with the DRD2 gene (which helps regulate dopamine receptors) and who have parents who are consistently attentive were able to

YOUNG LOVE IS THE BEST FOR MAKING BABY BRAINS

With any luck, your parents made you when they were in their twenties or only a bit older. We've known for a long time that a woman forty years old or older has an increased risk of bearing a child with Down's syndrome and other disorders.

Now it seems that the biological clock ticks for would-be-dads as well, especially when it comes to brains and being able to form relationships. Studies show that becoming a father after age forty (as many more men than women do) has the same risk of having a child with schizophrenia as a forty-year-old woman's risk of having a child with Down's syndrome, and even higher odds that his offspring will have autism compared to a child of a thirty-year-old dad. Children born to fathers forty or older had nearly a sixfold increase of autism; after age fifty, that jumps to a ninefold risk.

This advanced paternal age has also been linked in many countries around the world to an increased risk of birth defects, cleft lip and palate, water on the brain, dwarfism, miscarriage, and decreased intelligence. These are important concerns: birth rates for men older than forty have jumped as much as 40 percent since 1980, whereas birth rates for men younger than thirty have fallen by as much as 21 percent.

Researchers still don't know the reasons that increasing age brings the increased risks, but if you're deciding to have children, you might want to do it sooner rather than later, and men who decide to wait might want to consider having sperm stored when they're young.

respond normally to stress by the age of one year. The caretaking doesn't have to be a biological parent. Studies with rodents have shown that maternal affection from foster mothers can reverse the effects of prenatal stress on the brains of rats that developed while in their biological mothers' wombs and decrease the babies' secretion of stress-induced corticosterone.

Children (and parents) who are the product of (or who contributed to) less-than-perfect parenting also need not despair. So many conditions influence the brain in childhood and even later that we become the product of the total sum of everything we experience and continue to experience throughout life. Parenting is indeed a powerful influence, but it's just one of the many factors that affect you and the love in your life.

Love at First Sight: The Earliest Lessons in Love

When things go right—and they do most of the time—you are being primed for love from the moment you and your mother gaze deep into each other's eyes. Scientists don't yet understand the brain mechanisms behind the complex mother-infant bond, but mirror neurons must play a crucial role: almost from birth, infants mimic the expression of those who are holding them and respond to familiar facial expressions.

That deep gazing between mom and baby helps mothers excel at recognizing and interpreting the moods and emotions of their offspring—to even seem to know what their babies are thinking before they can speak. They smile when their baby smiles and frown when their baby is upset. Research suggests this emotional recognition helps with bonding and learning.

One of the most powerful forces at work here appears to be oxytocin. And no wonder: it's been flooding the maternal system (and thus yours) since your very beginning. It surged in your parents when they reached orgasm, was responsible for the birth contractions that pushed you into this world, and stimulated the release of breast milk that fed you. In short, mom and baby are suffused with this hormone.

And a good hormone it is. Scientists have established that the hormone oxytocin is a trigger for love and affection—the chemical stimulus for pair bonding, trust, generosity, and altruism. It creates

Five Great Things Oxytocin Does for Your Brain

We know oxytocin encourages bonding between child and parent and in romantic sexual love. But that's not the only good thing this essential and versatile neurohormone does for us.

1. *It helps us get along.* Oxytocin doesn't just promote bonding; it also helps us recognize and remember faces and improves our ability to infer the mental state of others by interpreting subtle social cues in a sort of mind reading.

2. *It boosts social skills in people with autism and other problems relating to others.* In a study where thirteen high-functioning adults with autism played a computerized ball-tossing game, researchers found that a dose of oxytocin helped them cooperate. Other studies have found that oxytocin increases autistic adults' ability to comprehend emotions in speech and tamps down repetitive behaviors, another common symptom of this disorder.

3. *It cures some headaches.* People with chronic daily headaches, including migraines, found relief using a daily nasal spray of oxytocin. So far there have been no side effects, not even an inappropriate urge to cuddle.

4. *It lowers stress and helps us sleep better.* This makes sense since it promotes feelings of comfort and security.

5. *It helps you remember your mom.* In a recent study, men who took whiffs of oxytocin had intensified fond thoughts of their mom if their relationship been positive. If not, it relieved some of the bad thoughts.

---

feelings of calm and closeness and appears to be vital for us to form loving connections: children and adults with low levels of oxytocin have been found to have difficulty forming attachments.

The oxytocin in your mom's body contributes to her attachment and the level of attention she paid to you as an infant. Studies have shown a correlation between the levels of oxytocin during pregnancy, the connection a mom makes with her infant, and the amount of time that mothers and infants spent gazing at one another. It makes a strong argument that not only are hormones preparing women to be loving mothers after giving birth, but they're also helping pregnant women defend their infants-to-be from the dangers in the world.

After your birth, oxytocin helps your mom interpret the intentions of others: from your needs to the intentions of those who might be a threat to you. And it makes the experience of breastfeeding so pleasurable and intimate for many that they are sorrowful when their babies outgrow the need.

This mind-to-mind bonding appears to be very important for establishing your secure relationship in infancy and in future relationships. Strong emotional bonds between mothers and infants increase children's willingness to explore the world—an effect that has been observed across the animal kingdom, from people to spiders. The more secure we are in our attachment to Mom, the more likely we are to try new things and take risks in life as well as in love.

Arginine vasopressin, which is released in males in orgasm, is also associated with social bonding, parental care, stress regulation, social communication, and emotional reactivity. Research has shown that vasopressin levels increase in both genders along with positive social bonding, also known as attachment and love.

Loving and consistent care affect us deeply. Several researchers propose that attachment in fact is the result of evolution: that babies who had people who cared deeply about them survived to pass on their genes. Some propose that the way we learned to attach to our parents and other caregivers in childhood carries over into our adult lives and romances. The late psychologist Mary Ainsworth and others have described three major attachment styles: secure attachment, which gives us the confidence to explore and find comfort in others; anxious, in which we are worried about losing the important other; and avoidant, in which we are indifferent to others, perhaps due to disappointed expectations.

If You Could Read My Mind: Moms Do

What's going on in the maternal mind when a mother looks at the smiles, pouts, and other facial expressions of her infant? Functional magnetic resonance imaging studies are giving us a better understanding of what happens. Not surprisingly, these show that just the sight of her baby prompts powerful feelings of love, joy, and attachment and accompanying brain activity.

Researchers at Baylor College of Medicine showed twenty-eight first-time mothers pictures of their seven month olds they had never seen before. The baby face pictures spanned a wide range of emotions and included images of the child making happy, sad, or neutral expressions. They were also shown similar images of an unknown infant. Seeing the happy baby face of her own infant activated all of the key areas in the mother's brain associated with reward processing, including the ventral tegmental area, substantia nigra, and striatum, suggesting that for mothers, the very sight of her smiling baby is a potent and a uniquely pleasurable reward experience.

Researchers found that happy faces led to more neural activity than neutral faces, and sad faces generated the least brain response. That is, the mom's reward areas seemed to directly mirror the emotions she saw on her baby. Positive sensory cues such as a smiling face, for example, stimulated dopamine release and a positive maternal response.

But babies aren't always smiling, as mothers know all too well. Since mothers must also learn to respond to infants in distress, the infant smile can't be the only motivation. In fact, a human mother's response to an infant in distress is a good indicator of how responsive she is to other infant cues. Studies also show that abusive and neglectful mothers show less empathy and more aversive feelings toward a crying infant when compared with nurturing mothers, suggesting that how a mother reacts to a baby when he or she is upset and not smiling is a crucial test of maternal behavior.

It's a complex neural love system. More recent work has shown that a mom's thinking and feeling brain is also tuned into her baby, with the orbitofrontal cortex and striatum more active when she looked at her own baby regardless of her baby's situation or mood.

A Mother's Everlasting Love

Do you love your mother? Regardless of the complexity (and even negativity) of your relationship, for most of us, the truthful answer will be yes. Your mom holds a special place in your heart and in your brain throughout your entire life. Even children who have been neglected or abused retain a need for their moms, perhaps based more on hope and dreams than any reality.

That first bond lasts apparently, forever. Battle-hardened warriors call out for their mothers when wounded, oldsters on deathbeds recall their mothers, and many of us call our moms in times of crisis and triumph and when we just need some soothing. A mere reminder of Mom's touch or the sound of her voice on the phone is enough to change people's minds and moods, affecting their decision making in measurable ways.

A study that looked at how adult brains responded to images of parents confirms that Mom holds the top place in most brains, even after years and surely hundreds of thousands (if not a million) of other faces, events, and relationships later.

Researchers at the University of Toronto examined fMRI brain activity in adults when they showed them images of the faces of their mothers and fathers, along with faces of celebrities and strangers. They found that pictures of both parents prompted more response than the faces of celebrities or strangers, but overall, it was Mom's face that drew the most activity. Fathers' faces did prompt activity but at a lower level than the reaction to Mom.

What's of special interest here is that the average age of the participants was thirty-five, long after the age when most of us have left the family nest. That this activity is seen even in adults who have lived away from their parents for many years suggests that the effect is very long lasting.

In another study, researchers wanted to see how or if college business students remembered that maternal touch. They gave students a stressful experiment where they had to choose between safe bets and risky gambles—an investment with a guaranteed 4 percent yearly return or a riskier stock option, for example. In half of the cases, researchers of both genders patted the students lightly on the back of the shoulder for about one second while providing instructions.

The male and female students who were touched by a female experimenter were far more likely to choose the risky alternative than were those who had not been touched or were patted by male researchers. Study authors speculate that the reassuring touch of a woman may have triggered early associations of a supportive mom, inspiring the same openness to exploration that is observed in young children of nurturing mothers.

Then the researchers did the experiment again. This time they asked a different group of undergraduates to make financial decisions after a writing exercise in which half wrote about a time they felt secure and supported and the other half wrote about feeling insecure and alone. The students got the same mixed-sex shoulder pats. Those writing about insecurity who got shoulder pats from female experimenters were much more willing to take a risk—just as a child leaving for a field trip might steal one last reassuring hug from Mom before stepping on the bus.

Touch is not the only source of remembered maternal comfort. In another study, researchers took samples of hormones from participants to prove it. Researchers from the University of Wisconsin–Madison stressed out a group of seven- to twelve-year-old girls by giving them math and public-speaking exercises. Then they reunited some girls with their moms but offered other girls only a phone call. The study found that girls who talked with their mothers on the phone released just as much oxytocin, the social bonding hormone, as those who got to hug their mothers. And both groups had similarly low levels of cortisol, a stress hormone.

All of which shows that mother love lasts and explains why so many of us, young and old alike, call our mothers when feeling blue.

How Parenting Primes Your Brain for Love

Having offspring isn't a one-way street: while parenting develops love in the brains of offspring, it also changes the brains of parents. The brains of both parents change and grow in competency and complexity as they relate to their baby, as what were once self-directed organisms devoted to their own needs and survival become instead focused on the care and well-being of their offspring.

Mothers, whose bodies undergo enormous changes during pregnancy, childbirth, and immediately afterward, endure a major hormonal upheaval that by itself is enough to convince mere observers that becoming a mom profoundly affects a woman's brain.

During pregnancy, the female brain is effectively revving up for the difficult tasks ahead. A mother-to-be may notice most her cravings for ice cream and pickles, but inside her brain, a transformation is afoot in fundamental functions, ranging from attention to memory.

Neurons in the medial preoptic area (mPOA), the part of the brain that largely regulates maternal behavior, grow impressively during late pregnancy, increasing the protein-synthesizing capabilities of the cell. These mPOA neurons are readying themselves to respond to a baby with appropriate and sensitized impulses.

In the hippocampus, which regulates memory and learning, neurons are undergoing changes leading to increases in the concentration of tiny projections on the surface of dendrites, the parts of brain cells that receive information. Called dendritic spines, these projections provide a more dense neuronal surface. This density suggests pregnancy is enhancing memory, particularly spatial memory that helps in navigating complex areas and finding food. In short, it makes a new mother a better hunter and forager.

The hormones estrogen and progesterone are also intensifying, helping a mother become more focused on the myriad cues and cries of her infant, preparing her for exposure to the ravening demands and the irresistible cuteness of a newborn.

Expectant mothers also undergo changes that make them better at reading faces in general. A research team showed mothers-to-be images of human faces throughout pregnancy and asked them to rate the emotions expressed on those faces. As the pregnancy progressed, the mothers became more efficient at recognizing the emotions on the faces of others—and the greatest recognition increase was of faces displaying dangerous expressions, such as fear (perhaps of a visible threat), disgust (contamination threat), and anger (direct physical threat). It appears a mother brain's increasing skill at reading emotions is yet another tool to help moms protect their children.

Parenting Rewires the Daddy Brain as Well

For years, social scientists considered fathers to be second-string parents, since there's no clear and constant physical connection between a father and his child—at least not like the one seen with Mom and baby.

That view is changing, partly as the result of research revealing that dads are anything but bit players in their children's lives. For one thing, the role of fatherhood has undergone a profound behavioral change in the past half-century. In 1965 fathers were spending 2.6 hours a week on child care; by 2000 that figure had reached 6.5 hours. Moreover, there are three times as many stay-at-home fathers today as there were at the start of the new century.

But the most astonishing news is what research shows the presence of a father in a newborn's life may be doing to both dad and baby brains. Research studies using rodents as subjects show that when dads stay in the familial nest and participate in child care, the brains of babies and fathers benefit, and when a father is absent, a baby brain can suffer. Perhaps neuroscientists have finally found the roots of the biological hook that makes sure a father sticks around after birth.

How Father Love Feeds Both Brains

We know that learning new things prompts the brain to constantly rewire itself and to create new brain cells—neurons—in a process called neurogenesis. Fatherhood appears to be one of those spurs. Research on rats and mice shows that in the first few days after birth, changes occur in the brains of both the dad and the babies, depending on whether the father is around or not.

A recent study has shown increased growth of new neurons in male mice in the first few days following the birth of their pups, but only if the mouse father stayed in the nest. One new set of brain cells formed in the olfactory bulb and were specifically tuned to recognize the smells of his pups. Another set of neurons grew in the hippocampus, a center in the brain crucial for memory, which helped to consolidate the smell of his pups into a long-term memory.

Yet smelling his pups was not enough alone to create more new neurons. It apparently takes touch as well. When researchers separated the father mouse from his pups by placing a mesh screen between them in the cage, he didn't grow as many new brain cells. In other words, if the dad mouse was removed on the day of the birth, nothing happened. The father had to be physically present in the nest in the early days after birth. The physical contact he had with his pups in the nest, coupled with the smells of his young, are what made the neurons grow.

Interestingly, the brain cells that formed when a father interacted with his offspring were regulated by prolactin, the same hormone responsible for producing breast milk in moms. It also seems to play a role in creating bonding between a father and his newborn offspring.

What's more, the brains of father mice, as well as those of foster fathers who cared for another male's pup for several days, contained more nerve fibers that were sensitive to oxytocin and vasopressin, the hormones associated with caregiving and bonding in humans. Daddy brains benefited in other ways too. Compared with bachelor rodents, fathers are better foragers—quicker to learn where food was located in a maze—and the dad mice were also more comfortable, showing less stress in strange situations.

The effect is lasting. After the birth bond was established, it persisted in both the parent and baby mouse brains. Being separated for a few weeks is usually long enough for adult mice to forget their cage mate pals. But these new neurons created by the dad's presence with his pups helped to form long-term memories and bonds. The mouse fathers easily recognized their offspring by smell even after they had been separated for a long period of time (in mouse terms).

Researchers wondered if a child is born with a brain that expects this parental bond to form in the first place. They looked at degu rats—rodents that split parenting duties between mother and father. Degu fathers behave just like loving human fathers. They spend the early days of their pups' lives helping with basic care, like warming and grooming. As the pups get older, the degu fathers begin playing with their toddler offspring.

Researchers then wondered: Would absent fathers in the degu nests create a social and emotional void for the babies just as a missing dad affects a human family? Indeed, yes. If a rodent father remained in the nest with his pups, his babies' brains developed normally. But if he was removed from the nest shortly after the birth of his pups, the brains of his newborns started to break down at the level of synapses (the minute junctions that allow brain cells to communicate with each other). The fatherless degu pups matured to have fewer synapses in both the orbitofrontal cortex, part of the prefrontal cortex that regulates decision making, reward, and emotion, and the somatosensory cortex, involved in processing touch.

Having fewer synapses or faulty connections in the orbitofrontal cortex could lead to processing problems. If these rodent studies can be extrapolated to humans, they may explain why we see some kids who grow up without a father or father figure wrestle with sometimes serious behavior problems.

Newer studies hint that similar changes do happen in the brains of primate fathers, which are closer to those of humans. Scientists working in the laboratory of neuroscientist Elizabeth Gould of Princeton University have found that when marmoset monkeys became fathers, neurons in the prefrontal cortex, a brain region dedicated to planning and decision making, became more densely connected and sprouted more receptors for vasopressin, suggesting an increase in the area's cognitive capacity.

So far these studies have been in animals, but these are mammals like ourselves, and the behavioral and biological changes are similar to those that researchers have observed in mothers, human and otherwise. Since changes in the mom's brain happen while she is pregnant or nursing, caregiving seemed to be connected with a flood of hormones during and after pregnancy.

The animal studies show that a father's brain is also significantly and beautifully intertwined with his offspring's. A father has direct influence on his child's neurodevelopment, and his own brain can benefit as well.

Postpartum Depression: Misery for Mom and Baby

Sometimes a new mother just isn't there emotionally or even physically, for reasons she can't help. She might be suffering from postpartum depression: baby blues.

Consider the changes she's been through. During pregnancy, a woman's body must ramp up many of its systems to support the growing fetus inside. The cardiovascular system has to pump 30 to 50 percent more blood, sending much of the extra blood supply directly to the uterus, which means more work for the kidneys and lungs.

The hormonal roller-coaster of pregnancy is even greater, and mood swings are common after the momentous and dramatic experience of birth. All of those hormones have a powerful effect on the brain, and bouts of crying and irritability affect 80 percent of new mothers for a few hours or days after delivery.

For most moms, it ends there. But for 10 to 20 percent of new mothers in the United States, postpartum depression can be disabling in the first year after childbirth and interfere with her ability to care for her baby. It's common around the world in other cultures too, with prevalence rates as high as 60 percent in some countries.

The specific causes aren't known, but a previous bout with depression is a huge risk factor for the postpartum variety, research shows. Women seem to be particularly vulnerable to depression during their reproductive years, with rates highest between the ages of twenty-five and forty-five.

The hormonal havoc in a new mother's body contributes. During pregnancy, a woman experiences a surge in blood levels of estrogen and progesterone. Then, in the first forty-eight hours after childbirth, the amount of these two hormones plummets almost fifty-fold, back to normal levels. This chemical seesaw could contribute to depression just as the smaller hormonal changes before a menstrual period may affect mood.

This can't be the only reason for the baby blues, since this biochemical oscillation occurs in all new mothers and yet only a small proportion of them become depressed. In addition, studies have shown that pregnancy hormone levels in a woman do not predict her risk of depression.

Whatever its cause, depression can weaken the brand-new and still-forming love bond between mother and baby. A baby's earliest days have the greater impact: three-month-old infants of depressed mothers look at their mothers less often and show fewer signs of positive emotion than do babies of mentally healthy moms. These toddlers may be more passive, insecure, and socially inhibited—something akin to learned helplessness, found University of Pennsylvania psychologist Martin E. P. Seligman and his colleagues.

But there is some good news: a mom's postpartum gloom usually does not affect her baby's thinking brain or intellectual development. Researchers did find some cognitive problems, however, in boys of low socioeconomic status who had chronically depressed mothers as compared with children whose mothers had less severe depression. Other work suggests that postpartum depression is connected with behavioral problems and negativity in children when they are older, but other factors may be involved too.

In the end, most mothers who receive appropriate treatment—often a combination of psychotherapy, medication, and self-help such as exercise—usually recover completely within about two months of starting treatment and can begin to build or repair the loving bond with baby.

Loving the One Who Hurts You: Why Children Cling to Abusers

The scenario is confusing and saddening: children who are abused develop an attachment to their abuser that keeps them from getting help or running away. There are many stories of children and young teens who were kidnapped and abused for years but who did not try to escape, even when they seemingly had the opportunity.

Experts have struggled to understand why. Fear of punishment of course plays a role, as does the Stockholm syndrome, in which captives develop positive feelings for their captors. But the underlying causes have remained hidden. Scientists who study attachment in rats offer insight into what may be happening in abused children's brains.

Rats are especially responsive to smells during infancy, which may help foster the parental bond. Psychologist Regina M. Sullivan of New York University showed in 2000 that young rats are drawn to almost any odor, even when the odor is associated with a stressful stimulus, such as a mild heat shock. In other words, baby rats are attracted to the very thing that hurts them rather than being repelled, as older rats would be.

What is happening in the young rats' brains to foster attachment instead of aversion or fear? In a new paper in *Nature Neuroscience,* Sullivan and Gordon Barr, a psychologist at the Children's Hospital of Philadelphia, found the answer in the rats' amygdala, a brain region associated with anxiety and fear that coordinates emotional behaviors. In the amygdala of rats attracted to the aversive odors, there were lower-than-normal levels of the neurotransmitter dopamine. This lack of dopamine activity may have turned off their brain's fear response, enabling attraction to take place instead.

A similar mechanism may occur in abused children, Sullivan says, although how much the amygdala is involved with early human attachment is unclear. Barr suggests this behavior probably evolved as a survival tactic. "The animal has to be able to survive, which means it has to be attached to its caregiver no matter what the quality of care," he says.

What If Things Went Wrong with That First Love?

Children's brains are resilient—and a good thing that is, since most of us didn't get ideal parenting and few of us give it to our own kids. We do the best we can, and that is usually plenty good enough. Most of us go on to form loving and meaningful relationships. But in extreme cases of abandonment, neglect, or abuse, children who didn't get that bonding grow up with problems attaching to others. When their needs are ignored or met with hostility or abuse before the age of three, they stop trying to connect and avoid social contact. When the rejection or abuse is extreme, the very young brain can have its capacity for love broken, perhaps permanently.

The hormone oxytocin is a trigger for love and affection, as is vasopressin. Children raised for their first two years in some orphanages where they were neglected (and may have been abused) do not produce the same levels of the hormones oxytocin and vasopressin as found in children raised in a family.

In experiments at the University of Wisconsin–Madison, eighteen adopted toddlers who had spent an average of sixteen months in orphanages in eastern Europe and Russia were studied along with twenty-one children with biological parents. Each toddler sat on his or her mother's lap while playing an interactive game that involved hugging and other touch; then they played the same game on the lap of a friendly female stranger. Urine samples showed that the adopted children had lower levels of arginine vasopressin than did the biological children. The biological children also showed a rise in oxytocin after playing with their own mother but not after playing with the female stranger. In the adopted children, there was no oxytocin increase in either.

Many (but by no means all) children adopted from some orphanages in eastern Europe and Russia, where they did not get early affection, have great trouble adjusting to family life and resist bonding with their new parents. In one dramatic case, an exhausted and exasperated adoptive mother in the United States put her seven-year-old adopted son on an airplane alone and sent him back to Russia.

The effects of childhood trauma can be measured. Even as adults, in several studies they show low levels of oxytocin, vasopressin, and serotonin, the neurotransmitters connected with reward, attachment, and mood regulation. Women who were abused in childhood (especially emotionally abused) have measurably lower levels of oxytocin in spinal fluid testing as adults.

It's worth repeating, however, that life experiences can and do change the brain. As the study authors wrote, "It is critical to note that not all children who experience early neglect develop the same kinds of problems, and children with lower hormonal reactivity may, over time, develop satisfactory interpersonal relationships."

In the End: Do Parents Matter?

With so much focused on the quality and importance of the early parent-child lessons in love, it's a good bet that many readers on both sides of that relationship are not feeling very good about themselves at this point. What if it wasn't ideal—or even adequate? There's plenty of guilt and regret to go around.

Sigmund Freud famously blamed the problems of the child on the parents, and he was especially hard on mothers. Behaviorists such as B. F. Skinner thought the parents were responsible, one way or the other, for whatever went wrong with a child.

While you're worrying about what parenting did to your ability to love (or what you did to your offspring), it's important to remember that the brain is amazingly plastic and startlingly resilient.

We know that new networks are created and disbanded in our brains all the time. Scientists are also finding that one of the ways the brain changes itself is by actually changing genes—or more correctly, the acting-out (or not) of certain genes—in a process called epigenesis. Your genome—the total deoxyribonucleic acid (DNA) that you inherit from your ancestors and that contains the instructions for making your unique body and brain—doesn't change. But there is another layer of information called the epigenome stored in the proteins and chemicals that surround and stick to your DNA (*epi* means above or beyond). It's a kind of chemical switch or volume control that determines which genes are activated (or not): it tells your genes what to do, where, when, and how much.

Researchers have discovered the epigenome can be affected by many things, from aging and diet to environmental toxins to even what you think and feel. This means even your experiences can literally change your mind by shutting down or revving up the production of proteins that affect your mental state.

So with the exception of truly extreme childhood trauma or injury, there's plenty of opportunity for other people and events to offset both the bad and the good parenting. Later life relationships are also very powerful.

Nurture researcher and textbook author Judith Rich Harris suggests parents don't matter as much as our current culture teaches. She posits that, ultimately, peers play a much more influential role. "There are many different ways to rear a child, and no convincing evidence exists that one way produces better results than another," she says.

For example, different cultures have different myths about the role of parents. The current view that parents have a great deal of power to determine how their children will turn out is actually a rather new idea, she says. It began around the middle of the twentieth century. Before that, parenting had a very different job description. "Parents didn't worry about boosting the self-esteem of their children—in fact, they often felt that too much attention and praise might spoil them and make them conceited," Harris says.

Things have changed dramatically in the past seventy years, but overall the changes haven't had the expected effects. People are the same as ever. Despite the reduction in physical punishment, today's adults are no less aggressive than their grandparents were, she says. Despite the increase in praise and physical affection, they are not happier or more self-confident or in better mental health.

This doesn't deny that parents have a great deal of power, especially when we are tiny and most powerless. But it reminds us of how the wide variety of influences in our lives will affect our ability to love and be loved. That helps take parents off the hook. But it also brings up a new area to worry about: Who are your kids (or you) hanging out with? And what are these peer relationships and influences teaching about living and loving?

It's always something.

CHAPTER THREE

His Brain, Her Brain, Gay Brain, and Other Brains

Much is said about gender differences: how men and woman are like Mars and Venus, yin and yang, oil and water, night and day—opposites all the way, and especially (the mythology goes) in love and sex.

Neuroscientists keep refining their search for male-female brain differences that will answer George Bernard Shaw's question, "Why can't a woman be more like a man?" (and vice versa), or even Freud's eternal lament: "What *do* women want?"

Research has confirmed that, yes, our male and female brains do differ somewhat in anatomy, function, chemistry, and apparently in desires. Unfortunately some people have taken that as license to proclaim superiority in one skill or attribute or another. In fact, newer research is showing that many of those oft-touted differences might not be so great—or matter so very much—after all.

How Real Are the Differences?

As recently as the nineteenth century, some scientists were saying that the inferiority of a woman's intellect could be seen in her lighter and smaller brain. Few people would make that assertion today (and certainly not out loud or in public). For while women's brains are indeed about 10 percent smaller than most male brains, that's in proportion to the smaller overall size of females and not related to intellect. In fact, we all start out as female: the female state is the default, and it's only the addition of the Y chromosome from a sperm that makes the man.

Indeed, many of the myths surrounding the supposed superiority of differences in male and female brains could be mostly the result of minor inherent differences that may be emphasized by conditioning rather than biology, says psychology professor Janet Shibley Hyde.

Girls don't have the same mathematical proclivity as boys? Not completely true. Men can't communicate as well as women can in relationships? Not so either. And it turns out that the self-esteem problems usually associated with teenage girls are just as pronounced in teenage boys, says Hyde, who reviewed forty-six major gender studies conducted over the past twenty years. She suggests that we too often tend to concentrate on our differences instead of our similarities, and to exaggerate scientific findings that might unveil minor contrasts. Humans like to categorize, Hyde says, and once we devise categories, we immediately start judging one as better than another.

Consider the sophisticated brain imaging tools that are revealing some fascinating and actual differences between male and female brains. Unfortunately, some researchers are linking these observed differences in brain structure and function to psychological behavior in ways that foster some unwarranted—and spectacularly speculative—conclusions. For instance, a 2005 twenty-person study using functional magnetic resonance imaging (fMRI) led some nonscientists to conclude that women have no sense of humor. The study found that for women, the left prefrontal cortex, a brain area associated with rational thought, was more active than in men when both genders were shown the same funny cartoons. This led to all kinds of interpretations by the media including a *Vanity Fair* article by Christopher Hitchens stating that women had to work harder to get jokes—if they got them at all. Hitchens also said that men worked harder than women to be funny, but that's beside the point, which is this: we should take generalizations of such findings with extreme caution, says a review in *Current Directions in Psychological Science.*

For one thing, most neuroimaging studies are conducted with small numbers of subjects (say, twenty), where differences could easily be due to chance. Although the new techniques are indeed marvelous, they are not yet totally precise, which could skew observations. Moreover, participants are not a truly representative group for several reasons: many can't endure the extreme claustrophobia and loud noises of the scanning machines, which in themselves can distort brain reactions, and many participants are college students who are not representative of the overall population in age, education, and other areas. And despite today's technology, we still have little understanding of how the neural structures (and any differences we see) actually influence complicated behaviors such as laughter, longing, and falling in and out of love.

Taking the politics out of the sex, what do the brains of men, women, heterosexuals, homosexuals, transsexuals, bisexuals—and even asexuals—look like in terms of love and sex? We do know that even small differences can have large impacts, says Lise Eliot, an associate professor of neuroscience at the Chicago Medical School of Rosalind Franklin University and author of *Pink Brain, Blue Brain: How Small Differences Grow into Troublesome Gaps—and What We Can Do About It*. But such research results should be handled with care, she says. For example, preference in sexual identity and partnerships is apparently irrevocably etched in the developing fetal brain and cannot be changed. Who we are sexually, and who and how we love sexually, seems in most cases to be hardwired, beginning even before birth. But that doesn't preclude some experimentation.

Five Genders of the Brain

Sexual partner preference seems to be more slippery than suspected.

While it's fair to say that many more people than reported have had at least one sexual encounter with a member of the same gender, it's even more slippery to try to pin down actual numbers or percentages since studies are based on what people say. This is not only suspect from the get-go, it has tended to change depending on the era and the asker.

Alfred Kinsey, who debuted sex as a science and shocked Americans in the 1950s with his studies of sexual activity, said that it was impossible to determine the number of persons who are "homosexual" or "heterosexual." It was possible only to determine behavior at any given time, and his and other more recent studies find a greater number of people engage in same-sex sexual activity than identify as homosexual or bisexual.

And how do we define sexual activity in the first place? Apparently it varies, as a recent American president demonstrated when he firmly avowed, "I never had sexual relations with that woman," even after he was revealed to have had several oral sex encounters with her.

Taking all of that into consideration, here are some rough statistics based on how people state their sexual preferences in partners:

1. *Heterosexual.* Kinsey personally interviewed more than ten thousand men and women about their sexual practices between 1948 and 1953, with most reporting they were heterosexual, and that remains so. In the 2010 National Survey of Sexual Health and Behavior (NSSHB) that surveyed six thousand people, 92.2 percent of men and 93.1 percent of women, identified themselves as heterosexual.

2. *Homosexual.* According to the Kinsey reports, 37 percent of males and 13 percent of females in 1950s America had at least one same-sex encounter to orgasm, and 10 percent of males and 2 to 6 percent of females were predominantly gay. In the NSSHB survey, about 7 percent of adult women and 8 percent of men identify as gay, lesbian, or bisexual, but 9 percent of men and 2 percent of women reported a same-sex partner during their most recent sexual event.

3. *Bisexual.* Many other animals indulge in sexual activity with both genders, and some theorize that bisexuality may be a natural state for most people. However, humans admit to being less flexible: in a 1993 study, 5 percent of men and 3 percent of women considered themselves bisexual, and in 2010 about 2.6 percent of men and 3.6 percent of women so define themselves.

4. *Transsexual.* When biological gender and gender identity don't fit, it can be painful. The American Psychological Association estimates that 2 to 3 percent of biological males engage in cross-dressing as females, at least occasionally, and transsexualism estimates are about one in ten thousand for biological males and one in thirty thousand for biological females. Some live as members of their preferred sexual identity, and some choose to have gender-changing surgeries and hormone therapies.

5. *Asexual.* People who have no interest in sex whatsoever are a rarity, and luckily so, since sex is still the most used and useful form of reproduction. Information is sketchy, but it's estimated that fewer than 1 percent identify as asexual.

His Brain, Her Brain: The Geography

Scientists agree that there are anatomical, chemical, and functional differences between the brains of men and women that could directly affect relationships—but not as much perhaps as mythology would tell us. And in many cases, nobody knows for sure what impact such differences have on behavior and relationships.

For openers, some areas crucial to relationships differ in size or activity or both. Several studies show the amygdala, our internal fight-or-flight sentry, is larger in men than in women (which, some might say, would explain flight behavior by some men when confronted with a request for a committed relationship and help explain why they can be more physically aggressive). Women have a larger hippocampus, which is crucial for memory storage as well as spatial mapping (and it may be why women remember birthdays and anniversaries and have a better sense of direction).

Other studies show an imbalance in the activation of the right and left amygdala in men and women. When they are recalling highly charged emotional scenes—the kind that trigger empathetic responses—women's left amygdala is more strongly activated than their right amygdala, whereas the reverse is true in men. These results are interesting, but apparently it's not known if this left-right difference is related to empathy—or in fact exactly what it means in terms of any behavior.

Female brains have symmetrical hemispheres and a larger percentage of gray matter areas with closely packed neurons and fast blood flow. Male brains have a higher volume of connecting white matter tissue, nerve fibers that are insulated by a white fatty protein called myelin—and more gray matter in the left hemisphere.

Again, what that means is being conjectured.

Imaging studies show that females perform better at language and other skills that call for symmetrical activation of brain hemispheres. Males perform better at tasks requiring activity in the visual cortex, such as video games (it is also active in sex). And even when both genders perform equally well at a task, they sometimes use different brain areas.

Depression, posttraumatic stress disorder (PTSD), and anxiety are much more prevalent among women, and a positron emission tomography (PET) scan shows one possible contributor: male brains produce 52 percent more of the mood-leveling neurotransmitter serotonin than those of females. That brings up the issue of how hormones and neurotransmitters affect the brain. The sex hormones testosterone and estrogen have powerful effects on brain development, function, and behavior and contribute to sexual characteristics and activities.

Others note that psychological gender differences are not especially large, nor are differences in intellectual performance or basic relationship abilities such as empathy and even most types of aggression. Although structural and biochemical brain differences between the sexes are real, many experts feel their impact on behavior is exaggerated. Cordelia Fine, author of *Delusions of Gender: How Our Minds, Society and Neurosexism Create Difference*, says many studies that purport to find differences between the brains of girls and boys are flawed. There is no convincing evidence that our brains are hardwired according to gender and no such thing as "biological destiny," she writes.

So What Does This Have to Do with Love?

Our male and female brains do behave differently in love and sex, studies show.

When men looked at a picture of their beloved, they showed activity in the visual cortex and also brain regions associated with sexual arousal. Women, on the other hand, showed more activity in the caudate nucleus and the septum—brain areas connected with motivation, attention, and pleasure—and in areas associated with retrieval of memories.

And during orgasm, the ever-alert amygdala is tamped down in both the male and female brains, and a large part of the female brain goes completely silent, indicating that a woman needs to turn off her inner sentry to let loose. (See Chapter Four, "That Old Black Magic.")

When it comes to being dumped, male and female brains react in different ways. Women worldwide are more likely to suffer a major depression when they are abandoned in love, whereas men turn to alcohol or risky business and are three to four times more likely to commit suicide after a love affair gone wrong. (See Chapter Seven, "You've Lost That Lovin' Feelin'.") Studies also show a gender difference in online sexual activities: men are more likely to watch pornography, and women are more likely to participate in sexual chatrooms, suggesting that they prefer sexual stimulation in the context of interaction.

But is this difference really due to biology? That is, when men and women (and their brains) appear to react differently in love, is that nature or nurture? Are we born with or do we learn these different reactions? What about brain differences that could affect relationships such as falling and staying in love?

Assumptions that such differences are hardwired are risky given all we've learned about the plasticity of the human brain. Our brains change every minute in reaction to what we experience, feel, and think and in response to life and our environment, and we all have individual experiences and brains.

At first glance, it seems that fMRI studies of very young male and female brains would offer a way out of this nature-nurture dilemma. Gender differences in behavior and development that appear in infancy or childhood suggest they are innate—the result of prenatal hormone exposure or genes, or both. Differences that grow larger through childhood into adulthood are likely shaped by social learning—a consequence of the very different impacts from lifestyle, culture, and training that boys and girls experience in every society. So researchers looked at how the human brain handles relationships, or what scientists call social cognition—the way people interact with one another and their environment, certainly a big part of how we form relationships.

A study of adult brains did find that one subdivision of the ventral prefrontal cortex—an area called the straight gyrus (SG), which is involved in social cognition and interpersonal judgment—is proportionally larger in women compared to men. Peg Nopoulos, Jessica Wood, and colleagues at the University of Iowa found the SG to be about 10 percent larger in the thirty women they studied. What's more, they found that the size of the SG correlated with a widely used test of social cognition, in that individuals (both male and female) who scored higher in interpersonal awareness also tended to have larger SGs.

As the researchers delved more deeply into this research, they found just how difficult it is to untangle nature and nurture, even at the level of brain structure. They speculated about the evolutionary basis for this sex difference. Perhaps, since women are the primary child rearers, their brains have become programmed to develop a larger SG to prepare them to be sensitive nurturers? Prenatal sex hormones are known to alter behavior and certain brain structures in other mammals. Perhaps such hormones—or sex-specific genes—may enhance the development of females' SG (or dampen the development of males') leading to inborn differences in social cognition.

Thinking the best way to test this hypothesis was to look at children, Wood and Nopoulos conducted a second study. They measured the same frontal lobe areas in children between seven and seventeen years of age to see if differences in the SG are present early in life. They were—but the results were unexpected: they found that the SG is actually *larger* in boys. What's more, the same test of interpersonal awareness showed that skill in this area correlated with a smaller SG, not a larger one as in adults.

And a twist in both studies showed even more problems when trying to interpret any finding about sex differences in the brain.

Instead of simply dividing their subjects by biological gender, the researchers had also given each subject a test of psychological gender: a questionnaire to assess each person's degree of masculinity versus femininity—regardless of their biological sex—based on their interests, abilities, and personality type. In both adults and children, this measure of gender identity also correlated with SG size: larger SG correlated with more feminine personality in adults but less feminine personality in children.

In other words, there does seem to be a relationship between SG size and social perception, but it is not a simple male-female difference. Rather, the SG appears to reflect a person's gender identity, such as "femininity," better than one's biological sex: women who are relatively less feminine show a correspondingly smaller SG compared to women who are more feminine, and the same is true for men.

Our Changeable Brains

Are you following this so far? Men and women are psychologically different and, yes, neuroscientists are uncovering new information in brain anatomy and physiology that seems to explain some of our behavioral differences. But just because a difference is biological doesn't mean it is unchangeable or hardwired. Individuals' gender traits—their preference for masculine or feminine clothes, careers, hobbies, and interpersonal styles—are inevitably shaped by rearing and experience, as well as their biological sex.

The brains that are ultimately producing all of this masculine or feminine behavior must be molded, at least to some degree, by the sum of their experiences as a boy or girl. Many researchers who emphasize brain differences between the genders are overlooking the basic facts of neuroplasticity. We know now that the human brain is capable of enormous changes as networks of neurons are created and disbanded and as the brain grows new cells (though we don't know

Love Me Tender

Sex isn't everything: a good cuddle is just as important for most of us, says Justin Garcia, a SUNY Fellow in the Laboratory of Evolutionary Anthropology and Health at Binghamton University. And, he says, the sexes aren't as different in their desires as we often think. "People want emotional intimacy," says Garcia, who recently completed a study showing that both men and women are driven to connect emotionally. Roughly 95 percent of men and women he queried say they like to cuddle, among other intimate behaviors. But, he added, the context of who they are cuddling matters. When in romantic relationships, 97 percent of both men and women report that they like to cuddle up close with their partner, but in uncommitted sexual hookups, only 52 percent of men and 61 percent of women say they like to cuddle.

The same general trend is true for a host of intimate behavior, he adds. "We quite often see that sex isn't always just about sex—it is often one of many ways to find someone to love."

---

yet if or where these new neurons fit in exactly). We also know now that even the effects of some genes can be changed through a process called epigenetics: they can be turned off or on or made more or less effective.

It's crucial to keep in mind this finding that brain structure correlates as well or better with psychological gender than with simple biological sex when considering any comparisons of the male and female brain. The research and observations challenge the idea that such brain differences are a simple product of the Y chromosome.

And so any time scientists report a difference between male and female brains, especially in adults, it should raise an eyebrow and some questions. In this case, is women's larger SG the cause of their social sensitivity, or the consequence of living a lifetime in a group that practices greater empathetic responding?

Wood and colleagues are among the few neuroscientists to analyze male-female brain differences for their relationship to gender type as opposed to strict biological sex. Their findings do not prove that social learning is the cause of male-female differences in the brain. "Most sex differences start out small—as mere biases in temperament and play style—but are amplified as children's pink- or blue-tinted brains meet our gender-infused culture," Eliot says. "Genes and hormones light the spark for most boy-girl differences, but the flame is strongly fanned by the essentially separate cultures in which boys and girls grow up."

Some Myths About Male and Female Brains: True or False?

What about the assumptions of male and female brains we take for granted, and for science. Are they true? Here's the latest research on some sex- and love-related behaviors.

Male Brains Are More Violent

Well, yes, but it's more likely testosterone acting on their brains. In 1995 the late psychologist David Lykken of the University of Minnesota wrote that if we could magically place all boys and men between the ages of twelve and twenty-eight in a cryogenic freeze, we would slash the rate of violent crime by two-thirds.

The data bear him out. In the United States, the rate of violent crime for girls and women aged ten and older is one in fifty-six; the corresponding figure among their male counterparts is one in nine. Men commit close to 90 percent of the murders in the United States and are responsible for more murders than women in all the countries researchers have examined, according to a 1999 report by psychologist Anne Campbell of Durham University in England.

The effect of testosterone on brain function contributes to violent behavior, along with male upbringing and cultural and personal models of how a man should act in a relationship. Males are the more belligerent sex in virtually all mammalian species that biologists have studied. Even the one marked exception to this trend, the spotted ("laughing") hyena, may prove the rule. The female hyena, which is more physically aggressive than her male counterpart, has higher testosterone levels than the male does. And studies of testosterone levels in female prison inmates found that the most aggressive women had the higher levels of testosterone.

In a 2004 mathematical synthesis of 196 studies (known as a meta-analysis), psychologist John Archer of the University of Central Lancashire in England found that men are more physically aggressive (by various measures) than women across all ages, with the difference peaking between the ages of twenty and thirty. This sex difference extended to all ten countries Archer examined, which included the United States, Finland, Spain, India, Japan, and New Zealand. Interestingly, researchers have found men to be more physically aggressive in their mental lives as well. Compared with women, men harbor more frequent and enduring homicidal fantasies, more often think about enacting revenge against their enemies, and report more physically aggressive dreams.

There is more evidence for the role of testosterone on aggression: when males compete, testosterone levels in the losing males drop. Since testosterone is linked to aggression and risk taking, changes in testosterone levels after competition can help both winners and losers in all species, explains Steven Stanton, lead author of a study from Duke University and the University of Michigan at Ann Arbor. Victors may be motivated to pursue further gains, whereas also-rans are encouraged to back down so as not to press onward and potentially get injured.

The study used the 2008 U.S. presidential election results as an example of a competitive experience and looked at testosterone in male voters. They found that those who backed a losing candidate had a drop in the hormone. Female voters showed no significant testosterone changes after victory or defeat of their candidate.

Men Are More Violent Than Women in Matters of Sex and Love

It's a toss-up. When it comes to romantic or domestic arrangements, women can be violent too. They are just as likely as men to express hostility physically in a romantic relationship.

Indeed, investigators have consistently found that men exhibit more frequent and more extreme levels of physical aggression with one exception: in domestic disputes, the tables are often turned. The popular stereotype of a domestic abuser is a man who habitually harms his female partner. Research by Archer and sociologist Murray Straus of the University of New Hampshire demonstrates that men and women exhibit roughly equal rates of violence within relationships, and some studies hint that women's rates of physical aggression are slightly higher. This apparent equality is not solely a result of women fighting back, because it holds even for altercations that women start.

Still, domestic abuse within intimate relationships is a greater threat to women than to men. Women suffer close to two-thirds of the injuries, largely because men are stronger on average than women. In addition, women and men differ in the severity of their actions; women are more likely to scratch or slap their partners, and men more commonly punch or choke their partners.

Women Love More Than Men Do

This is probably true. Studies are showing that women may be more susceptible to many kinds of addiction, including drugs, alcohol, and sex, and so they may get hooked on love more than men do. It's all about the estrogen. Just as male brains are skewered by testosterone, so estrogen affects women. Scientists believe that estrogen spurs addiction by stimulating the brain's reward pathways, enhancing the highs.

National Institutes of Health research on gender and addiction noted that women more quickly escalate to heavy drug use than men do. Even female rats obsessively self-administer addictive drugs more readily than do male rodents.

The brains of women are especially vulnerable to the allures of addiction at certain times in their monthly cycle (another reason to call it "The Curse"?). As levels of estrogen and progesterone naturally wax and wane over the menstrual cycle, a woman's response to drugs varies also. Pleasurable things give far more pleasure to women during the estrogen-dominated follicular phase, which occupies the approximately two weeks from the onset of a woman's period until she ovulates, than during the luteal phase after ovulation, when both estrogen and progesterone are high. A study that looked at women smokers trying to quit found that 34 percent succeeded during the second part of their cycles, when progesterone levels are high, compared with only 14 percent of those who tried to stop smoking when progesterone levels were low.

Short of a chemical fix, paying attention to the calendar could help women succeed at kicking addictions to smoking, drinking, drugs, or a miserable lover. Conversely, she can calendar in her sexual encounters to take advantage of the highs. In the mix of hormones, brain chemicals, and desire—as in many other parts of life—timing may be everything.

Jealousy: Men Care About Sex; Women Care About Love

Well, it's not that simple. The theory is that men are more likely to be jealous of sexual betrayal because of the ancient urge to be certain an offspring is their own and that women value emotional fidelity because they want a partner to help raise their children.

So men value sex, and women value love. That's why the genders experience jealousy in different ways, right? Or is this an example of sexual stereotyping? It could be. A recent study from Pennsylvania State University suggests it may be time to rethink why individuals respond differently to infidelity in a partner.

In a study of more than four hundred people, clinical psychologists Kenneth Levy and Kristen Kelly found that jealousy patterns may be explained by individual personality differences that stem from a person's childhood experiences. The pair asked subjects what would be more upsetting: their partner having sex with someone else or forming a strong emotional bond with another person. Both men and women with an insecure attachment condition called dismissing—typical of people who had inconsistent or insensitive parents and learned to shun intimacy and become hyperindependent—were the most likely to report being jealous of sexual infidelity.

More men than women have a dismissing attachment style. This may relate in part to our cultural notions of what constitutes "manly" behavior. Levy says this understanding of personality formation, known as the attachment model, seems to explain both the average differences between men and women in what makes them most jealous, as well as why some people better fit the jealousy profile of their opposite sex.

Toujours Gay: The Gay Brain Is Born That Way

Researchers are confirming what most homosexuals have known all their lives: sexual orientation is neither a choice nor something in the way people are brought up. It's something influenced by genes and perhaps prenatal factors, and people are born that way.

Many gay men and lesbians say they knew they preferred the same sex from the time they were children. Brain scan research suggests that's probably true. In a recent study, brain scans show that the

---

SCENT OF A GENDER: SNIFFERS PREFER THEIR GENDER PREFERENCE

Sniffing may let us pick out partners of a preferred sexual orientation, and gay men apparently have a distinctive odor for reasons that are as yet largely speculative.

In a 2005 study, psychologist Yolanda Martins and sensory neuroscientist Charles Wysocki of the Monell Chemical Senses Center asked six heterosexual men, six gay men, six heterosexual women, and six lesbians to wear cotton gauze pads under their armpits for three days. After collecting the pads, Martins and Wysocki had eighty volunteers—of both sexes, gay and straight—take a big sniff of the gauze (whose wearers were not identified) and to report which pads smelled best. They found that heterosexual men and women and lesbians preferred the odor of the heterosexual men and women to that of gay men, whereas gay men favored the odor of other gay men. Heterosexuals of both sexes and lesbians also liked the scents of lesbians better than those of gay males.

---

brains of gay men are similar to those of straight women and that the brains of heterosexual men and lesbians are similar. The brain characteristics they scanned are those that develop in the womb or in early infancy, meaning that psychological or environmental factors played little or no role, said researchers at the Stockholm Brain Institute in Sweden.

The researchers used MRI scans to look at the brains of ninety volunteers—twenty-five straight and twenty gay members of each sex. They found that the straight men and gay women had asymmetrical brains; that is, the cerebrum was larger on the right hemisphere of the brain than on the left. They also found that the brains of straight women and gay men had symmetrical cerebrums.

The team next used PET scans to measure the blood flow to the amygdala, the seat of emotion, fear, and aggression. They scanned the brains when at rest to minimize external and learned influences, and they found that in gay men and straight women, the blood flowed to areas involved in fear and anxiety—but in straight men and lesbians, it tended to flow to pockets linked to aggression.

The question about whether sexual partner preference is genetic or if genes are involved at all is unresolved. But it's known that the chances of being homosexual (or heterosexual) increase if other family members also share that sexual preference. Studies of twins raised together, twins raised apart, and family trees suggest that, at least for males, the more genes that are shared with a homosexual relative, the more likely a person is to be homosexual.

No advances in science will ever completely resolve the moral, cultural, and philosophical issues around sexual orientation. Enormous pressures push most of us toward the straight end of the sexual orientation continuum from the time we are very young. Also, some religious and other groups claim gays can switch to straight if they really want to. While that may be true for some, most gays can't switch—or don't feel very comfortable about it if they do.

Most heterosexuals also feel very definite and fairly rigid about their sexual identity. Yet in some cultures, young people experiment with same-gender sex before settling down with an opposite-sex partner to raise children. And in the animal kingdom at large, bisexuality—sex acts with either gender—is common.

Can Animals Be Gay? Better to Call It Bisexual

Two penguins native to Antarctica met one spring day in 1998 in a tank at the Central Park Zoo in midtown Manhattan. They took turns diving in and out of the clear water, entwined necks, called to each other, and mated. They then built a nest together to prepare for an egg. But no egg was forthcoming because Roy and Silo were both male.

After a keeper at the zoo watched the chinstrap penguin pair roll a rock into their nest and sit on it, he found an egg from another pair of penguins that was having difficulty hatching and slipped it into Roy and Silo's nest. The loving couple took turns warming the egg with their blubbery underbellies. After thirty-four days, a female chick pecked her way into the world. Roy and Silo were devoted parents to the gray, fuzzy chick that was named Tango.

The penguin's same-sex pairing was a surprise to humans and stirred up quite a bit of controversy. Like most other animal species, penguins tend to pair with the opposite sex, for the obvious reproductive reason, and that's the way the largely heterosexual population seems to like it. But researchers are finding that same-sex couplings are surprisingly widespread in the animal kingdom. Roy and Silo belong to one of as many as fifteen hundred species of wild and captive animals, from insects to apes, that have been observed engaging in homosexual activity.

Researchers have seen such same-sex goings-on in male and female, old and young, and social and solitary creatures on all branches of the evolutionary tree. Unlike most humans, however, animals generally don't stick to either gay or straight categories. An animal that engages in a same-sex flirtation or partnership does not necessarily shun heterosexual encounters, and vice versa. That is, there are probably no strictly gay critters, just bisexual ones.

Researchers speculate that animals engage in same-sex couplings for diverse reasons—to make peace, diffuse social tensions, better protect or support their young, because opposite-sex partners are unavailable—or simply because it's fun. "Animals don't do sexual identity. They just do sex," says sociologist Eric Anderson of the University of Bath in England.

This evidence suggests to some that bisexuality is a natural state among animals, including, perhaps, *Homo sapiens*, despite the sexual orientation boundaries most of us take for granted and rigidly enforce.

Homosexuality among some species, including penguins and people, appears to be far more common in captivity or in enclosed environments than in the wild. Captivity may bring out gay behaviors in part because of a scarcity of opposite-sex mates or because being confined boosts stress levels, leading to a greater urge to relieve the stress through sex. Some of the same influences may encourage what some researchers call situational homosexuality in humans in same-sex settings such as prisons, the military, or sports teams.

I Am What I Am

Studies and reports of animal homosexuality date to the late nineteenth century and the first half of the 1900s. Back then, scientists generally considered homosexual acts among animals to be abnormal. In some cases, they "treated" the animals by castrating them or giving them lobotomies. A 1914 report, however, eased tensions and gave insight into possible reasons for behavior when a psychopathologist practicing in Montecito, California, reported that same-sex behavior in twenty Japanese macaques and two baboons occurred largely as a way of making peace with would-be foes. He observed that female macaques offered sex to the more dominant macaques of the same sex, while homosexual alliances between mature and immature males seemed to ensure the younger male an adult defender in the event of an attack.

More recently, some researchers studying bonobos (close relatives of the chimpanzee and notorious for their promiscuity) have noted that about half their sexual activity involves same-sex partners— again, behavior that seems to ease social tensions. Conflict between two adults of the same gender is often resolved by sex, suggesting that these homosexual acts may be a sensible peacekeeping strategy (and perhaps an example to humans for resolving crises?).

"The more homosexuality, the more peaceful the species," asserts Petter Böckman, an academic adviser at the University of Oslo's Museum of Natural History in Norway. Homosexual bonding and even polygamous trios among animals can also be a sensible life strategy, fostering cooperative parenting that produces more offspring and protects them better against predators. Other animals may turn to homosexuality when there are no opposite-sex partners available, to maintain reproductive fitness and an interest in sex. In males, this benefit is obvious: sexual behavior, homosexual or heterosexual, stimulates the continued production of seminal fluid and sperm.

And many animals do it simply "because they want to," Böckman adds. "People view animals as robots who behave as their genes say, but animals have feelings, and they react to those feelings. . . . As long as they feel the urge [for sex], they'll go for it."

In a study published in 2008 in the journal *Sex Roles*, Eric Anderson found that 40 percent of forty-nine heterosexual former high school football players attending various U.S. universities had had at least one homosexual encounter. These ranged from kissing to oral sex to threesomes that included a woman.

In fact, in team sports, homosexuality is "no big deal, and it increases cohesion among members of that team," Anderson claims. "It feels good, and [the athletes] bond." In stressful same-sex environments such as prisons or a war zone, heterosexuals who allege to hate gays may engage in homosexual behavior in part to relieve tension. It could be interesting to see what, if any, effect there will be from the change that now allows gays to serve openly in the U.S. armed forces.

"Homosexuality appears mostly in social species," Böckman says. "It makes flock life easier, and jail flock life is very difficult."

In recent decades, zoo officials have tried to minimize the stresses of captivity by making their enclosures more like animals' natural habitats. Zoo homes have become more hospitable, with more open space and more objects for animals to play with. Researchers hope such improvements might affect animal behavior, making it more

LET THEM BE GAY—OR WHATEVER

Some were incensed when Roy and Silo, the coupled penguins at the Central Park Zoo in Manhattan, formed a loving relationship and, when given a fertilized egg, hatched and raised a female baby named Tango. Articles about their relationship caused a furor. A children's book about the unusual family, *And Tango Makes Three*, won many awards but was attacked by conservative religious groups: the American Library Association reports it was the most challenged book of 2006, 2007, and 2008 and the most banned book of 2009.

Conversely, when workers at Bremerhaven's Zoo on the Sea in Germany discovered that three of their five endangered Humboldt penguin couples were of the same sex, keepers brought in four female Humboldt penguins from Sweden in hopes of tempting the males to reproduce. That action angered gay and lesbian groups around the world. A group of European gay activists protested what they called "organized and forced harassment through female seductresses."

In the end, the males were not swayed. "The males have scarcely thrown the females a single glance," said zoo director Heike Kück. So more males were flown in to keep the Swedish females company. As for Roy and Silo, that union ended when Silo deserted Roy after six years to be with a newly arrived female penguin from California. C'est l'amour.

like what occurs in the wild, including reflecting the lower rate of homosexuality in wild members of the same species. Some people, however, contest the notion that zookeepers should prevent or discourage homosexual behavior among the animals they care for.

Perhaps certain environments bring out normal tendencies suppressed in other settings, for humans as well as animals. In other words, some experts argue that humans are naturally bisexual, because the idea of exclusive homosexuality or heterosexuality isn't really accurate, biologist Joan E. Roughgarden says. "Homosexuality is mixed in with heterosexuality across cultures and history."

ARE PEOPLE REALLY BISEXUAL?

Is bisexuality a distinct sexual preference in humans—or just an excuse for some who are homosexual to eschew that label?

In 2005, a paper in *Psychological Science* debunked the idea that men have bisexual attraction. It concluded they're either gay or straight. That may still be up for debate for men, but apparently not for women. Researchers say that bisexuality legitimately exists in women. In 2008, the American Psychological Association published the first longitudinal study of female bisexuality. Lisa Diamond studied seventy-nine women over a ten-year period in an attempt to define female bisexuality. She found no evidence for the commonly held view that bisexuality is an experimental phase, en route to lesbianism or heterosexuality. Rather, she found that bisexuality in women is a distinct and consistent sexual orientation. Interestingly, she also found that as women age, they become more aware of their sexual fluidity and thus tend to turn more toward bisexuality than away from it.

And although bisexuals continue to be attracted to both sexes as they age, they are more likely than heterosexuals or lesbians to settle into monogamous relationships.

The Third Gender: When Gender and Sex Do Not Align

Scientists have realized that biological sex, gender identity, and sexual orientation are three distinct, independent variables. In transsexuality, a person feels an unhappy mismatch between his or her biological sex and gender identity.

Biological sex is perhaps the most straightforward of the three variables at the heart of the science of transsexuality. We all have a set of sex chromosomes that identifies each of us as either a genetic male

(XY) or a genetic female (XX). There are many genetic disorders in which sex chromosomes are either missing or redundant (for example, XYY), and birth defects can occur in which infants are born with ambiguous genitalia or genitalia of both genders. But in general, researchers who study gender identity disorder—the clinical term for what we colloquially know as transsexuality—say transsexuals are people with normal chromosomes who are biologically male or female but who feel psychologically like the opposite sex.

This brings us to the concept of gender, which is meaningfully different from biological sex. Gender identity is a subjective feeling of "maleness" and "femaleness." In most cases, biological (genetic) males have a male gender identity, and biological females have a female gender identity.

When there's a disconnection between a person's biological sex and his or her gender identity, there can be an uncomfortable gender dysphoria—a persistent negative emotional state that's often a factor in the momentous decision to undergo sex reassignment surgery, which some transsexuals choose. The third variable related to sex and gender is sexual orientation. Most biological males are attracted to biological females, and vice versa. Yet the very fact that homosexuals (and bisexuals) exist and, more important, are represented by such a wide stereotype-shattering spectrum of individuals that includes both "lipstick lesbians" and very masculine gay men, shows clearly that sexual orientation too is different from both biological sex and gender identity. However, homosexuality itself is not a transsexual behavior: gay men in general do not want to become women. Transsexual people can be straight or gay.

Even within the transsexual community, there is much diversity. For example, a biological male who experiences gender dysphoria, and thus "feels" like a female, can be either gay or straight when it comes to his sexual orientation and partner preference. And beyond the mixing and matching that occurs between sex, gender, and sexual orientation, a huge array of psychological and cultural factors seems to underlie or affect transsexuality. Scientists are only starting to unravel these many influences. As we say, it's complicated.

A good example of gender dysphoria and its complications is Chaz, formerly Chastity Bono, offspring of entertainers Sonny and Cher, who is biologically female but psychologically male. After living most of her adult life as a lesbian, Bono announced in mid-2008 that he was in fact a transsexual and had begun to transition from the lesbian "Chastity" to the straight male identity of "Chaz." Chaz is just as attracted to his girlfriend, Jennifer, as Chastity was before the transition, only given Bono's physical metamorphosis, theirs is arguably no longer a same-sex relationship.

"Gender is between your ears and not between your legs," Bono said during a 2009 interview with ABC's *Good Morning America*.

Are There Asexuals Among Us? On the Possibility of a Fourth Sexual Orientation

Some scientists believe that there may be a fourth sexual orientation in our species that has absolutely no desire and sexual interest in males or females. In fact, those who are asexual have a complete and lifelong lack of sexual attraction toward any human (or nonhuman) being. Unlike bisexuals, who are attracted to both males and females, asexuals are equally indifferent to and uninterested in having sex with either gender. These individuals aren't simply celibate, which is a lifestyle choice. Rather, sex to them is boring, writes *Scientific American* blogger Jesse Bering.

Bering quotes Brock University psychologist Anthony Bogaert who says there may be more genuine asexuals than we realize. In 2004 Bogaert analyzed survey data from more than eighteen thousand British residents and found that the number of people (185, or about 1 percent) in this study population who described themselves as "never having a sexual attraction to anyone" was not much lower than those who identified in that study as being attracted to the same sex (3 percent). Since this discovery, a handful of academic researchers have been trying to determine whether asexuality is a true biological phenomenon or a slippery social label that for various reasons some people may prefer.

Sexual desire in the brains of most of us may wax and wane or, as many people on antidepressants have experienced, become virtually nonexistent due to medications, disease, chromosomal abnormalities (such as Turner syndrome in which females have an incomplete or missing X chromosome), or childhood sexual trauma. But if it exists as a fourth orientation, true asexuality would be due to none of these.

Not much is known about the reason (Bogaert speculates it may be traced to prenatal alterations of the hypothalamus), and most asexual people are normal, healthy, hormonally balanced, and sexually mature adults who, for still-uncertain reasons, have always found sex to be one big, bland yawn.

Asexuality appears to be like other sexual orientations in the sense that it is not acquired but rather an essential part of one's biological makeup. Just as a straight man or a lesbian can't easily change preferences, neither could a person (in principle, anyway) "become" asexual.

But the story of asexuality is very complicated. The AVEN (Asexuality and Visibility Education Network) Web site forums show a tremendous variation in the sexual inclinations of those who consider themselves asexual. Some masturbate; some don't. Some are interested in nonsexual romantic relationships (including cuddling and kissing but no genital contact), while others aren't. Some consider themselves to be "hetero-asexual" (having a nonsexual aesthetic or romantic preference for those of the opposite sex), while others see themselves as "homo-" or "bi-asexuals." There's even a matchmaking Web site for sexless love called asexualpals.com with the tagline, "Because there is so much more to life!"

Many asexuals are also perfectly willing to have sex if their partners want it. It's not awkward or painful for them, but, rather like making toast or emptying the trash, they just don't personally derive pleasure from the act. Thus, while many asexuals are virgins, others are, ironically, even more experienced than traditionally sexual people. Some want children through artificial means such as in vitro fertilization; others are willing to have them the old-fashioned way or don't want children at all.

If some asexuals masturbate in the absence of sexual fantasy or porn, then what exactly is it that's getting them physically aroused? And how does one have an orgasm, as some asexuals apparently do, without experiencing pleasure?

Scientists have just scratched the surface in studying human asexuality: You can count the number of studies on the subject on one hand. Does asexuality, like homosexuality, have heritable components? Certainly it's plausible. After all, historically, female asexuals would have probably had offspring with their male sexual partners, thus ensuring continuity of the genetic bases of asexuality.

If sex is nature's feel-good ruse to get our genes out there, could there be a natural category of human beings that is immune to evolution's greatest gag?

CHAPTER FOUR

That Old Black Magic
Your Brain in Love

Romantic love—hot, mad, sexual, passionate love—can shake us to our very foundations.

Aflame with desire, we ache and tremble in a fever of lust and ecstasy. We burn, we yearn, we thrill. We crave the object of our affection above all others, night and day, and the hunger for the beloved replaces other appetites: we lose sleep, we don't eat. Sometimes we feel our very heart has been ripped out and given away.

Obsessed, we long to possess every atom of the other, to be consumed. The beloved has become the sun and the moon—the everything—and we are willing to risk everything to be together, even life.

How long has this been going on? Writings from thousands of years ago echo these same passions we express today. How can romantic love have such powerful and universal effects?

If this is the first chapter you turned to—the one you really want to read—no wonder. We're all looking for our own true loves, our other halves, the perfect meeting, mating, and merging of two adults who each fulfill what's missing in the other, and that includes sexual union.

Mature romantic love embodies our deepest wish: to be totally united with another, mind and body, heart and soul. It is the crown jewel of loving, fulfilling our yearning to be completed, and at its best, it combines all of our other loves: that of the child, the parent, the friend, and even the spiritual, as many people speak of finding the divine in the loved one. It goes beyond the passion of lust—but come to think of it, the lust part is pretty good too.

The very word *erotic* takes its name from Eros, the Greek god of love, usually portrayed as a mischievous winged cherub who shoots arrows of desire into the hearts of the unsuspecting, engendering in them an immediate burning passion for the loved object. You know what that's like: love at first sight, or as the French call it, *coup de foudre*—a thunderbolt.

In *The Brain in Love*, neuroscientist Daniel G. Amen describes that magic flash point of sexual connection: "As you walk by me, millions of nerve cells spark in my brain and I have to turn to look at you again. You look back at me and a soft, brief smile forms on your lips. . . . Your smile triggers an adrenaline release that causes my heart to leap with excitement. Chemicals send increased blood flow to sensitive areas as thoughts of you light the emotional fire centers of my mind. For a brief moment you literally live in my skin."

Such sexual passion remains the stuff of our hopes and dreams, played out in novels, films, operas (classical and soap), popular songs, and gossip. Biologists, sociologists, psychologists, and neuroscientists have long been mesmerized by sexual passion, as well as by the act (and, we suspect, not merely in an academic way).

The effects of sexual arousal, response, and orgasm were obvious, but the physiology wasn't well understood until the early 1960s when researchers William H. Masters and Virginia E. Johnson took a keen

YOU COMPLETE ME: WHY WE LOOK FOR
OUR OTHER HALF

We say it all the time: we're looking for (or the lucky ones have found) our "other half."

Two thousand years ago, the Greeks had some ideas about why we yearn for love, and a theory about that missing half. The great Greek poet and playwright Aristophanes explained half-humorously why we incessantly and sometimes obsessively yearn for the Other who will complete us.

Once, he told students in a famous symposium with the philosopher Plato, all humans were composed of two entities connected back-to-back to make one creature with four arms, four legs, and two heads. He posited three kinds of these beings: the all male, the all female, and the androgynous, which was half-man, half-woman.

Alas, these beings became prideful, challenging the very gods. And when they angered Zeus by trying to scale the heights of heaven, he cast thunderbolts that split them in two. Ever since, we have been longing to find that other half, whether in eros, philia, or agape.

Aristophanes proposed this theory in jest, but for many of us, it rings so very true, as myriad popular songs confirm. The human brain can get very lonely sitting in its fortress of bone, and yearns to connect with another.

interest. Thanks to their exhaustive laboratory research observing people having sex in more than ten thousand cycles from arousal to completion in many interesting and sometimes novel ways, we know much more about what are coyly called the man parts and the lady parts, as well as about what happens in their union. (Masters and Johnson also showed that women are multiorgasmic, wrote two best-sellers, and eventually divorced their spouses and married each other.)

But it took brain imaging to begin to unveil the deepest mystery of sexual passion. Scientists now know for sure what we always suspected: sex is acted out with the genitals, but desire, arousal, and orgasm happen in the brain—in several places in the brain, in fact. And while we often talk about how lust leads our bodies to take over our brains, it's more a case of our emotional brain parts taking over our prefrontal cortex—our thinking brain.

How Love and Sex Are Good for Your Brain

Being in love makes you feel good, or even better than good. So does sex. You go around in a haze of euphoria, well-being, and preoccupation with the beloved.

Now science shows that love and sex do more than just make you feel great. They're good for your heart, brain, and mind. They ease pain, can improve your thinking and creativity, and can even spur the creation of new brain cells.

Sex lowers blood pressure (eventually) and thus heart attack and stroke risk: men who report having orgasms twice a week had a lower risk of heart attack. Sex even encourages the brain to reproduce itself: Scientists who have been studying neurogenesis report in a 2010 study that regular sex can prompt the brain to make new neurons (in rats at least).

Just the thought of love or sex can improve brain performance, but in different ways. Thoughts about the two states have different impacts on performance: Love makes us creative, whereas sex makes us analytical, report authors of a 2009 study intriguingly titled, "Why Love Has Wings and Sex Has Not: How Reminders of Love and Sex Influence Creative and Analytic Thinking."

Previous research suggested that love, a broad, long-term emotion, triggers global brain processing and creative thinking: the state in which we see the big picture, make broad associations, and connect disparate ideas. Sex, a more specific "right now" activity, prompts analytical thinking and local processing in which the brain zooms in and focuses on the details. Indeed.

The researchers wondered whether these brain states could be put to work to improve specific performance. They asked thirty people to imagine a long, loving walk with their partners and asked thirty others to think of casual sex with someone they didn't love. Then they gave the subjects cognitive tests. The creative task involved solving a problem about the provenance of an antique coin that involved a leap in reasoning; the analytical section consisted of logical mathematical questions from the Graduate Record Examination. As predicted, the love-primed subjects performed much better on creative tasks and scored worse on analytical questions, while the reverse was true of those who thought only about sex. When researchers primed another group to think about love or sex, they got similar results. However, the authors noted, when the dust settles, most neuroscientists seem to agree that all of the brain systems for passionate love, sexual desire, and attachment in fact communicate and coordinate with one another.

Love can also trump pain when it activates the brain's reward system. Brain researchers at two institutions—pain specialist Sean Mackey at Stanford and love specialist Arthur Aron at Stony Brook University—teamed up to look at pain and love in the brain.

Stanford researchers recruited fifteen undergraduates in the early euphoric throes of a love relationship. The volunteers had photos of the romantic partner and an attractive acquaintance. As they looked at the photos, their palms were (safely) heated to the point of mild pain. Since previous research found that almost any distraction can ease pain, they did the experiment with both the love object photos and with other less charged tasks such as asking volunteers to think of sports that don't use balls.

That may not have been as interesting as sex. But both the mundane distraction and the pictures of the new lovers reduced pain, although in different ways. Viewing the love photo had a greater pain-relieving effect and acted in an area of the brain not associated with distraction-induced analgesia: the primitive reward system where addictive drugs (and sex) work and pain-relieving opioid drugs do their magic.

When Love Occupies Your Brain

Not surprisingly, the same parts of your brain that sit up and sing when you are in love or sexually excited are the ones activated by heroin and music: sex, drugs, and rock and roll do go together, after all. In fact, sexual pleasure rides our reward system as much as any drug: it has been said that orgasm is the most powerful legal high you can get without a prescription.

The reward system is powerful because it's one of our best survival tools: it makes pleasurable what we need to do to propagate for our species to survive. Indeed, propagation must be very high on the list, since the pleasures of sex can be so extremely satisfying and also because the act itself is so downright dangerous: orgasm requires a quieting of our inner sentry, the amygdala, and thus a weakening of our defenses to attack or disaster. (And, porn movies aside, it also looks fairly ridiculous when we ordinary middling-attractive people are not in the throes of participation, but that's another issue entirely.)

Many researchers have described sexual love as a drive, an urge, and even a hunger. A small multi-institute study confirms it: that powerful rush we feel when newly in love is not really an emotion. It's a reward produced by ancient brain pathways that similarly motivate eating and drinking.

The study indicates that during the intoxicating early stages of a relationship, "we are driven," says Lucy L. Brown, a neuroscientist at the Albert Einstein College of Medicine and a coauthor of the study. The brain encourages an intense focus on the beloved through the reward system. "The person we are in love with becomes a goal in our lives."

This is not exactly news, but scientists need to prove their theories. Brown and her colleagues recruited seventeen subjects who were eighteen to twenty-six years old and had been smitten for one to seventeen months. The researchers used functional magnetic resonance (fMRI) imaging to see how the subjects' brains responded to a picture of their beloved, in contrast with an image of an acquaintance.

For every lovebird, gazing at his or her sweetheart activated the unconscious neural system associated with reward, which experts believe arose early in our mammalian evolution to encourage vital behaviors. Other neural activity varied; for example, some individuals who had been in love for more than eight months had stronger signals in cortical areas involved in cognition and emotion. That has been confirmed by later studies that show longer-lasting love does involve our thinking brains.

Their findings led Brown and others to conclude that early romantic love is not an emotion at all but a motivational state. The brain encourages an intense focus on the beloved through the reward system. Then, thanks to the many neural systems linked to our reward circuitry, we experience other feelings.

Her group also studied what happens to the brain when personally rejected by showing subjects a picture of a recent ex-boyfriend or ex-girlfriend. This, Brown noted, "was not so rewarding." (See Chapter Seven, "You've Lost That Lovin' Feelin', for a description of that unhappy research.)

Who Do You Love? And Who Loves Ya, Baby?

How do we choose our lovers and mates—and how do they choose us?

One concept suggests we have constructed elaborate "love maps" and look for the person (or persons) to fit them. The late John Money, professor of medical psychology and pediatrics at Johns Hopkins University, is credited with coining the term. In a 1988 book of that name, Money says he developed the idea of love maps as a shorthand expression to describe for students "an idealized and highly idiosyncratic image" of a desirable other. "Everyone knew immediately exactly what I was talking about," he wrote.

And you probably do too. It's a blueprint of your idealized lover, against which you measure and rate all prospective mates. It includes your likes and dislikes and preferences in hair and eye color, voice, smell, body build and personality type, and possibly profession and income. Everyone has an idealized love, he thought, and we aren't born with them but learn and develop them over time.

That may be so. Psychologists have many other wide-ranging theories about who our brains choose to love. In her book, *Why We Love*, anthropologist and love expert Helen Fisher presents a summary of various theories from several noted experts of why we choose who we choose to fall in love with. They include, not surprisingly, more than a nod to our first great loves: our parents. Our attachment style—the way we learned to attach to our parents and other caregivers in childhood—seems to carry over into our adult lives and romances.

Take your choice of these scenarios. We seek attachments that: mirror our relationship with our moms or our dads; with partners who suffered similar childhood traumas; with partners who have qualities we lack or who satisfy a need; with those who have the same level of independence or who handle anxiety the same way we do; with those who are similar to the parent with which we have an unresolved childhood issue—or with someone we think absolutely, totally, and completely loves us.

CAN MEDITATION MAKE YOU A BETTER LOVER?

Most likely. Studies have shown that meditation can lower blood pressure and reduce stress. Recent findings suggest that meditation may actually change the physical structure of the brain in areas that are important for sensory, cognitive, and emotional processing and improve the ability to pay attention and improve compassion—all qualities important for making love and bonding.

Neuroscientist Richard J. Davidson of the University of Wisconsin–Madison has been active in many meditation studies. In research that shows meditation can increase concentration, he and his colleagues asked seventeen people who had received three months of intensive training in meditation and twenty-three meditation novices to perform an attention task in which they had to successively pick out two numbers embedded in a series of letters. The novices did what most other people do, the investigators announced in June: they missed the second number because they were still focusing on the first—a phenomenon called attentional blink. In contrast, all the trained meditators consistently picked out both numbers, indicating that practicing meditation can improve focus—the ability to pay attention to the very moment, whatever you are doing—and focus is very good for making love.

Davidson and his colleagues also compared expert meditators with novices and found that meditation can increase compassion. When long-time meditators engaged in compassionate meditation, the brain region known as the insula burst into action when they heard the sound of a woman in distress. The insula has been associated with the visceral feeling of emotion, a key part of empathizing with another's emotional state. And when these experts heard the female screams or the sound of a baby laughing, their brains showed more activity than the novices in areas like the right temporal parietal juncture, which plays a role in understanding another's emotion.

Another recent new study (rather alarmingly but reasonably) suggests that we prefer mates who resemble our opposite-sex parent. A Hungarian team found correlations of facial proportions between men and their partner's father and between women and their partner's mother. The findings support a sexual imprinting hypothesis: children shape a mental template of their opposite-sex parent and search for a partner who looks like it.

What about the old rule in physics that opposites attract? Popular culture has grabbed on to that and applied it to romance. Think of Hollywood movies and TV sitcoms: *Harold and Maude*, *Pretty Woman*, *The Ugly Truth*. Alas, research busts this myth—for the long haul at least. Psychologist Donn Byrne has found that we are twice as likely to be attracted to someone when we agree on six out of ten issues than we are to someone with whom we agree with on only three out of ten issues. But don't overlook sexual chemistry: at least for the short (very short) haul, we are likely to respond to a very, very attractive other regardless of mutual agreement on life's main political, social, and moral issues.

For example, a 2006 University of Pennsylvania study of speed dating found that daters said they wanted someone who had a similar background in education, religion, and economic status and shared personality traits. Yet when they were in the midst of the one-minute date, they made choices based on more immediate cues such as physical attraction. In the speed-dating environment—a bar surrounded by singles, under the pressure of a ticking clock—daters made choices based on what researchers euphemistically called short-term mating criteria that were more likely to lead to fast hookups, but not necessarily long-lived love.

That quick appeal may not last: the attractiveness of shared interests applies to long-term relationships. So if it's the long haul you're searching for, look beyond the cute face and hot body and see if you can carry the conversation beyond sixty seconds.

Can't Take My Eyes Off of You

When your loved one claims to "only have eyes for you," it might be truer than you think. When in love, we don't look at others than the beloved—or at least not in the same way. Attractive faces of others, it seems, hold no power over people in love.

Research shows that people in a committed relationship who have been thinking about their partner actually avert their eyes from attractive members of the opposite sex without even being aware they are doing so.

Psychologist Jon Maner of Florida State University and his colleagues put this to the test. They knew from earlier research that people who see attractive faces of the opposite sex on a computer screen take longer to shift their attention away to a less interesting object, such as a square or circle. Maner took subjects who were married or living together monogamously and asked half of them to write about feelings of love for their partner and asked the other half to write about a happy experience. They then flashed pictures of faces on a computer screen for half a second, following each immediately with a square or circle, and they asked participants to identify the shape by pushing the correct button.

Those who wrote about being in love actually turned their attention away from attractive members of the opposite sex even more quickly than they looked away from average-looking people. Subjects who wrote about being happy, however, remained distracted by a pretty face.

Psychologists speculate that this unconscious attentional bias probably evolved to help men and women stay in monogamous relationships, which in humans tend to have a reproductive advantage. Maner says: "This whole research area is guided largely by an evolutionary perspective. These biases have been built into our psychology to enhance people's reproductive success."

So if your beloved appears to be grazing—er, *gazing*—elsewhere, it might be time to put some new life in your love.

You've Got That Lovin' Feelin', But What Turns You On?

The specifics of sexual arousal are as individual as we are (and perhaps say more about us than we want anyone who is not sharing our bed and bod to know). But the overall biology igniting our brain's sex drive is darn near universal and something we share with all mammals. What we see and smell are our sexiest turn-ons, even before we get to the touching part.

"Wine comes in at the mouth, love comes in at the eyes," wrote poet William Butler Yeats. And for humans, he was right. Just one look may be all it takes: visual cues help us determine in less than a second if we find another person attractive.

Stephanie Ortigue and Francesco Bianchi-Demicheli, who have been studying where love works in the brain among other aspects of relationships and neuroscience, say we can tell in a fifth of a second if someone is attractive to us. "In other words: your brain knows in a blink of an eye whether you desire someone or not," Ortigue says.

Visual simulation is especially key for men, which might explain the popularity of pornographic videos, strip clubs, leather, and high heels. Some French scientists even showed that the mirror neurons of men who were viewing sexy videos activated in correspondence with the magnitude of their erections.

You Go to My Nose: The Power of Smell over Sex

Scent may be as powerful as visual stimulation in sex. We've long known that smell is a key to unlocking powerful memories, especially sense memory, and that it's involved in sexual arousal in humans as well as in other animals.

Smell is one of our oldest senses and is more strongly connected with emotions, which also evolved early, than with reasoning. Business knows the power of smell. Perfume is a billion-dollar industry based on scent and sexual attraction, and many other products trade on our sense of smell, from new cars to fabric softener.

Scientists have found that the information our brain gets from our sense of smell directs and defines our social, romantic, and sexual relationships. Our brains react strongly to scent, even very subtle scent. We subconsciously use smell to assess another's likability, sexual attractiveness, emotional state, and genetic compatibility. Through scent, we can tell stranger from friend, male from female, and even gay from straight. We can tell if someone is afraid, has an immune problem, is too closely related genetically to make a good reproductive match, and is sexually available. In mice, the scent of an alpha male spurs the growth of new brain cells in the female smeller. Problems with the sense of smell could contribute to social isolation (as well as a diminished sex drive) and often accompany schizo-phrenia. People with Alzheimer's disease typically lose their ability to smell.

Smell has been devalued for centuries in so-called civilized soci-eties as a bestial, "animalistic" sense. These cultures lean heavily on the bath, the perfume, and the absence of authentic body odor. It's a puri-tanical hangover from a Victorian attitude about civilization—that people who are civilized should be scent free. In fact, women and men are attracted to the real smell of their mates, not the perfume or after-shave.

The messages we get from olfactory bulbs in our brains are essen-tial, research is showing. Look at nature: every living organism has some form of chemosensory detection mechanism that enables it to sense threats at a distance, says neuroscientist Johan Lundström of the Monell Chemical Senses Center in Philadelphia.

True, humans don't have the olfactory equipment of a blood-hound. We do, however, have a remarkably sophisticated apparatus that our brain depends on to both guide us to pleasures and warn us of dangers.

How the Nose Knows

When we inhale, air currents infused with chemicals swirl up the nose, passing over the moist olfactory tissues on the roof of the nasal cavity and its roughly 12 million odor-detecting cells. Tiny hair-like cilia on each olfactory cell are covered with proteins that grasp odor molecules as they enter the nose. Each odor-detecting cell bears one of about 350 different olfactory receptor proteins and is specialized for sensing a limited number of odorant molecules. These receptor proteins work in different combinations to enable people to detect at least ten thousand scents. Sensory nerves carry signals from the odor-detecting cells to the brain's olfactory bulb, which in turn relays information about the inhaled odors to other areas of the brain.

We sometimes wonder why a certain person lights us up while another turns us off. We seem to use odors—in most cases, subconsciously—to evaluate potential mates. Each of us has a unique scent: milky exudates of various glands, including the apocrine glands, which are located around the nipples, genitals, and armpits and contain roughly two hundred chemicals. The ratio of these chemicals, which are metabolized into an aromatic brew by skin-dwelling bacteria, varies from person to person. Men and women, for example, have distinct odors governed by different ratios of sex hormones.

The neurons that convey odors from the nose to the brain's olfactory bulb have close connections with the oldest areas of the human brain: the limbic system, the region that includes the amygdala, our emotional gatekeeper, and the hippocampus, which controls memory making. Odors trigger subconscious emotional responses before they ever arrive at the brain's outermost and thinking section, the cerebral cortex, for conscious assessment.

This means a great deal of the processing of odors is done on a nonconscious basis. For all our deliberate parsing of our fellow humans' speech and our careful guesswork in decoding their intents from their expressions, we may be more bound (or repelled) by chemistry than we have imagined. Consider the recent news that the chemicals in a woman's tears are a sexual turn-off for men, who can apparently detect a warning in their very subtle odor—and not just any tears, but emotional tears. The men in the experiment said they smelled no odor, but both their testosterone level and sexual response dropped when they were exposed to a woman's emotional tears. The study shows we can communicate on a molecular level to send a chemical message that others can't resist. Interestingly, the first proof of this is a message that says, "Hold off."

The Sweet Smell of Sex—and Danger

Many sniffing studies involve whiffing smelly T-shirts, armpits, and pads doused in human odors, all in the name of science. The research has yielded some very interesting results.

One sexually related trait you may be subconsciously evaluating is another's immune system status. Some studies suggest that variations in the major histocompatibility complex (MHC)—a gene region coding for cell-surface proteins that help our immune system distinguish our own cells from those of invaders—can influence body odor. In a classic experiment in 1995, biologist Claus Wedekind of the University of Lausanne in Switzerland and his colleagues demonstrated that women can determine the status of a man's immune system by sniffing his body odor.

When women rated the odors of T-shirts that men had slept in for two nights, they consistently preferred the scents of the men whose MHC genes differed significantly from their own. Men can also differentiate MHC genes by smell. Researchers theorize that this tendency may be a way of promoting genetic diversity: a mixing of differing MHC genes through mating may lead to a more robust immune system in the resulting children than would occur from the mixing of similar MHC genes (see "Your Hormones May Drive You Apart," in Chapter Six, "Only You Can Make My Dreams Come True") for how oral contraceptives may skewer this sense and your love life).

In a study that showed female mice grew new brain cells after getting a sniff of a dominant male's urine, these neurons were generated both in the olfactory bulb and in the hippocampus, an area important for memory formation, perhaps ensuring that she will remember him. Scientists speculate that the ability to recognize and remember subtle chemical sex signatures could be important for regulating mating behavior in female mice, which prefer to mate with dominant males. While this hasn't been shown in humans, one study noted that some women reach orgasm more easily with wealthier men.

But are such particular human odors sexy? That is, are they a turn-on? Other animals secrete chemicals called pheromones that evoke a sexual response. For example, the compound androstenone can drive female pigs into a frenzy of lust. Such an extreme effect from an odor has never been documented in humans.

But not so fast: at least two nongaseous compounds, one exuded by men and one by women, seem to prompt distinctive brain activity patterns in men and women, indicating a possible difference in their meaning to each sex, according to recent findings by neuroscientist Ivanka Savic of Karolinska University Hospital in Stockholm and her colleagues.

Androstadienone, which is found in male sweat and semen, may help put women in the mood. In 2007 neuroscientists Claire Wyart of the University of California, Berkeley, and Noam Sobel, now at the Weizmann Institute of Science in Israel, reported that the smell of androstadienone was more likely than whiffing baker's yeast to improve mood and increase sexual arousal in twenty-one heterosexual women. Androstadienone also boosted levels of cortisol, a stress hormone, in the women's saliva. "It's the first report to my knowledge showing that smelling a specific component of male sweat was inducing significant changes in the hormonal balance of women," Wyart says.

Anytime You Call My Name: Are Women Always Ready?

Almost all female mammals have a distinct period when they are fertile and sexually available, called estrus (that is, when they are in heat). Anyone who has lived with an unneutered female animal has seen the powerful effects of this biological fact.

Human females have been believed to be unique: we are sexually available and ready to go anytime we please. Or so we thought. Now evidence is mounting that humans also go through estrus, but perhaps in a more subtle way—or perhaps it's not all that subtle.

A number of recent studies have shown that ovulating women appear—and even smell—more attractive to men. A recent University of New Mexico study found that female strippers earn up to twice as much tip money during their most fertile period as compared with other times.

But while men may clamor for a woman when they sense she is fertile, Meghan P. Provost, a psychologist at Mount Saint Vincent University in Halifax, says that women in heat become choosier: they are not interested in just any man. And in fact, their way of walking—a public advertisement of attractiveness—is sexier when they are not ovulating.

Psychologist Geoffrey Miller, who led the New Mexico study, notes that this pickiness does not make us so different from our primate relatives. "It's a common misconception that females are always promiscuous during heat," he says. In most species, females may advertise, but they are very choosy about who they accept.

Smell enables us to avoid various types of danger: to detect rotting food or toxic gases or even, as a 2007 study showed, the odor of a stranger. Researchers used positron emission tomography (PET) to peer into the brains of fifteen healthy nonsmoking women while they sniffed each of three aromas: their own body odor, the body odor of a long-time friend, and the odor of a stranger (each scent had been accumulated in cotton pads and then encased in glass bottles for sniffing purposes).

The participants could indeed identify their friend's scent: after sniffing each of the three odor-containing bottles, they correctly chose the one containing the friend's odor, and they picked the one emitting their own aroma with similar accuracy. They registered the difference between friends and strangers and rated the smell of a stranger as more intense and less pleasant than that of their friend: it activated the amygdala and the insula, which process fear and disgust, among other emotions.

A Kiss Is (More Than) Just a Kiss

We kiss hello and goodbye, we kiss when happy or sad, we kiss when aroused and when suffused with tenderness. In some cultures, we eschew the lips to kiss the air, or buss cheeks two or three times in a row; in others, we don't kiss at all. But in most of the Western world, osculation has been raised to an art form, with lovers locking lips at every opportunity. Indeed, a passionate kiss is the perfect happy ending—or a beginning.

But a kiss is more than just a kiss: it's an intimate exchange of scents, tastes, textures, secrets, and emotions. The touch of lips to lips triggers a cascade of neural messages and chemicals that transmit tactile sensations, sexual excitement, feelings of closeness, motivation, and even euphoria. Indeed, the fusion of lips dispatches powerful communiqués to your partner about the status and future of a relationship—

so much, in fact, that, according to recent research, a first kiss gone bad can stop an otherwise promising relationship dead in its tracks.

Kissing may have evolved from primate mothers' practice of chewing food for their young and then feeding them mouth-to-mouth. Some scientists believe that the fusing of lips evolved because it facilitates mate selection, since it involves a complicated exchange of information about the degree to which people are genetically compatible.

Silent chemical messengers called pheromones could have sped the evolution of the intimate kiss. Many animals and plants use pheromones to communicate with other members of the same species, but whether humans sense pheromones is controversial. Nevertheless, biologist Sarah Woodley of Duquesne University suggests that we might be able to sense pheromones with our nose, located conveniently just above those kissing lips.

Kissing seems to be addictive. That may be because human lips enjoy the slimmest layer of skin on the human body and are among the most densely populated with sensory neurons of any body region. When we kiss, these neurons, along with those in the tongue and mouth, rocket messages to the brain and body, setting off delightful sensations, intense emotions, and physical reactions. Of the twelve or thirteen cranial nerves that affect cerebral function, five are at work when we kiss, shuttling messages from our lips, tongue, cheeks, and nose to a brain that snatches information about the temperature, taste, smell, and movements of the entire affair.

Some of that information arrives in the somatosensory cortex, a swath of tissue on the surface of the brain that represents tactile information that can be represented in a map of the body. In that map, the lips loom large because the size of each represented body region is proportional to the density of its nerve endings (see the "Kiss and Tell" illustration in the color insert). Kissing unleashes a cocktail of chemicals that govern human stress, motivation, social bonding, and sexual stimulation.

Not all kissing goes well. It can also be a signal of betrayal, as in the film *The Godfather* and in Judas's betrayal of Christ. It can also be the end of a promising relationship. A survey by Gordon G. Gallup and colleagues at the State University of New York at Albany found that 59 percent of 58 men and 66 percent of 122 women admitted there had been times when they were attracted to someone, only to find that their interest evaporated after their first kiss. The "bad" kisses had no particular flaws; they simply did not feel right, and they ended the romantic relationship then and there—literally a kiss of death for that coupling. The reason a kiss carries such weight, Gallup theorizes, is that it conveys subconscious information about the genetic compatibility of a prospective mate. His hypothesis is consistent with the idea that kissing evolved as a courtship strategy because it helps us rate potential partners.

That said, kissing is probably not strictly necessary from an evolutionary point of view. Most other animals do not smooch and yet manage to produce plenty of offspring. Not even all humans kiss. In fact, some experts estimate that up to 10 percent of humanity does not touch lips. Some even consider it unsanitary, unsavory—or worse. Too bad for them.

You Light Up My Brain

Desire starts with a thought, a scent, a touch, or the sight of an object of desire, and this is as true for women as it is for men. But scientists still haven't figured out everything that happens in your brain or your body between that first tweak and orgasm.

When we are smitten by lust, it may seem that we've been blind-sided by desire. It's often difficult to figure out what's happening in our body, let alone our brain. Sometimes it seems as if our brains aren't involved at all when it comes to sex—that we've been hijacked by our genitals. But the fact is that your brain, not your body, calls the shots (literally). The sex organ between your ears is driving your body. But why are we wired to so crave sex?

The need for male orgasm is obvious: sperm have to be produced and ejaculated to meet up with an egg to create a new being. But scientists are still stymied about what survival role a woman's orgasm plays. It may help make babies. There's physiological evidence that female orgasm helps retain more or better-quality sperm. And a woman's desire to conceive may lead to more frequent orgasms during sex, which are also most likely to occur during the most fertile period of the menstrual cycle. Moreover, better orgasms are likely to leave her wanting more sex, again increasing chances of conception.

Researchers are trying to crack this riddle by probing brain activity during arousal and orgasm, and they're finding that the sexes aren't so different here. Preliminary evidence suggests that the control center of sexual functions in men and women is remarkably similar. The same neurochemicals fuel the flames of desire, and many of the same brain parts light up under imaging scans. Women also have nocturnal "erections"—a swelling arousal of the labia, vagina, and clitoris—four or five times a night during rapid eye movement (REM) sleep.

The so-called higher brain centers get involved in both genders, but we know less about how this happens. PET studies show that parts of the cerebral cortex associated with emotional experiences are activated when men are aroused, and its functions of memory and desire can direct erections. Women may have better orgasms when they are in love. (See "What's Love Got to Do with It?" later in this chapter.) And both genders are vulnerable to sexual dysfunction when taking some medications, including antidepressants.

Thanks to new imaging techniques and cooperative subjects willing to perform many kinds of sexual activities under observation, researchers are collecting a lot of sometimes surprising information about what goes on in the brain during orgasm. They're finding that the arousal-to-orgasm trip winds through many parts of your brain and that men and woman tend to be turned on by a lot of the same

Five Great Things Orgasm Does for Your Brain

1. *Nourishes it.* Sexual activity increases blood flow, pulse rate, and respiration. In short, it is a cardio workout that bathes your brain in oxygen.

2. *Relaxes it.* Relieves stress and depression.

3. *Eases pain.*

4. *Quiets your anxiety-ridden amygdala.* In fact, it has to tune way down for you to have an orgasm.

5. *Renews it.* Orgasm may prompt the growth of new brain cells.

things. (Viewing others having sex is one example: women get turned on in this way as much as men do, a finding that surprised some researchers.) They're also finding that some brain parts have to get turned off for us to get really turned on. Orgasm requires a release of inhibitions, a shutdown of the brain's center of vigilance in both sexes, and what looks like a widespread neural power failure in females. The amygdala seems to swoon when either sex has an orgasm. And the pleasure centers tend to light up brightly in the brain scans of both sexes, especially in those of males.

Neuroscientist Gert Holstege of the University of Groningen in the Netherlands and his colleagues discovered these brain actions while scanning both men and women as they reached orgasm. They had female partners of eleven men stimulate their partner's penis until he ejaculated while they scanned each man's brain using PET.

During ejaculation, activity in the men's amygdala declined while there was extraordinarily intense activation in a major hub of the brain's reward circuitry, the ventral tegmental area. Brain regions involved in memory-related imagery and in vision also turned on, and the anterior part of the cerebellum, which is involved in emotional processing, switched into high gear.

The team then used PET scans to see what orgasm looked like in the brains of twelve women while each one's partner stimulated her clitoris to climax. When she reached orgasm, brain activity fell in her amygdala too. But then something unexpected happened: much of her brain went silent. Some of the most muted neurons sat in the left lateral orbitofrontal cortex, which may govern self-control over basic desires such as sex. Decreased activity there, the researchers suggest, might correspond to a release of tension and inhibition. The scientists also saw a dip in excitation in the dorsomedial prefrontal cortex, a brain section that has an apparent role in moral reasoning and social judgment—a change that may be tied to a suspension of judgment and reflection (and explains why smart women can make dumb choices in men).

In another study of women and orgasm, brains told a different story. Brain activation was imaged during orgasm in five women with spinal cord injuries that left them without sensation in their lower extremities. These women reached "deep," or nonclitoral, orgasm through mechanical stimulation (using a laboratory device) of the vagina and cervix. But contrary to Holstege's results, this team found that orgasm was accompanied by a general activation of the limbic system, the brain's seat of emotion, including the amygdala. Also activated was the hypothalamus, which releases both dopamine and oxytocin. The love and bonding hormone levels jump fourfold at orgasm. The researchers found heightened activity in the nucleus accumbens, a critical part of the brain's reward circuit, and in the anterior cingulate cortex and the insula, two brain areas some researchers have found associated with the later stages of love relationships.

In fact, the chemicals of toe-curling sex are pretty much the same for men and women. The thrill comes from a cascade of pleasure-producing hormones and neurotransmitters that tickle the reward center in both sexes, setting off a rainbow rush of good feelings and, perhaps, a desire to stay together.

Dopamine, the neurochemical of all addictions and desires, sets off the reward system by triggering the release of testosterone, the hormone that drives the libido in both men and women and surges in orgasm. The hormone prolactin gives sexual gratification and helps lower the arousal effects of dopamine, opening the door for arginine vasopressin and oxytocin, associated with pair bonding. Oxytocin is perhaps the true love potion, called the "cuddle hormone" because it promotes that postclimax loving feeling. But it's different in men than in women: in women, estrogen adds to the oxytocin loving effects, while in men, testosterone tends to offset some oxytocin effects.

Of course, there are also dramatic differences between men and women in sex. There is a delay between orgasms for men, and the ability to get and sustain an erection weakens with age. Women can have multiple orgasms, and sexual arousal and function doesn't fade with time.

What's Love Got to Do with It? Plenty It Turns Out—for Women

Women can certainly have orgasms without love, but research confirms that a woman in love has better orgasms, suggesting the feelings a woman has for her sexual partner are tied to how good her orgasms are.

Researchers at Geneva University in Switzerland and the University of California, Santa Barbara, asked twenty-nine head-over-heels-in-love heterosexual women to rate the intensity of their love as well as the quality, ease, and frequency of orgasms with their partner. Then they mapped brain activity with fMRI while the women focused on an unrelated thinking task. As the women worked, their lover's name flashed on screens in front of them too quickly to be noticed consciously but slowly enough to evoke a subliminal response from the brain—a technique that has been shown to reveal the neural networks involved in partner recognition and related emotions.

The more "in love" the subjects reported being, the greater activity the name flash triggered in the left angular gyrus, a brain region involved in memories of events and emotions. The most smitten subjects also reported having orgasms more easily—and far better ones too—with ease and quality linked to a region involved in reward and addiction.

"The more they were satisfied by their sexual relationship in terms of orgasm, the more this brain area was activated," says psychologist and study coauthor Stephanie Ortigue. However, there was no link between intensity of love and how often the women climaxed.

Need Some Love Potion? Try a Bit of Oxytocin Spray

You might be able to increase the odds that someone will find you attractive (or remember you from last night) with a whiff of a powerful, and legal, oxytocin spray available without a prescription.

For sale, and unregulated, are spray containers of the hormone of bonding and trust. "Imagine for a moment that everyone trusted you," the online ad voice-over intones. "You would sell more, love more . . . Now you can have the world in the palm of your hand. Trust is power."

Some advertised products include androstenone, a known aphrodisiac pheromone for many mammals. Spray it on yourself, and people you meet will respond with trust—or maybe lust, although oxytocin is more known as the cuddle hormone and androstenone hasn't been known to excite humans.

It sounds like the stuff of science fiction, but scientists at the University of Zurich discovered that a whiff of oxytocin makes people more willing to trust others with their money. No wonder: oxytocin in nonhuman mammals is associated with social attachment, as well as a number of physiological functions related to reproduction. As such, it is believed to help animals overcome their natural tendency to avoid proximity and allow others to approach them.

Hypothesizing that oxytocin might have a comparable effect on humans, Michael Kosfeld and colleagues devised a double-blind study to look at oxytocin and trust. They found that after participants receive a single dose of the hormone, trust increased markedly, with 45 percent of the oxytocin group exhibiting the highest trust level compared to just 21 percent of the placebo group. Oxytocin didn't seem to promote risk taking in general, but rather social risk taking specifically: when the participants playing an investment game were paired with a computer instead of a human, they did not take such risks.

When the study was released, Kosfeld and collaborators acknowledged that their findings could be misused for personal gain. They add, however, that the work could ultimately help patients with mental disorders, such as autism or social phobia. In fact, recent research has shown that a sniff of oxytocin does seem to help those with autism or Asperger's syndrome relate to others.

I'll Have What She's Having: What Makes a Better Female Orgasm?

The purpose of the female orgasm remains in doubt, but there's no debate about its pleasure. However, some women seem to have more (and perhaps better, although that may be in debate) orgasms. Writing for *Scientific American* online, blogger Jesse Bering has the following observations about women and orgasms.

Clue 1: It's in your genes. Twin-based evidence shows that orgasm frequency has a modest hereditable component. Hereditary factors account for only a third of the population-level variance in female orgasm, however, but that's something.

Clue 2: It's about loving yourself (literally). Most women report that they are more likely to experience an orgasm while masturbating than during sexual intercourse with a male partner, and such masturbatory orgasms do not always hinge on simulating intercourse-type penile-vaginal sex.

Clue 3: It's about education. Educated women are more likely to report having orgasms with masturbation, but they are no more likely to have orgasm through intercourse than less educated women are. However, religious women tend to have less frequent orgasms than nonreligious ones (or at least they report having fewer).

Clue 4: It's about his beauty. Using self-reported data collected from college-aged American females, researchers have found the frequency of orgasm is related to the physical attractiveness of male partners, with attractiveness being measured by subjective ratings as well as by indexes of facial symmetry. Recall that in genetic fitness terms, attractiveness tends to relate to health and overall genetic value.

Clue 5: It's about his wealth. Wealthy men spur more orgasms—in China, anyway. A study at the University of Groningen found that Chinese women who were dating or married to wealthy male partners reported having orgasms more frequently than women whose partners made less. This income effect panned out even after the authors ruled out a host of extraneous variables, including health, happiness, education, the woman's personal income, and Westernization. Researchers speculate that female orgasm may be linked to male income because money is a reliable indicator of the male's ability for long-term investing in offspring, and it may also reflect desirable underlying genetic characteristics. In this light, female orgasm may serve an emotional bonding role, motivating sexual behavior, and hence conception, with high-status males. (Not to be cynical, but it could also mean she reported more orgasms to keep her wealthy partner happy.)

IS SEX REALLY NECESSARY?

Approximately 2 billion years ago, a pair of single-celled organisms made a terrible mistake: they had sex. We're still living with the consequences.

Sexual reproduction is the preferred method for an overwhelming portion of the planet's species, and yet from the standpoint of evolution, it leaves much to be desired. Finding and wooing a prospective mate takes time and energy that could be better spent directly on one's offspring. And having sex is not necessarily the best way for a species to attain Darwinian fitness. During the act, many animals are distracted and vulnerable to attack, and if the evolutionary goal of each individual is to get as many genes into the next generation as possible, making a clone would be simpler and easier.

The truth is, nobody really knows why people—and other animals, plants, and fungi—prefer sex to, say, budding. There are more than forty theories on why sex is so popular. Each has its shortcomings, but the current front-runner seems to be the Red Queen hypothesis. It gets its name from a race in Lewis Carroll's *Through the Looking Glass* in which Alice has to keep running to stay in the same place. Organisms have to keep changing their genetic makeup to stay one step ahead of parasites, and sexual reproduction allows them to shuffle their genetic deck by adding different genes with each generation.

That's not to say that sex is forever. When resources and mates are scarce, almost all types of animals have been known to revert to reproducing asexually. However, so far, mammals, including humans, appear to have been denied the cloning option. Our lives seem fated to include plenty of sex, in good times and in bad.

Does the Penis Have a Brain of Its Own?

It certainly seems so at times. The penis may insist on attention in inconvenient circumstances or refuse to participate when its owner asks. So in a way: yes, it does have a brain of its own—though we can't really call it a brain. It's more of an erection-generating reflex that responds to nerve signals created by physical stimulation. It appears that the penis and its purposes are so vital to the survival of our species that there are backups and safeguards to protect reproductive function if something goes wrong in the brain.

The penis and brain do stay in contact, sending each other messages along the spinal cord where they influence nerve pathways. But the penis can function very well, thank you, without the brain. Men can have erections and ejaculations without involvement of the brain function. It's common for men to awake with an erection without any stimulation or even sexy dream.

An erection does not even require an intact spinal cord, as researchers have discovered from men who have damaged or even severed spinal cords and nevertheless father children. In fact, when the brain is disconnected from the penis, erections are more frequent.

It seems there is an erection-generating section—a kind of penis brain—located in the sacral segments of the spinal cord, just above the tailbone in men. Physical stimulation of the penis sends sensory signals to this erection center, which activates a cascade of messages to tell the penile blood vessels it's time to boot up.

An erect penis appears to be the default state. One of the important functions of the brain is to suppress erections most of the time, so that men can go about other business—and also to protect the blood vessels from damage from being constantly engorged. When a man is not sexually aroused, parts of the sympathetic nervous system actively limit blood flow to the penis, keeping it limp. Sildenafil (the generic name for Viagra) works by slowing the breakdown of one of the chemicals that keeps the muscles relaxed, thus holding blood in the penis.

Studies have also shown that men can learn to have erections on demand using only their brains, in response to mental imagery or nonsexual cues or through the use of imagery and fantasy. This

Addicted to Love: Is There Really a Sex Addiction?

There is no doubt that sex acts like a drug in the brain. Heck, it *is* a drug in the brain, and lost love feels like withdrawal.

But whether love or the urge for sex are bona-fide addictions is another question, which seems to depend on who you ask as well as the definition of addiction. Some experts contend it can be addictive, but scientists debate whether *addiction* is an appropriate term for behaviors such as excessive gambling, shopping, and compulsive sexual activity.

Those in favor of recognizing so-called behavioral addictions argue that such excessive actions share core characteristics with alcohol and drug addiction: these include extreme indulgence and continued use despite a negative effect on the user. Skeptics counter, however, that although people may engage excessively in sexual activities and sometimes suffer detrimental consequences, they rarely develop tolerance or obvious withdrawal symptoms—two hallmarks of addiction.

And it could be that your genes are spurring your brain on to the risky business that comes with an insatiable desire for sex. New research is showing that a propensity for one-night stands is connected with the genetic variation DRD4—that same bad-boy gene associated with a host of behaviors such as risk taking, liberal attitudes, and attachment disorder.

explains why an astounding number of fetish objects—such as high-heeled shoes, leather whips, and flimsy lingerie—can be a turn-on for men.

Higher brain centers are involved in male erections as well, particularly learning and memory, but we know much less about them.

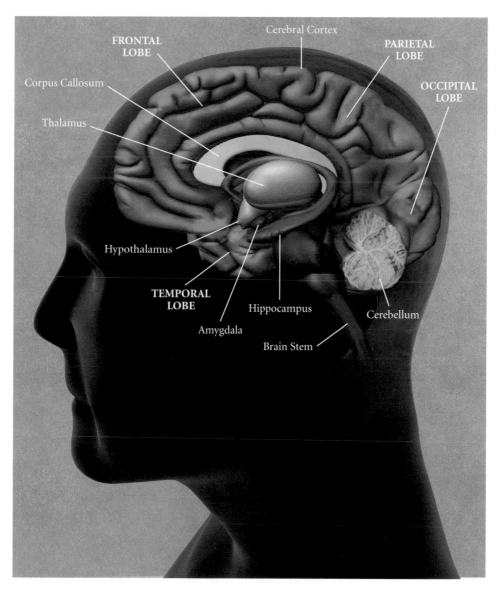

Some of Your Brain's Most Important Parts

If I Could Read Your Mind

In some ways, you do. Mirror neurons are a fairly new discovery: they are specialized brain cells that are activated when we perform an action—and also exactly the same way when we see another perform the same action. Originally called "monkey see, monkey do" by discoverers who first observed it in monkeys wired up for an experiment, these specialized neurons go a long way toward explaining empathy and our ability to understand and interpret the actions and intentions of others. Our brains are capable of "reading" not just the actions but also intentions. This illustration shows how a brain distinguishes between the grasping actions in two images that suggest two different intentions—drinking on the left and cleaning up on the right. The three images of the human brain as it observes the actions show different views of mirror neurons in the area activated by both, the inferior frontal cortex. They don't, however, show the degree of difference in brain activity between the two observations: the drinking intention provokes twice as much activity as cleaning up.

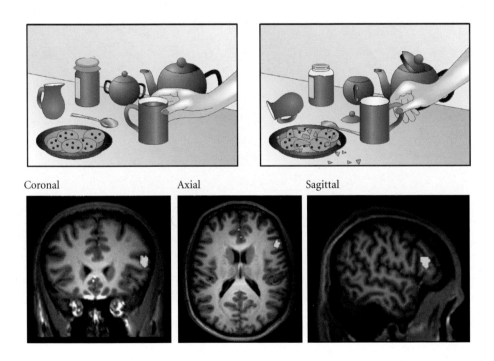

Coronal   Axial   Sagittal

Epigenetics: Volume Control for Your Genes

Your genes are powerful, but they are not your destiny: epigenetics can change the actions of your DNA. The very name *epigenetics* (from *epi*, meaning over, and *genome*, referring to your DNA) describes chemical attachments to your DNA (or to the histone proteins that control its shape within the chromosomes). This epigenetic information of several kinds can act like volume knobs to amplify or mute the effect of genes (gene expression). Your epigenome can be affected by your environment, your actions, and even your thoughts and feelings, and those changes can be inherited by your offspring.

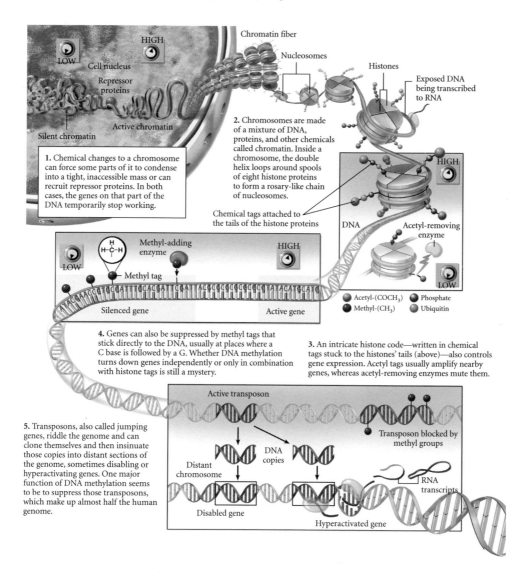

Chromatin fiber

Nucleosomes

Histones

Exposed DNA being transcribed to RNA

Cell nucleus

Repressor proteins

Active chromatin

Silent chromatin

1. Chemical changes to a chromosome can force some parts of it to condense into a tight, inaccessible mass or can recruit repressor proteins. In both cases, the genes on that part of the DNA temporarily stop working.

2. Chromosomes are made of a mixture of DNA, proteins, and other chemicals called chromatin. Inside a chromosome, the double helix loops around spools of eight histone proteins to form a rosary-like chain of nucleosomes.

Chemical tags attached to the tails of the histone proteins

DNA

Acetyl-removing enzyme

Methyl-adding enzyme

Methyl tag

Silenced gene

Active gene

Acetyl-(COCH₃)   Phosphate
Methyl-(CH₃)   Ubiquitin

4. Genes can also be suppressed by methyl tags that stick directly to the DNA, usually at places where a C base is followed by a G. Whether DNA methylation turns down genes independently or only in combination with histone tags is still a mystery.

3. An intricate histone code—written in chemical tags stuck to the histones' tails (above)—also controls gene expression. Acetyl tags usually amplify nearby genes, whereas acetyl-removing enzymes mute them.

Active transposon

5. Transposons, also called jumping genes, riddle the genome and can clone themselves and then insinuate those copies into distant sections of the genome, sometimes disabling or hyperactivating genes. One major function of DNA methylation seems to be to suppress those transposons, which make up almost half the human genome.

Distant chromosome

DNA copies

Disabled gene

Transposon blocked by methyl groups

RNA transcripts

Hyperactivated gene

Thinking for Two

Pregnancy and motherhood change the structure of a woman's brain, making mothers attentive to their young and better at caring for them. In fact, studies with rats show that mother rats always beat out virgin rats in tasks requiring multitasking.

During pregnancy, the ovaries and placenta produce large amounts of estrogens and progesterone, the female reproductive hormones. The hypothalamus and pituitary gland secrete oxytocin (which triggers birth contractions), prolactin (which stimulates the mammary glands), and endorphins (which may ease the pain of birth). Estrogen and progesterone appear to enlarge the cell bodies of neurons in the medial preoptic area (mPOA) of the hypothalamus, which regulates basic maternal responses, as well as increase the surface area of neuronal branches in the hippocampus, which governs memory and learning. Oxytocin also stimulates the hippocampus. Other brain regions apparently involved in maternal behavior include the cingulate cortex, the prefrontal and orbitofrontal cortices, the nucleus accumbens, the amygdala, the lateral habenula, and the periaqueductal gray. Several of these areas have also been found to be involved in unconditional love.

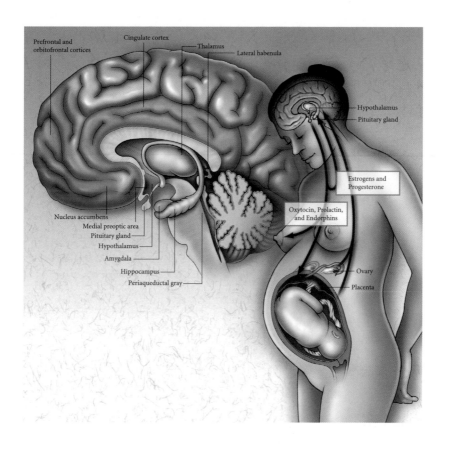

Oxytocin and the Brain

Oxytocin—the neurochemical of love, trust, and mother's milk—involves several of your brain structures (highlighted in green). These areas share three features: they have dense fields of oxytocin receptors, which convey oxytocin's "messages" to nerve cells; they control emotions and social behavior; and they modulate midbrain dopamine release, which makes people feel good and thus rewards and reinforces specific behaviors. This image also shows how some brain cells secrete oxytocin into the bloodstream (detail at bottom left) to influence the uterus and mammary glands.

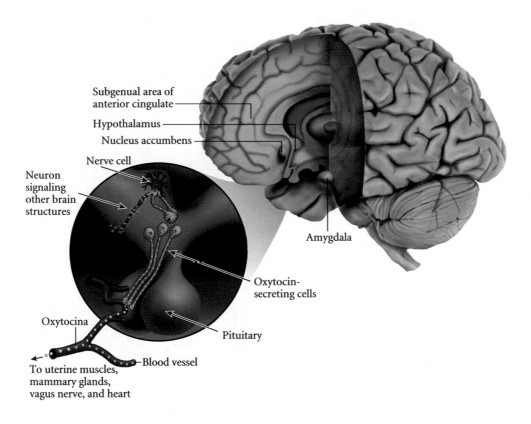

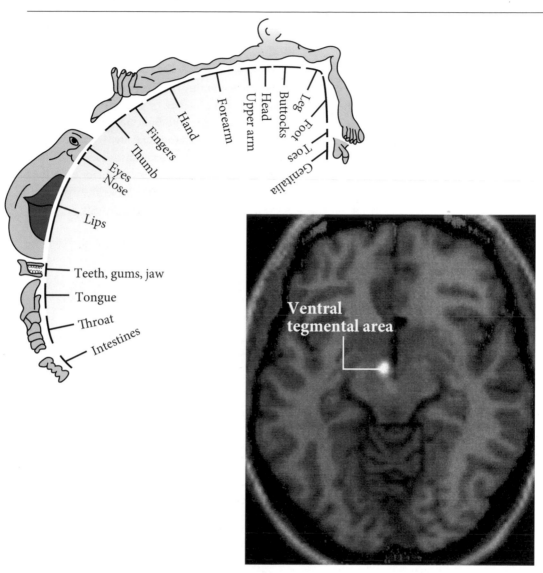

Kiss and Tell

A kiss on the lips tells a lot about the kissee and the kisser: it can trigger a cascade of neural messages and chemicals that convey important information about the status and future of a relationship—and a bad first kiss may even put the brakes on any future romance.

The lips are disproportionately large on this map (above, called a sensory homunculus, which reflects your brain's sensory reception area). That's because human lips enjoy the slimmest layer of skin on the human body and are among the most densely populated with sensory neurons.

When we kiss, these neurons, along with those in the tongue and mouth, rocket messages to the brain (see above, right; a brain ignited by love) and to the body, setting off delightful sensations, intense emotions, and physical reactions.

Your Brain in Love

Men and women can now thank a dozen brain regions for their experience of love. Researchers have revealed the fonts of desire by comparing functional magnetic resonance imaging studies of people who indicated they were experiencing passionate love, maternal love, or unconditional love—and there are many similarities. Together, the regions release neurotransmitters and other chemicals in the brain and blood that prompt greater euphoric sensations such as attraction and pleasure. And there is hope for the brokenhearted: psychiatrists might someday help individuals who become dangerously depressed after a heartbreak by adjusting those chemicals.

Passion also heightens several cognitive functions as the brain regions and chemicals surge. "It's all about how that network interacts," says Stephanie Ortigue, an assistant professor of psychology at Syracuse University, who led the study. The cognitive functions, in turn, "are triggers that fully activate the love network." Tell that to your loved one.

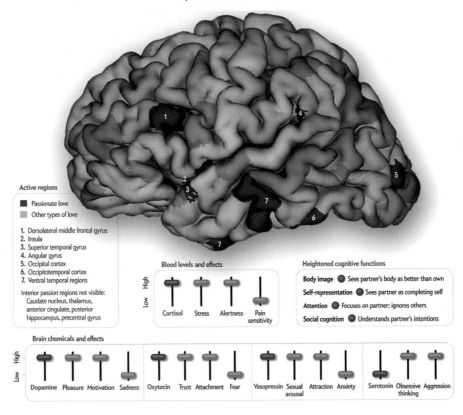

Active regions

- ■ Passionate love
- ▨ Other types of love

1. Dorsolateral middle frontal gyrus
2. Insula
3. Superior temporal gyrus
4. Angular gyrus
5. Occipital cortex
6. Occipitotemporal cortex
7. Ventral temporal regions

Interior passion regions not visible: Caudate nucleus, thalamus, anterior cingulate, posterior hippocampus, precentral gyrus

Blood levels and effects

High / Low

| Cortisol | Stress | Alertness | Pain sensitivity |

Heightened cognitive functions

Body image ● Sees partner's body as better than own
Self-representation ● Sees partner as completing self
Attention ● Focuses on partner; ignores others
Social cognition ● Understands partner's intentions

Brain chemicals and effects

High / Low

| Dopamine | Pleasure | Motivation | Sadness | Oxytocin | Trust | Attachment | Fear | Vasopressin | Sexual arousal | Attraction | Anxiety | Serotonin | Obsessive thinking | Aggression |

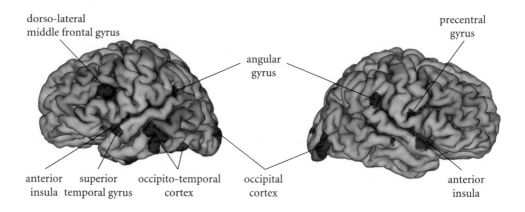

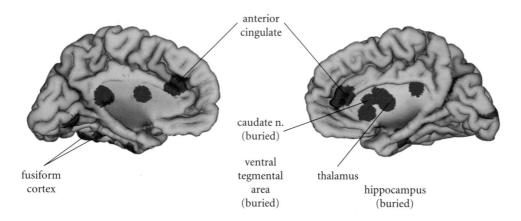

Twelve Areas of Love in the Brain

These images better show the dozen brain regions, working together, that create and nurture feelings of love in its several guises. Ortigue and her colleagues worldwide compared MRI studies of people who indicated they were either in love or were experiencing maternal or unconditional love to reveal a "passion network"—the red regions shown here at various angles. The network releases neurotransmitters and other chemicals in the brain and blood that create the sensations of attraction, arousal, pleasure . . . and obsession.

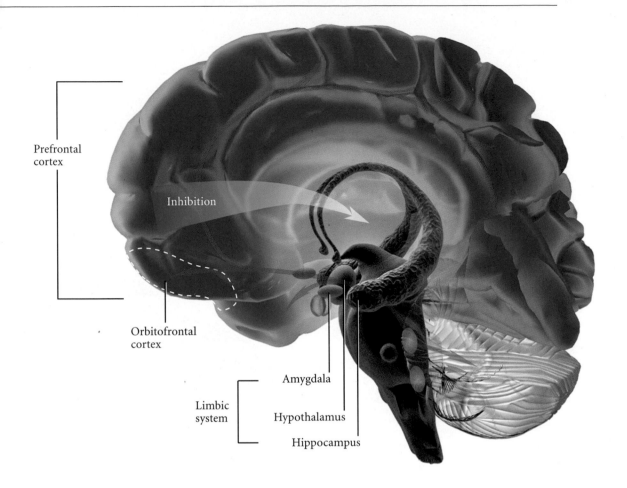

Prefrontal cortex

Inhibition

Orbitofrontal cortex

Amygdala

Limbic system

Hypothalamus

Hippocampus

A Brain Unable to Love

Imaging is showing that the brains of some criminals are different. Abnormalities or injuries in the thinking brain (the prefrontal cortex) may handicap some people, making it difficult for them to show restraint or to feel tender emotions. Some scientists hypothesize that a person might not be able to control emotional reactions if a defect blocks communication between the orbitofrontal cortex (an area involved in decision making) and regions in the limbic system—specifically the hypothalamus and the amygdala, where fear and aggression arise. Damage to the hippocampus may also interfere with the brain's processing of emotional information—and in some instances, a malfunction of the amygdala may underlie violent behavior. This theory could explain the lack of fear, empathy, and regret that is characteristic of criminals who plan their acts and commit them in cold blood.

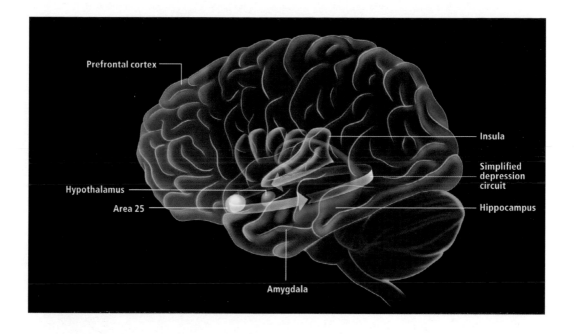

Prefrontal cortex

Insula

Simplified depression circuit

Hypothalamus

Area 25

Hippocampus

Amygdala

The Depression Circuit

Depression can come on the heels of heartbreak or even a happy event such as childbirth. But hormones and neurochemicals aren't the only reasons: depression seems to be connected in some with a faulty circuit in the brain.

Since sufferers have low energy and mood and their reaction times and memory formation are inhibited, it seems as though normal brain activity levels are being suppressed. Yet common symptoms, such as anxiety and sleep disturbances, suggest rather that certain brain areas are overactive. Imaging of the brain regions most disrupted in depression points to the source of such imbalances as a tiny brain structure called area 25, which acts as a hub for a depression circuit. Area 25 connects directly to brain areas such as the amygdala, which mediates fear and anxiety, and the hypothalamus, involved in stress responses. Those regions, in turn, exchange signals with the hippocampus (a center of memory processing) and the insula (where sensory perceptions and emotions are processed). A smaller-than-normal area 25 is suspected of contributing to a higher risk of depression in people with a gene variant that inhibits serotonin processing.

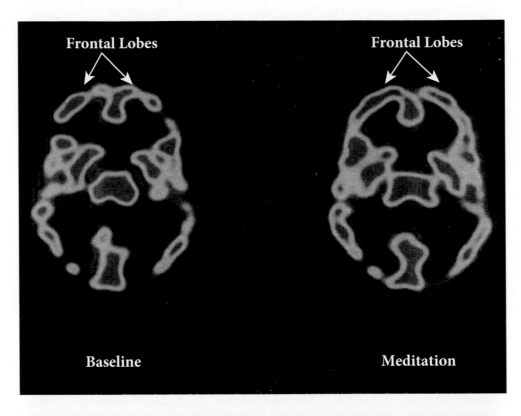

Baseline

Meditation

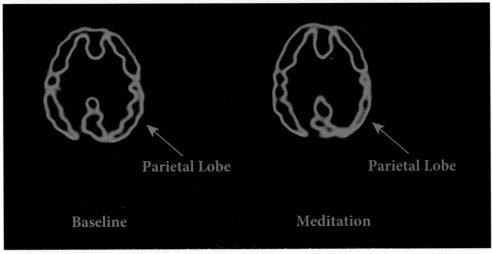

Can Meditation Make You a Better Lover?

Could be. Studies of longtime meditators show it can change the brain: meditation can improve the ability to pay attention, withhold judgment, and increase compassion, empathy, and calmness—all qualities that increase the likelihood of bonding in lovemaking.

The images here are from an ongoing study of the brains of longtime Tibetan Buddhist meditators. A brain-imaging technology called single photon emission computed tomography (SPECT) shows active areas by measuring increases in blood flow. These two sets of images, showing slightly different parts of the brain, captured the results from a baseline scan of the brain at rest (left) and during a "peak" of meditation (right).

The first set of images shows that the front part of the brain, which is usually involved in focusing attention and concentration, is more active during meditation. This makes sense, since meditation requires a high degree of concentration.

The second set shows decreased activity in the parietal lobe, an area of the brain that is responsible for giving us a sense of our orientation in space and time (lower right shows up as yellow rather than the red on the left image). The blocking of all sensory and thought into this area during meditation is connected with the sense of being beyond space and time, which is so often described in meditation.

Andrew Newberg, who provided the images, and Eugene d'Aquili give a more detailed explanation of their findings in their book, *Why God Won't Go Away: Brain Science and the Biology of Belief* (New York: Ballantine Books, 2001).

Where Emotions Rule

Our emotional and primitive brain center—the limbic system—has a powerful effect on the thinking brain, the cerebral cortex. The amygdala rules here: an almond-shaped nucleus at the center of the limbic system, it generates and processes unconscious emotions and experiences, especially those from our environment that are frightening or could be dangerous. It could also deal with curiosity and the will to action.

Emotions of desire, satisfaction, and contentment are related to the mesolimbic system, which contains the nucleus accumbens and the ventral tegmental area—components of the reward circuit that become activated when you feel love or desire. These use dopamine to alert the rest of your brain when a positive or desirable circumstance presents itself. Memory, which is mediated by the hippocampus, is vital to consciousness and helps you recall that special someone. The cingulate cortex, which sits midway between the limbic system and the cerebral cortex, controls alertness and the emotional coloring of perception. It also helps us recognize and correct mistakes.

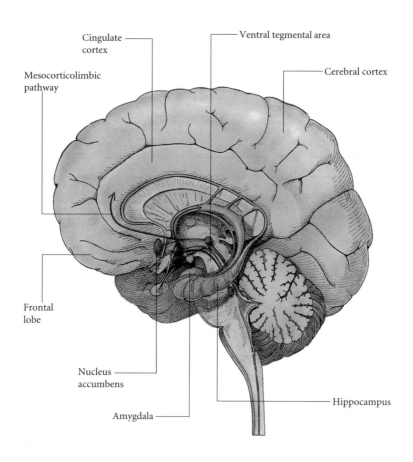

Cingulate cortex

Ventral tegmental area

Mesocorticolimbic pathway

Cerebral cortex

Frontal lobe

Nucleus accumbens

Amygdala

Hippocampus

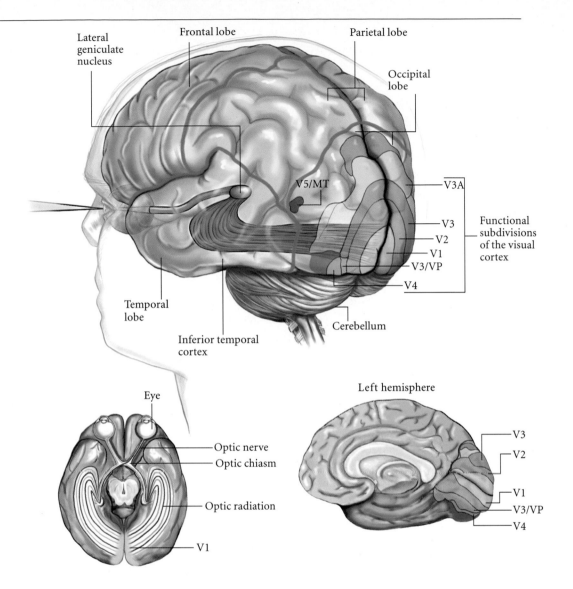

Lateral geniculate nucleus

Frontal lobe

Parietal lobe

Occipital lobe

V5/MT

V3A

V3

V2

V1

V3/VP

V4

Functional subdivisions of the visual cortex

Temporal lobe

Cerebellum

Inferior temporal cortex

Eye

Left hemisphere

Optic nerve

Optic chiasm

Optic radiation

V1

V3

V2

V1

V3/VP

V4

Structures for Seeing

Just one look. That's all it takes to tell if we find another attractive. Indeed, sight (and scent) rule our most powerful turn-ons: visual stimulation is exciting for men and women alike. Seeing begins with the eyes, of course, but travels through several parts of the brain before it comes to the primary visual cortex (see V1, V2, and so on). The optic nerves cross over partially (at the optic chasm) so that each hemisphere of the brain receives input from both eyes, which it will combine for three-dimensional vision. Information is filtered by the layers of cells in the lateral geniculate nucleus, which respond only to stimuli from one eye. Other brain parts are involved as well, including the parietal and temporal lobes that interpret what the brain is "seeing."

When Things Go Wrong: A Fine Romance

Sometimes, no matter what, it seems sex just can't—or won't—happen. Men can't get erections, women can't get aroused, and no one gets to orgasm. In fact, nobody can even get interested in the idea of sex, with others or by themselves.

It's called sexual dysfunction, and a surprisingly large number of people of both genders and various sexual orientations have it occasionally or more often. The reasons are legion: they could be biological, hormonal, situational, psychological, social, or due to injury, illness, or old age. But it could be that the brain is distracted, injured, or just not interested.

It has long been acknowledged that sexual response and interest in women is more complex than that of men, and that more women than men have issues with sex. More than 40 percent of women ages eighteen to fifty-nine say they have sexual dysfunction, with lack of interest in sex being the most commonly reported complaint. But men can also just not be interested: researchers find that nearly a third of men can't get in the mood at least some of the time.

Lack of interest in sex has a name (and a clinical diagnosis): hypoactive sexual desire disorder (HSDD). And as scientists scan both male and female brains, it appears the brains may be putting on the brakes in those with HSDD.

It is known from brain scans that the amygdala (our internal sentry that controls fight or flight) has to be tamped down in men and women for us to let go and let orgasms happen. It seems we also need to turn down other parts of the brain to get aroused. Brain scans are demonstrating that when both men and women are shown erotic images, brain activity in those with HSDD is different, mainly in revealing that the mind just can't let go and go with the flow.

A small Stanford University study reports that women with low sex desire had more activity in brain areas that contribute to a heightened attention to one's own and others' mental state (the medial frontal gyrus) and in one involved in suppressing emotional response (the right inferior frontal gyrus). Researchers say this suggests that paying too much attention to your own responses to erotic stimuli (or thinking too much) plays some part in inhibiting sexual arousal. This is not exactly an original idea to any women who has tried to get herself excited while her children are waking up in the next room and about to start hammering on the bedroom door.

But as the researchers point out, correlation is not cause and effect. The study could be showing how paying too much attention inhibits sexual desire or how the lack of desire in a sexual situation causes heightened self-consciousness.

Interestingly the brains of heterosexual men with HSDD are also different when exposed to erotica, but in a different way. A small French study used a PET scan to compare seven men with HSDD with a control group of eight men without issues, noting their cerebral blood flow responses as they viewed sexually stimulating images of various intensity. In the control group, there was less activity in the medial orbitofrontal cortex, a brain area involved in inhibiting motivated behavior. But in the HSDD patients, there was an abnormally maintained activity of this region. Similar conflicting reactions took place in other parts of the brain that control emotional and motor imagery and related processes, which seem to indicate that men with HDSS also have trouble dropping control.

When You Just Can't Get in the Mood for Love

Brain research seems to refute the promise of the pharmaceutical company ads that tell us a man can be "ready" anytime just by popping a pill. A little-acknowledged statistic is that pharmaceuticals fail to help from 25 to 33 percent of men with erectile dysfunction. Also, side effects keep many men from using these drugs. Does that mean millions of males, and their partners, are simply out of luck? Not necessarily.

We've seen that erections begin (or never get started) in the brain, the most important sex organ, and that's where at least some erection problems and solutions lie. As many as 28 percent of men who don't get an erection may actually have a lack of sexual interest that has been incorrectly diagnosed as erectile dysfunction. Their brain can't take a rest. In other cases, many men feel an anxiety to perform that can be exaggerated with increasing age and normally decreasing sex hormones and potency. A variety of psychological treatments may help overcome the mental triggers and stutters that interfere with sex.

It may help to know that, unlike what most men believe, a male erection and orgasm is a carefully orchestrated event.

Erectile dysfunction (ED, the term that is preferred over *impotence*) affects more than 50 percent of American men ages forty to seventy at least occasionally, and the episodes increase with age. Issues with medications and physical conditions can contribute to ED. But even a man in peak health can stumble over emotional blocks in brain and bed that can keep him from rising to the occasion occasionally and can lead to a vicious circle.

Anxiety that he can't satisfy his partner's sexual desires can ruin all sense of play in lovemaking, creating an even greater chance of physical problems. And while women claim they are frequently pressured into sex, men are also pressured to perform by societal expectations of an ever-ready erection. Pressure for sexual performance and potency is itself a large contributor to impotence. Advertising is rife with sexually charged images and symbols, selling men everything from automobiles to razor blades and beer. Talk about "good" or "better" sex is also ubiquitous in the media, as if bad sex (whatever that means) were the best a guy could hope for without special effort.

IT'S NOT ALWAYS YOUR BRAIN:
MEDICAL REASONS FOR ERECTILE DYSFUNCTION

Issues with illnesses (and the medications that treat them) can contribute to ED. Among the ailments that can trigger male impotence are heart disease, high blood pressure, hardening of the arteries, smoking, alcoholism, diabetes, hormonal imbalances, damage to nerve impulses, pituitary gland damage, and the side effects of various prescription medications.

True, many conditions cause impotence by reducing blood flow to the penis, which ED drugs can help. But these medications may not be the best, or even a viable, option. A more long-lasting approach may be to improve the underlying condition that originally caused the erection problem. Something as simple as a change in treatment or medication could help. Antidepressant drugs, for example, are known to lower libido, so getting off them is known to help ED.

Beyond that, there are other treatments, including penile implants, vacuum erection devices, urethral suppositories, and even injections. Testosterone or other hormone treatments might help. The bottom line is to consult a doctor with all the details about physical health and circumstances, and not to expect to find a better sex life simply by popping a little pill.

Unrealistic myths about sexual performance begin in adolescence and continue into adulthood. Men end up scoring their sexuality by how often they can "do it" and for how long. There is no place for sensuality, much less weakness or fear—or the reality that sexuality is multidimensional, involving anticipation, desire, love, and attachment and not just a firm member.

Studies by the late sexual psychologist and popular author Bernie Zilbergeld showed that most men with erection problems believe in the potency myth of being always ready, able, and willing. Men also often overestimate the level and type of women's sexual demands: in fact, many women have quite good orgasms without penetration. As a result, as soon as sex is in the offing, many men begin to observe and assess the situation as if they were outsiders, rating what they think is expected against what they can deliver. Zilbergeld called this phenomenon "spectatoring."

Stress puts the brakes on sex, but not exactly as many think. If a man who is stressed at work has trouble getting an erection—say, the night before a very important meeting—the problem is probably not work stress itself: he's usually transferring to his sex life the pressure to perform that he feels generally in his job. This turns the love act from a dance of desire into another grueling job that must be completed.

When She Doesn't Have That Loving Feeling: The Search for a Female Sex Drug

Sex drugs work for many men. Why not a female version of ED and similar drugs for women? Pharmaceutical companies, which found a blockbuster in Viagra when it's strange but pleasing side effect was noted by men in blood pressure trials, have been eager to find a similar drug for women.

Researchers have promising leads, but the results so far have been less than desired. First, ED drugs and their cousins don't provoke desire: they just (as it were) shore up the equipment to allow an erection. Desire has to come first. Both men and women can have trouble allowing sexual desire to arise in the brain, and if that doesn't happen, nothing else will, contrary to popular myths.

A transdermal testosterone patch is approved for HSDD in several European countries, and a promising new pill is under study to help rev up women who suffer from chronically low levels of sexual desire. Like Viagra, which was originally developed as a hypertension drug, fibanserin was not born as a sex-enhancing drug: it came about as an antidepressant. When it failed to alter mood in trials, researchers noticed it seemed to be helping women with low sex drives.

In a review of three clinical trials, scientists found that after twenty-four weeks of treatment with the drug fibanserin, women reported significantly more sexual desire and an increase in satisfactory sexual encounters. How the drug works is not yet entirely clear, but it is known to alter the levels of serotonin in the brain and appeared to be the first drug demonstrated to treat low libido in women by targeting the brain.

Unfortunately, fibanserin is also connected with depression, anxiety, irritability, and dizziness. Nearly 15 percent of trial participants discontinued treatment early due to an adverse event (compared to 6.8 percent of those taking a placebo). The Food and Drug Administration hasn't given its approval.

There is also controversy about whether low sexual desire in men or women is a medical condition requiring treatment. Under debate is the issue of what constitutes a normal range of sexual desire among women, with critics saying that drug companies are trying to turn a low libido into a medical pathology.

CHAPTER FIVE

Friendship, Such a Perfect Blendship

Or, with a Little Help from My Friends

Pity poor friendship: it just doesn't get enough respect. Romantic love takes center stage in our relationships every time, in lip-service at the very least. The dreaded words, "Let's just be friends," often signal the end of a romance and, for many of us, the end of a meaningful and deep connection.

Too bad. Research shows that, after your mother, friendship may be the most meaningful type of love in your life. Among its many benefits is that it doesn't deny other relationships or demand exclusiveness, it forgives many trespasses, and it often deepens with age. Moreover, meaningful friendships can be with your lover, your mother, your spouse, your ex-spouse, your kids, your social companions, your work companions, your companions from childhood or schooldays.

Friendship offers itself in many guises and times, and it may be your truest type of love.

Couples newly in love seek only each other's company, but those mated for many years know they need more than each other for a rich life and (in fact) to support their very union. That loving companionship is often referred to as a close circle of friends—a perfect term, implying, as it does, a protective surround.

Research shows that close friendship is just that. It protects your health, your happiness, your very brain. A traditional African saying, quoted by inspirational writer Alan Cohen, sums it up:

> A friend is someone who knows your song and sings it to you when you have forgotten it. Those who love you are not fooled by mistakes you have made or dark images you hold about yourself. They remember your beauty when you feel ugly; your wholeness when you are broken; your innocence when you feel guilty; and your purpose when you are confused.

Think about it: Many great literary works, songs, films, and some of the longest-running TV sitcoms are all about friendship. One was even called *Friends*: it ran for ten years and is still broadcast in reruns. *Cheers*, an eleven-year veteran, was about regulars who met and melded in a neighborhood. It had a subtitle that grabbed us all: "A place where everybody knows your name."

The word *friend* has fallen into wide use as a verb since the advent of Facebook, as in "to friend" someone, along with another verb newly in use, to "defriend" someone. Defriending describes one of the worst Internet insults (and most troublesome in its backlash): to cut someone out of your cyber–social network.

Many people have hundreds of Facebook friends and may subscribe to other such virtual networks as LinkedIn and Twitter. Some actively and persistently recruit cyber others, collecting hundreds of contacts. But despite the hyperconnectivity of texting, e-mail, and social networking, isolation is on the rise. It looks as if that close circle of friends is shrinking.

Is Friendship Declining?

Friendship may be endangered today in spite of the growth of social networks (or possibly because of them). According to a study from the *American Sociological Review*, Americans have been suffering a loss in the quality and quantity of close friendships since at least 1985. The study says 25 percent of Americans have no close confidants, and the average total number of confidants per citizen has dropped from four to two.

An analysis of studies shows, in fact, that more people than not report not having a single person they feel that they can confide in—up threefold from twenty years ago. According to the study, as the list of friends got shorter and shorter, dependence on immediate family as a safety net went up from 57 to 80 percent, and dependence on a partner or spouse went up from 5 to 9 percent.

How can this be? We humans are naturally social. We have a deep need for companionship, as powerful as hunger or thirst. Indeed, our intense use of social networks proves the need.

Blame it on the times. Modern life in industrialized countries is greatly reducing the quantity and quality of social relationships, possibly because of the fewer opportunities to get together—actually physically together. Many people in these countries no longer live in extended families or even near each other. Instead, they often live on the other side of the country or scattered across the world from their relatives and friends. They move frequently, following careers and opportunities, in contrast to a century ago when people worldwide tended to be born, work, and die in the same community. Many are now also delaying marriage and having children, or not even having children at all: birth rates have fallen in many countries. In addition,

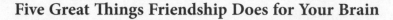

Five Great Things Friendship Does for Your Brain

Friendship is a great investment for brain and body. It also helps your soul and spirit, and that includes relationship with your animal friends. Consider these benefits:

1. Lowers your blood pressure and inflammation, and thus heart disease and risk of stroke.
2. Improves your immune system functioning.
3. Helps you take better care of your health, for their sake if not for your own.
4. Lowers or delays your risk of memory loss or Alzheimer's disease.
5. Relieves pain. Just holding hands with someone you care about lowers pain perception.

more and more people of all ages in developed countries are living alone, and loneliness is becoming increasingly common.

In the United Kingdom, according to a recent survey by the Mental Health Foundation, 10 percent of people often feel lonely, a third have a close friend or relative they think is very lonely, and half think that people in general are getting lonelier. Similarly, over the past two decades, there has been a threefold increase in the number of Americans who say they have no close friends to confide in.

This isolation is bad for our brains, as well as our bodies. University of Chicago psychologist John Cacioppo, who has been studying social isolation as it affects the brain and the rest of the body, finds it disconcertingly associated with mental and physical illness. He finds that lonely people take more risks, are more impulsive, and tend to eat more comfort (read: unhealthy) foods. Those who feel disconnected from others live with a low-level feeling of threat, among other ills. That type of stress contributes to higher blood pressure— and what's bad for the heart is bad for the brain.

Are You Lonesome Tonight? 60 Million Other Americans Are

It is no fluke that solitary confinement is one of the worst punishments. Our brains are so exquisitely calibrated to read and relate to those around us that we can hardly survive alone. And being all alone can be hell. Chronic loneliness, says John Cacioppo, is a hunger that refuses to be fed. "We have evolved to connect deeply with other human beings," he argues in his book, *Loneliness: Human Nature and the Need for Social Connection*.

He suggests that our social structures—pairs, families, groups, whole cities, and civilizations—evolved hand-in-hand with our brain's genetic, neural, and hormonal mechanisms to support them. We are all wired for connection and social living and ignore this fact at our own risk. When we don't, or can't, connect, we can fall into a spiral of isolation that can contribute to any number of health issues. Cacioppo estimates that a startling 60 million Americans suffer from a hidden epidemic of loneliness.

Cacioppo has discovered that lonely people tend to be more sensitive to cues from others, but have a harder time reading them accurately. So even as they crave human contact, lonely people are demanding and withdrawn, awkward socially, and easily victimized: they are willing to accept unfair treatment that others will not. In addition to feeling unhappy, lonely people don't feel safe: they are more likely to perceive others as threatening.

Feeling lonely can trigger a change in gene activity that can lead to illness. The initial results of a University of California, Los Angeles, study found that people who scored in the top 15 percent of a psychiatric questionnaire for measuring loneliness showed increased gene activity linked to inflammation and reduced gene activity associated with antibody production and antiviral responses. Patterns of gene expression were specifically related to the brain's feelings of loneliness, not to other negative feelings such as depression.

But what could cause these changes? In a study of 1,023 Taiwanese adults, researcher Steven Cole analyzed data from a range of lonely people and found that the stress hormone cortisol was not doing its job of suppressing the genes associated with inflammation. Inflammation is a known risk factor for a variety of serious illnesses, such as heart disease and cancer. Recent animal studies from Cole's group confirm the link: cortisol receptors stopped working in rhesus monkeys that were socially stressed.

In another study, Cacioppo and colleagues found that the ventral striatum—a region of the brain associated with rewards and activated by drugs and pleasure—is much less active in lonely people when they view pictures of others enjoying themselves or in pleasant settings. Also, the temporoparietal junction—a region associated with taking the perspective of another person—is much less active among the lonely than in the nonlonely when viewing pictures of people in unpleasant settings.

Many questions remain. Could loneliness be a result of a brain problem—of low activity in the ventral striatum—rather than the cause of it? Do all lonely people have some brain or stress damage, or is there some threshold, some measure of loneliness, at which feeling isolated starts affecting the body? Researchers are still working to see how different degrees of loneliness affect health. "We're just touching the tip of the iceberg in our understanding of loneliness," says Cacioppo.

You've Got a Friend—or You Should!

The good effects of companionship are so profound that an active social life may be the next prescription from your doctor, who, in the not-too-distant future, may tell you to "find two more friends, and call me in the morning."

It could be, as studies increasingly reveal, that having a wide range of social relationships improves longevity. More than a century's worth of research shows that having a healthy social life is important to staying mentally and physically healthy. Overall, social support increases survival by some 50 percent, concluded the authors behind a new meta-analysis, Julianne Holt-Lunstad, Timothy Smith, and J. Bradley Layton. Therefore, a long lunch with coworkers, a night out with your same-sex friends, or a late-night conversation with a close family member might be just what the doctor ordered.

Sometimes we view these events as a distraction from other healthy habits, such as going to the gym or getting a good night's sleep. Or we may regard them as poor substitutes for romantic relationships. But the benefit of friends, family, and even colleagues turns out to be just as good for long-term survival as giving up a fifteen-cigarette-a-day smoking habit. And by the study's numbers, interpersonal social networks are more crucial to physical health than exercising or beating obesity. When they looked at studies that asked more detailed and nuanced questions, such as how involved a person is with many others, rather than just asking if a person is living with someone, researchers found that having real-life and complex social networks increased survival rates by 91 percent.

Friendship may also protect your aging brain. Several studies have connected an active social life with a lower risk of dementia, and a 2008 Harvard University study found that older folks with an active social life have a slower rate of memory decline. The study looked at data gathered from the Health and Retirement Study over the years between 1998 and 2004, beginning when all participants were over the age of fifty. Participants were given memory tests at four different times and were queried about their social and volunteer activities, marital status, and contact with relatives, neighbors, and friends. And voilà: those with the highest level of social interactions had the slowest rate of memory decline over the years—less than half the rate of those who were the least socially active. A Kaiser Permanente study in Southern California found similar results among 2,249 elderly women tested over the years. The women were all older than seventy-eight when the

THE IDEAL CIRCLE OF FRIENDS

Your social circles may seem chaotic. But they actually form regular hierarchical structures—in the shape of concentric rings—according to evolutionary psychologist Robin Dunbar of the University of Liverpool in England.

Our very closest intimates form an innermost hoop of three or four, or at most five, people. We feel our greatest emotional connection to them, and we share with them common interests, values, and opinions. In crises they help us, and they advise us on personal, emotional, and financial matters. Generally we are in contact with members of our "support group" at least once a week.

The next circle holds between twelve and twenty. Our relationship with these individuals is less strong, but we maintain a caring mutual interest. The subsequent level contains between thirty and fifty people; our attachment to them is considerably looser, although we still have regular, if only occasional, contact. Dunbar believes that this third set corresponds to a band in traditional hunter-gatherer societies.

At each step in our growing circle of friends and acquaintances, the number of individuals increases by approximately a factor of three, Dunbar discovered. For example, in the armed forces of many countries, the smallest battle unit consists of 10 to 15 soldiers, a platoon of 35, and a company of 120 to 150. This magical maximum has cropped up again and again for millennia. The Roman army's basic unit, the maniple, had 150 soldiers. Today the size of most companies fluctuates between 120 and 150.

study began in 2001 and free of dementia. In the follow-up studies over the years, those with the larger and more active social networks had the lowest rate of dementia.

Previous research has pointed to happiness as a key to longevity, but apparently our relationships don't even have to be good to boost our health. In most of the studies, social connections weren't classified in terms of their quality: most likely negative associations were lumped in with positive ones. This means the benefit of our positive social connections is likely to be even higher.

In fact, a 2008 study in *Social Science and Medicine* found that people with chronic illnesses actually had a lower mortality rate if they had negative—or at least more demanding—relationships with family members. Researchers speculated that those near and dear to sick people might be nagging them about unhealthy habits and urging them to take their medication and that more demands may be seen as a sign of more caring.

And the greater the number of friendships, the lower the risks. Many researchers thought "you're at risk if you're socially isolated, but as long as you have one person, you're okay," says Julianne Holt-Lunstad, lead author of the meta-analysis. The decades of research that she and her colleagues examined showed that in fact, social support and survival operate on a continuum: more, it seems, is better. "The greater the extent of the relationships, the lower the risk," she says.

Widening the Social Circle

Health professionals might be better able to find people at risk if they knew to look more deeply at an individual's social environment. Rather than focusing only on those who seem to be entirely isolated, health care workers could encourage friendship and personal connectedness for a larger number of people—perhaps boosting overall population survival rates.

But when doctors do prescribe social interaction for those who seem to be severely isolated, it often comes in the form of a paid companion. That's not always effective, Holt-Lunstad says: "A naturally-occurring friendship is very different than someone who has been hired to be your buddy or your friend." Research has shown that friends "provide a sense of meaning or purpose in our lives," she says. A "professional friend" such as a hired companion might be helpful, but "might not be able to provide the emotional benefits." The same is true for online social interactions, Holt-Lunstad says. Although online connections might be better than nothing, time in front of a screen is likely not as beneficial as a phone call or face-to-face conversation. Although social and physical health are intimately linked, Holt-Lunstad does not see it as a purely medical issue. She suggests a range of avenues to address the social fitness of the population: from school curriculum emphasizing good social skills, to city planning that reinforces community building, to workplaces that accentuate human interaction.

Imaginary Friends: TV Characters Can Ease Your Pain

Okay, loneliness hurts and is bad for your health. But what should you do about it when you are alone and feeling blue and there is no one dear or near to call, see, or even e-mail? Wait! Remember *Friends*?

New psychological research suggests that loneliness can be eased by simply turning on your favorite TV show. In the same way that a snack can satiate hunger in lieu of a meal, it seems that watching your favorite characters on your favorite TV shows can give your brain the experience of belonging without a true (that is, in-person) interaction.

For decades, psychologists have been interested in understanding how we make and keep social relationships and ward off isolation and loneliness. The vast majority of this research has focused on actual humans as they interact face-to-face. Recent research has widened this focus from real to faux, or what are called parasocial relationships.

Parasocial relationships are the kind of one-sided pseudo-relationships we develop over time with people or characters we might see on TV or in the movies. So just as a friendship evolves through spending time together and sharing personal thoughts and opinions, parasocial relationships evolve by watching characters on favorite TV shows. We become involved with their personal lives, idiosyncrasies, and experiences just as if we were spending time with a friend.

In a recent article published in the *Journal of Experimental Social Psychology*, Jaye Derrick and Shira Gabriel of the University of Buffalo and Kurt Hugenberg of Miami University discussed their findings after testing what they call the "social surrogacy hypothesis." Starting with the theory that loneliness motivates us to seek relationships, even if those relationships are not real, the researchers discovered that participants were more likely to report watching a favorite TV show when they were feeling lonely and reported being less likely to feel lonely while watching. This preliminary evidence suggests that people seek out social surrogates when real interactions aren't available. The authors also found that those who recalled a fight with a close person in their lives wrote significantly more about their favorite TV show than a nonfavored TV show. It appears that a lack of belonging actually caused people to revel in their favorite TV shows, as though the TV characters replaced the flawed real-life relationships.

A threat to interpersonal relationships, such as a fight or social rejection, is often followed by lowered self-esteem and negative mood. However, the researchers found that study participants who had a relationship threat and then watched their favorite TV show were buffered against the blow to self-esteem, negative mood, and feelings of rejection.

At the core of this research is our fundamental need to belong. We humans are social animals, driven by the need to be accepted and to form and maintain relationships. When that desire to connect is met with consistent, meaningful interactions, the craving subsides, but when it goes unmet, it intensifies just like a hunger.

Research has shown that threats to belonging provoke a wide array of thoughts and behaviors directed at trying to maintain social connections. One particularly intriguing finding is that people seem to become highly sensitive to social cues after a social rejection or when lonely. For example, those with a heightened need to belong are better at decoding the emotional facial expressions of others and have a longer memory for socially relevant information compared to the less socially needy.

So in much the same way as a person on a restrictive diet may salivate while watching someone else eat a juicy, warm apple pie à la mode, those who have few or fragile relationships undergo a perceptual shift, making them more sensitive to the source of their hunger. They become more sensitive to interpersonal cues, and that might cause a parasocial relationship with a TV character to feel even more "real" or satisfying.

Unfortunately, the main advantage of a parasocial relationship is also its greatest drawback: its one-sidedness. Sure, social surrogates are the safest of social connections. They can provide the psychological experience of a connection with none of the drawbacks of a real relationship: no painful slights, time-consuming maintenance, or personal sacrifices. A social surrogate is consistently and dependably available at the same time, on the same channel, from week to week, or maybe on your computer hard drive. As time becomes more limited by work and obligations, it seems much easier to flip on the TV than to spend time cultivating new friendships and thereby risk rejection. In fact, the average American home has more TVs than people, with the average American watching more than four and a half hours of TV a day. Using TV to satisfy that need to belong may come at the expense of real relationships, where the risks are greater but the potential rewards are greater as well.

However, it seems no relationship is totally safe. Parasocial relationships may offer a quick and easy fix for the unmet need to belong, but individuals counting on these may not be spared the pain and anguish of a lost relationship: even very popular TV shows eventually go off the air. A study published in the *Journal of Social and Personal Relationships* found that viewers expecting to "lose" their favorite characters anticipated going through the same negative reactions that they experience when their real social relationships dissolve.

It could be that social surrogacy is like a candy bar in the vending machine, which briefly satiates the hunger of real belonging but ultimately leaves a person still hungry, instead of replacing real relationships in some lasting way. "There ain't nothing like the real thing," Marvin Gaye and Tammi Terrell sang.

Until the Real Thing Comes Along: Your Brain on Facebook

Virtual friending on Facebook, MySpace, Twitter, and other social networks is different from face-to-face contact, but not *that* different, you might say: sure, it's cyberspace, but it's a connection with a real person. Perhaps. The effect of virtual social networks is yet to be determined. But they are a mighty force. If Facebook were a country, it would be the fourth most populous in the world, just behind the United States, and very active: almost half of Facebook's users visit every day.

It's true that as social networks proliferate, they're changing the way people think about the Internet—from a tool used in solitary anonymity to an interactive medium—in ways that touch on questions about human nature and identity. Nielsen Online reports that social networking (and associated blogging) is now the fourth most popular online activity. Time spent on social networking sites is growing at three times the rate of overall Internet use, accounting for almost 10 percent of total time spent online.

Social networks can lessen loneliness and boost self-esteem. But they can also have the opposite effect, depending on who you are and how you use these forums. When connecting us to those we know face-to-face, they can ease loneliness. But when used as a substitute for relationships, they can lead to more feelings of isolation. For example, in a 2009 functional magnetic resonance imaging study by Cacioppo and his colleagues, the heightened ability to read social cues, especially negative cues, can be seen in the brains of lonely people; that can be a liability to lonely people who use social networks.

"When you're lonely, your brain is in a heightened state of alertness for social threats, even if you're not explicitly looking for them," Cacioppo explains. Insults, snubs, alienation, and gossip all elicit much higher levels of stress in the lonely, measurable in part by elevated production of the stress hormone cortisol. The effect is amplified online because social threats are more difficult to anticipate there. A long silence between replies during an online chat can spawn fears that others are locking you out of the conversation and gossiping behind your back—and the very number (or lack) of contacts can leave the lonely feeling even further out of touch. You can't even know for sure who really is on the other end of the Internet connection; cyberbullying, stalking, and hacking over the Internet have become problems. Before we completely bash virtual social networks, however, consider the not-so-distant past: long-distance friending is not so very new. In older times—as recently as the 1980s, before everyone jumped on the Net—people separated by distance communicated quite a bit by actual post office paper letters in the mail and by telephone. Letter writing sustained many relationships of the past, when distances were too great for frequent meetings, and there were many courtships by mail where letters sparked love and kept it alive.

Letters, like e-mail today, enabled people to communicate fairly anonymously as well. *The Shop Around the Corner,* a book and film, details the development by mail of such a friendship between two people who could not stand each other in person (it was revamped to twenty-first-century Internet standards as the film *You've Got Mail*). Similarly, as war veteran and politician John McCain describes, he and other Vietnam prisoners of war in solitary confinement kept sane by communicating with taps and code. Perhaps any communication is better than none.

For the disabled and others who can't get out and around or for those who may have difficulty speaking, the Internet has been a boon. And being glued to texting is not such a bad thing for awkward or shy teens who often find face-to-face socializing excruciating. At least they're reaching out.

The key (for now) appears to be having offline relationships as a base. In a 2009 study of loneliness and Facebook membership, psychologist Laura Freberg of California Polytechnic State University and her team found that college students who are socially connected in their face-to-face lives bring that persona online and really do derive benefits, but the lonely became lonelier. A 2007 study of older adults in Australia found similar results: using social networks diminishes loneliness when online social contacts are also offline contacts. When older adults try to use social networks to meet new people, however, they consistently feel lonelier than they did before.

Work, the "Other Love" in Your Life

Work takes the better part of most days for most of our lives, so it's no wonder that we form deep attachments to not only our coworkers but to the very place we work.

Most of us don't love our bosses (or we are discreet about it if we do), but all of us have a complex connection to those we work for and with. When that relationship is good, it gives us deep satisfaction—so much so that former coworkers may continue to meet long after retirement. When it goes wrong, people can react just like jilted lovers, as stories of workplace violence by fired or passed-over employees show. Your place and people of work can also be a great and deep source of well-being and enjoyment—or not.

Your brain tells you when it's unhappy on the job. Now the University of Chicago's General Social Survey can help you predict which jobs your brain will like. Researchers looked at who was satisfied with their jobs and who was happy, and found that a good bet was a career involving helping people. Your brain likes helping others: altruism makes us feel good. The survey asked people how satisfied they were with their jobs and how happy they were in general and correlated the results. On average, 47 percent of people were very satisfied with their jobs, and 33 percent said they were very happy. On the job front, clergy topped the lists: 87 percent of clergy surveyed said they were very satisfied with their calling, and 67 percent said they were very happy. Next, 80 percent of firefighters really like their work, and 57 percent said they were very happy.

The no-satisfaction list was topped by roofers, only a quarter of whom said the job was satisfying. And only 14 percent of roofers said they were happy (and their knees may be even less happy than they are). The people in what are usually called "service jobs" but can feel more like "servant jobs"—waiters, bartenders, cashiers, and various kinds of retail salespeople—also didn't like their work much. A satisfying career and happy life may involve working at something that helps other people.

Can Animals Love? Yes, and More

The bond between humans and our companion animals is a powerful force in numbers alone. One estimate puts the number of pets in U.S. households at 1.2 billion, and that may be low.

Our love of animals helps us fend off depression and even mental illness. A close relationship with a pet reduces almost all the signs of stress—high blood pressure, heart rate, respiratory rate, anxiety, and tension—and leaves us happier. They seem to know when we need a reassuring snuggle, and are welcome in many hospitals, nursing homes, and psychiatric units. Pets can sense the onset of an epileptic seizure and seek help. In fact, service animals are now approved for people with emotional and psychological issues as they have traditionally been for those with physical impairments such as blindness and deafness.

We love our animal companions. But do they love us? Or is our relationship all about dominance and food? Are animals substitutes for other people or even children? Can we have a real relationship with an animal?

Many scientists (and others) say equating human motives to animal behaviors is anthropomorphizing, and they don't mean that in a nice way. But is that so? Are we only projecting our own love onto creatures who have none in their hearts (or brains)?

Nope. Researchers are discovering that animals display what looks like many of the same feelings we humans do, and they behave much as we do in situations involving sex, love, pain, empathy, sorrow, and jealousy. No wonder: we share many of the same DNA with many mammals. Chimpanzees are famously close to the human genome (although new research shows not quite as close as the oft-quoted 98.5 percent; it's more like 96 percent). But guess who else is sharing our DNA? Fido.

The dog apparently shares 94 percent of its genetic sequence with humans and mice, despite having a substantially smaller genome. And dog lovers will be happy to know that humans have more in common genetically with dogs than with mice, despite sharing a more recent common ancestor with the latter.

Animals famously show affection, longing, and even sorrow about their human companions. Among themselves, many animals display what looks very much like human love and empathy. Recently, when an elderly chimpanzee was dying in a U.K. zoo, her long-time companion, daughter, and son stayed with her in the nest, soothing her as she passed away, and they mourned her for days afterward.

Even rodents show the related human traits of empathy and altruism. It's tempting to dismiss such behavior in animals that we believe don't have much brain power by arguing that the sight of a suffering fellow mouse simply evokes an automatic fear reaction in the watcher. But a study undermined that explanation by finding that mice showed empathetic reactions only with cage mates. The mice seem to go far beyond being frightened by injury to accounting for whether the injured party is friend, family, foe, or stranger. This response is a significantly humanlike social feeling—caring for acquaintances more than for strangers, just as our empathy for someone who is hurt differs depending on whether the person is a foreigner, a national compatriot, a school chum, or an immediate family member.

A research team at the University of Bern in Switzerland trained rats to deliver food for one another by pulling a stick. Then they divided the animals into two groups: some rats received food from other animals, while others did not. The research team noted that rats that had received help were more likely to pull the stick for other, unfamiliar animals—going one step beyond the well-documented, "You scratch my back, and I'll scratch yours," reciprocity that is seen in many species.

Studies show humans have this kind of altruism toward strangers, termed generalized reciprocity. One experiment showed that people who found money in a telephone booth were more likely to help a stranger pick up dropped papers. But scientists have not yet figured out whether cultural experience or natural selection explains such acts of kindness. The fact that rats show generalized reciprocity hints at an evolutionary mechanism, the researchers say.

Our pets can show another human emotion: jealousy. Scientists have confirmed what dog owners have always suspected: our pooches may pout when they sense another pup is getting favorable treatment.

Dogs may be like our human best buddies: they get jealous if they feel we're treating another dog better, researchers at the University of Vienna in Austria reported in the *Proceedings of the National Academy of Sciences of the United States of America*. In a series of experiments with dogs, Friederike Range and her colleagues found that the canines were happy to "shake hands" whether or not they were rewarded (at least for a while). But that all changed if one pup got a treat and the other got none.

The scientists worked with fourteen well-trained dogs that either lived together or knew one another. A familiar human companion remained on the scene during the research with the animals. Range and her colleagues put the dogs through a series of experiments to determine how long each one would follow commands in different circumstances: when rewarded or not, solo or with another pooch on hand.

For a long time, scientists believed a sense of equity was a purely human trait. Scientists have learned in the past decade that primates have a sense of fairness. In 2003 researchers discovered that capuchin monkeys complied with requests in return for cucumber slices, but they got their backs up when they saw another monkey getting grapes, which they perceived as sweeter, better treats.

The dogs apparently weren't quite as picky. They were eager to please their human experimenters as long as they got something—be it a piece of bread or sausage—in acknowledgment of their effort. But they became visibly stressed and stopped playing along if they shook hands and got nothing, especially if another dog was rewarded for doing the same thing. And they cooperated longer if their canine companions also were stiffed or if they were being tested alone. And while all of the dogs preferred the sausage to the bread, they didn't protest if their neighbors got the better prize as long as they got a tidbit too.

So animals do seem to feel emotions quite a bit as we do, or at least express them that way. And while this may not resolve the age-old question of whether animals love us for ourselves, we know that we love our animal companions—and that having them around and caring for them improves our health and our life.

How to Make Friends

Some people seem to have the gift of friendship: their phones are always ringing, and their calendar is full. But most of the rest of us aren't so fortunate.

Making friends is easier when we are young: we meet people in school, at work, and then in the activities of our children. But as we grow older, opportunities for finding friends aren't so available.

It takes some courage to get out there, put on a friendly smile, and possibly face rejection. But as the song from *Cabaret* goes, "What good is sitting alone in your room?" Psychologists, self-help writers, and successful socializers offer tips on where and how to friend (to use the verb form of today). Here's a summary of some practical advice:

Five Ways to Make Friends

1. *Show up, and pay attention.* Accept all invitations (within reason)—even the one for your second cousin's son's graduation party. Attend art gallery openings, fundraising events, community celebrations—even if you have to go alone. Check out neighborhood yard sales (and the neighbors). You can't meet people if you don't get out. And the more you do it, the easier it gets.

2. *Join a group, take a class, volunteer.* Take an art course or tai chi course, join a gym, sign up for a lecture series, find a walking group, or volunteer at the library, museum, or other nonprofit. Many social groups are connected to church. If you haven't been a church-goer, consider a nondenominational group such as the Unitarians. Soon you'll be seeing the same people week after week, and friendly encounters will follow.

3. *Befriend friends of friends.* Someone you like a lot probably has friends you'll also like. Invite a friend and one of that person's friends to join you for lunch or dinner, a movie or a play. Tell friends you are looking to expand your social circle.

4. *Turn off the computer, or at least leave it off for awhile.* It's easy for online and virtual relationships to take the place of real contact. Use your computer to find local activities, but not as a substitute for friendship.

5. *Consider a pet or fostering a pet.* Our animal companions offer lots of love, and they're also great icebreakers, as every dog walker knows. If you can't or don't want a full-time pet, volunteer at an animal shelter or foster pets in your home. Pet rescue organizations and those who train service animals are looking for animal lovers for short-term sheltering.

CHAPTER SIX

Only You Can Make My Dreams Come True

Let's Get Married

Marriage is good for us. Studies confirm it, long-time couples sing its praises, and gay and interracial couples have gone to court to have the right to it.

Marriage is the choice of an overwhelming majority of us: 94 percent of living Americans have tried marriage at least once by age sixty-five (and many of us more often).

We know why our brains like sex, but why do our brains like marriage, also known as pair bonding? Why do we choose one person over another or hold out entirely until we find what we believe is the perfect mate? And what makes us stick together after that first hot passion? Most animals are not monogamous (and apparently many people are not either, whatever they say), yet we humans hold it up as an ideal.

Grow Old Along with Me: The Marriage Benefits

Being married or mated brings benefits sociologists and psychologists have been tallying up for years. There are many obvious immediate economic and sexual benefits and long-term health advantages, including emotional support and a sense of belonging, which act as buffers against depression. Being mated lowers stress hormones and generally improves health, and that's true even for those who are happily and tightly mated even if not married.

Overall, monogamous mating benefits the lives and brains of both partners (and their children as well), but men benefit more than women. Studies show that being married adds more years to a man's life than to a woman's. Marriage seems to most support men's health since wives provide social support and connections to the broader social world—characteristics increasingly found to contribute to longevity and better brain health. Wives also tend to wean men away from risky business—what are often called "stupid bachelor tricks." Husbands typically forgo drunken nights out and the motorcycle, stop using illegal drugs, eat regular meals, get a job, and buckle up—all of which help to prolong their life.

Many men remarry fairly quickly after the loss of a spouse from death or divorce (an interesting switch on the popular perception that women are more eager for marriage). And that's a good move for them, compared to women. Recent analysis of an eight-decades-long Stanford University longevity study show that fewer than a third of divorced men reached old age, whereas single women or women who were married once and divorced outlived them.

The older you get, the better marriage seems to be for you. Some studies show that very elderly persons who are still married are likely to be healthier—76 percent reported being in good or excellent health—compared to their peers who are widowed, divorced and living with a partner, or never married. A study titled "'Til Death Do Us Part" analyzed what happened to more than eleven thousand men and women in and out of marital relationships from 1968 to 1988. Although the study is two decades old, much of what was found remains true today and has been confirmed by subsequent studies. The researchers found that the friendship and companionship that spouses provide make a body—your body, and presumably your brain—feel good. The nearness of a familiar person can improve health, boost immune function, relieve depression, and lower heart rate, especially for men.

However, the quality of the marriage does matter, according to a 2008 analysis from the National Healthy Marriage Resource Center. An article titled, "What Is the Relationship of Marriage to Physical Health?" summarizes research that shows marriage can have both negative and positive effects depending on the quality of the relationship—and that women suffer more than men do from discord and a negative marriage. The article cites a national survey showing that an unhappy marriage eliminates the health benefits of being married: living in a negative marriage contributes to stress that under-mines health and happiness.

But it doesn't have to be a great marriage to have advantages. Research also shows a good-enough healthy marriage, one that's low in negativity, can give lifelong protection against chronic illness and premature death for men and women, as well as greatly increasing the chances of healthy children. "And these benefits increase as couples grow old together," the article concludes.

You Make Me Feel So Good: Romance Lowers Stress

Couples don't have to be legally married to benefit from being together. A recent study suggests that those in a committed, long-term relation-ship, married or not, have lower levels of the stress hormone cortisol than their single peers. And when stressed, they also had lower levels of testosterone, which is related to being less aggressive.

Researchers at the University of Chicago put a bunch of business students to a test intended to raise stress: they had them play computer games based on economic behavior, telling them (falsely) that the test was a course requirement and that the outcome would affect their future. Then they sampled the subjects' saliva. Cortisol levels jumped in all the students, but increased the most in the women and, especially, the unpaired or unmarried students. The single students also had higher testosterone levels, but these dropped in the men who were mated.

Another saliva study found that couples tend to share the same stress level, for better or worse—but those who say they have a very satisfactory marriage tend to be less affected when their partner has a negative mood. University of California, Los Angeles, researchers had thirty couples note their mood states and collect saliva four times a day for three days to document levels of cortisol, the stress hormone. The couples had been married an average of thirteen years, and both spouses worked. They found, to no one's surprise, that the stress level in one spouse is linked to the amount of stress the partner is feeling. However, the more satisfactory they say the marriage is overall, the less each is affected by the other's negative moods.

Finding That Special Someone: Looking for Love in All the Wrong Places?

But where to find that special someone? Research shows that people traditionally mate and marry with those only a few degrees of separation away, connected by the neighborhood, friends, family, or even a matchmaker.

At least that's the way it used to be. Social change and the Internet are starting to affect all that. Gone are the days of wooing and wedding the girl (or boy) next door. We increasingly meet our partners through social networks that are much less constrained by geography—if at all—than they have been in the past. So while it's still true that you "love the one you're with" and tend to mate with those connected to those we know, that connection doesn't have to be in person.

A French study showed that from 1914 to 1960, 15 to 20 percent of people reported meeting their future spouses in the neighborhood; by 1984 this figure was down to 3 percent, wrote Nicholas A. Christakis and James H. Fowler, authors of *Connected: The Surprising Power of Our Social Networks and How They Shape Our Lives.*

Back in 1992, Christakis and Fowler write, the National Health and Social Life Survey sampled 3,432 people aged eighteen to fifty-nine at that time. Among the findings were that 68 percent of the people sampled met their spouses after being introduced by someone they knew. Less that half that number—32 percent—met by "self-introduction." Even for short-term sexual partners, such as one-night stands, 53 percent were introduced by someone else.

Flash-forward to 2006. Christakis and Fowler report that about 16 million adults, or one in nine American adults using the Internet, say they used an online dating Web site or other site. Nearly half of these—43 percent, or 7 million adults—had gone on actual dates with men or women they met online.

Facebook, which started in 2004, was barely a toddler when this study was done in 2006. Since then it has connected millions of old friends and old (and new) lovers. Today, with 500 million active users who spend over 700 billion minutes per month on Facebook, it's surely connecting even more couples. An international survey of twenty-four thousand people published in 2011 found that one in three who use the Internet have visited online dating sites, and that's not just the very young: middle-aged men report using them the most, and 36 percent of these men say that had found their current partners online.

Indeed, a 2010 *New York Times* article says there are now fifteen hundred online dating services and cites a study by IBIS World Marketing that estimates 20 million Americans are using such dating services, double the number of five years ago.

Falling and Staying in Love

We've all heard the statistic: about half of first marriages in the United States fail, and practice does not make perfect: two-thirds of second marriages and three-quarters of third marriages also fail. Yet arranged marriages, practiced by more than half of the rest of the world, succeed.

Some conjecture that we fail in large part because of our highly unrealistic expectations of relationships and our poor skills for maintaining them. Studies of arranged marriages, in which love has grown over time, hint that commitment, communication, accommodation, and vulnerability are key components of a successful relationship. Other research indicates that sharing adventures, secrets, personal space, and jokes can also build intimacy and love with your partner.

More than eighty scientific studies help to reveal how people learn to love each other and how to keep love alive. Here are some key findings for building strong relationships:

○ *Arousal helps us bond.* Studies by researchers such as psychologist Arthur Aron of Stony Brook University show that people tend to bond emotionally when aroused through exercise, adventures, or exposure to dangerous situations.

○ *Novelty heightens the senses and also makes people feel vulnerable.* Psychologist Greg Strong of Florida State University, Aron, and others have shown that people tend to grow closer when they are doing something new.

○ *Proximity and familiarity tend to produce positive feelings.* Studies by Stanford University social psychologists Leon Festinger and Robert Zajonc and others conclude that simply being around someone fosters intimacy, and when two people consciously and deliberately allow each other to invade their personal space, feelings of intimacy can grow quickly.

○ *Similarity increases closeness.* Opposites sometimes attract. But research by behavioral economist Dan Ariely of Duke University and MIT and others shows that people usually tend to pair off with those who are similar to themselves in intelligence, background, and level of attractiveness. Some research even suggests that merely imitating someone can increase closeness.

○ *Humor makes us happy.* Marriage counselors and researchers Jeanette and Robert Lauer showed in 1986 that in long-term, happy relationships, partners make each other laugh a lot. Other research reveals that women often seek male partners who can make them laugh—possibly because when we are laughing, we feel vulnerable.

○ *Loosening inhibitions and some self-disclosure lets the other in.* Countless millions of relationships have probably started with a glass of wine. Inhibitions block feelings of vulnerability, so lowering inhibitions can indeed help people bond (but getting drunk is self-defeating). Research by Aron, Sprecher, and others indicates that people tend to bond when they share secrets with each other.

○ *Kindness, accommodation, and forgiveness fuel bonding.* A variety of studies confirm that we tend to bond to people who are kind, sensitive, and thoughtful. Feelings of love can emerge especially quickly when someone deliberately changes his or her behavior—say, by giving up smoking or drinking—to accommodate our needs. Forgiveness often causes mutual bonding, because when one forgives, one shows vulnerability.

○ *Touch and sexuality produce warm, positive feelings, and a back rub can work wonders.* Even getting very near someone without actually touching can have an effect. Studies by social psychologist Susan Sprecher of Illinois State University, among others, also show that sexuality can make people feel closer emotionally, especially for women. There is danger, however, of confusing sexual attraction with feelings of love (as many of us have found to our regret).

○ *Commitment is a key.* We are not that good at honoring our relationship commitments in the United States, but studies by researchers such as psychologist Ximena Arriaga of Purdue University suggest that commitment is an essential element in building love.

I've Grown Accustomed to Your Face

We dream of fairytale romance, but more than half of the marriages on our globe are brokered by parents or professional matchmakers whose main concerns are long-term suitability and family harmony. In India an estimated 95 percent of the marriages are arranged, and although divorce is legal, India has one of the lowest divorce rates in the world. (This is starting to change as Western ways encroach on traditional society.)

Young couples in India generally have a choice about whether to proceed with a proposed marriage, and the combination of choice and sound guidance probably accounts for the fact that studies of arranged marriages in India indicate that they measure up well against Western marriages in longevity, satisfaction, and love. Indeed, the love experienced by Indian couples in arranged marriages appears to be even more robust than the love people experience in "love marriages."

In a 1982 study, psychologists Usha Gupta and Pushpa Singh of the University of Rajasthan in Jaipur, India, used the Rubin Love Scale, which gauges intense, romantic, Western-style love. They thought they would find that love in love marriages in India does exactly what it does in love marriages in the United States: starts high and declines fairly rapidly. But not so. Love in the arranged marriages they examined started out low and gradually increased, surpassing the love in the so-called love marriage in about five years. Ten years into the marriage, the love was nearly twice as strong. How do they do it? How do people in some arranged marriages build love deliberately over time, and can others do it too?

It seems we could. A study presented at the November 2009 meeting of the National Council on Family Relations included thirty individuals from nine countries of origin and five different religions who said their love had grown, on average, from 3.9 to 8.5 on a 10-point scale in marriages lasting an average of 19.4 years. They identified eleven factors that contributed to the growth of their love.

The most important factor was commitment, followed by good communication skills. The couples also listed sharing secrets as well as accommodation—altering behavior to meet the other person's needs—and seeing a spouse in a vulnerable state. Several said their love grew when they had children with their spouse, unlike Americans. Studies in the United States routinely find parenting to be a threat to feelings of spousal love, perhaps another sign of the unrealistic expectations of a marriage.

Americans want it all: the freedom to choose a partner and the deep, lasting love of fantasies and fairy tales. And it's possible we can have it all. By adopting some of the practices and techniques (and patience) that science and arranged marriages show build love over time, we may be able to achieve that kind of lasting love.

My One and Only Love: Are We Monogamous?

Monogamy is apparently not a natural practice for mammals. Some studies put the percentage of mammals that mate for life at between 3 and 5 percent (they did not give a breakdown of the percentage of human mammals).

So considering that monogamy is not the usual animal state, what's going on in our brains that makes so many of us want to bond—and stay mated 'til death do us part? Or at least hold that up as the relationship ideal? It's our brain, of course.

Researchers got insights from the laboratory stars for studying love-for-life: monogamous prairie voles with their strong pair bonds. Male prairie voles are upstanding citizens: they typically cohabit with their mates for life, live in social groups, and are attentive fathers. In contrast, their cousins the male montane voles are cads: promiscuous, solitary, and indifferent to their offspring.

Researchers have found that the differences between the social behaviors in these vole species are connected with the locations in their brain of receptors for oxytocin, the love hormone, and arginine vasopressin, the neuromodulator connected with courtship. In prairie voles, those receptors are concentrated in brain regions that make monogamy rewarding—in midbrain areas that modulate release of the neurotransmitter dopamine, which we know makes us feel very good about love, cohabiting, and caring for offspring.

But those are rodents. What goes on in the brain of primates like ourselves? It seems to be a similar process. A couple of year ago, scientists at the University of California, Davis, took a look at the brains of monogamous monkeys and found a primate model of monogamy they believe will be more relevant to us for uncovering the basis of human affection. The researchers used positron emission tomography (PET) scans to examine the brain activity in males of small South American monkeys, called titis, which form strong relationships with their mates. They discovered that lone, unpaired male titis had strikingly different patterns of brain activity than did males in long-term monogamous partnerships. These differences were found primarily in two brain circuits also active in those monogamous prairie voles: one involved in reward processing and another that plays a part in social recognition.

The scientists also studied the brains of lone males who had recently been introduced to new mates. Although the average of the monkeys' brain activity was somewhere in between that of unpaired males and that of those in long-term partnerships, testing showed tremendous individual variation in both behavior and brain activity.

Other factors may drive us human primates toward monogamy. It appears to be on the upswing since the free-wheeling free love pre-AIDS era of the 1960s and 1970s that followed the introduction of oral contraceptives. Couples in 2000 reported having fewer affairs than they were reporting in the 1970s. Extramarital (and extrapartnership) sex was way down, and discussion about the topic within couples is way up, according to a study from the 2009 annual convention of the

American Psychological Association. This was true across sexual groups: gay or straight, they reported fewer affairs in the Alliant International University in San Francisco studies. And the percentage of couples who were decidedly closed to having sex outside the relationship—those who decided that "under no circumstances is it all right"—just about doubled in every group (from around 43 percent in 1975 to around 80 percent in 2000) except in gay men, among whom it more than tripled (13 to 44 percent). "It was surprising to us that in all groups, the trend is toward monogamy," said Gabrielle Gotta, lead author of the study.

The temper of the times certainly affects this trend, much as the free love atmosphere of the 1970s did. There is more awareness about HIV and other sexually transmitted diseases, speculate the authors, and the economy might play a part: in bad times when cash is tight, we tend to stick closer to home.

Granny's Got to Have It

However, not everyone is opposed to a little fling on the side. Some spouses do cheat. And guess which group of swingers is on the upswing? It's grandma and grandpa—and maybe grandma more often.

A look at national survey responses in 2010 that compared infidelity rates from the more conservative (compared to the 1970s) year 1991 reveals that men's rates of infidelity didn't change much in that decade. Roughly a fifth to a quarter of men surveyed then and now admit to cheating—but women's admissions of an affair rose from 11 to 17 percent during the last decade and a half.

And the age group that's doing its part to close the infidelity gap? More people over age sixty are cheating than they were in 1991, possibly related to the recent popularity of—you guessed it—drugs for erectile dysfunction. Being able to be up for sex apparently makes it more attractive for both genders of a certain age.

DOES DOMESTIC BLISS DEPEND ON SEX?

Many psychotherapists, such as Esther Perel, say that sexual gratification is vital to a healthy relationship. She emphasizes the importance of eroticism and orgasm in marriage in her book, *Mating in Captivity*, and says the disintegration of a couple's sex life is typical when their love bond becomes politically correct and excessively domesticated. To avoid sexual staleness and make your partner more mysterious and exciting, Perel advocates some separateness—developing different interests and groups of friends from those of your partner, for example—instead of closeness. She also suggests looking for creative ways to let fantasy, X-rated playfulness, and even a little craziness thrive in a long-term relationship.

Other psychologists disagree. They advise against placing too much emphasis on orgasm in a mature relationship. In her book, *Peace Between the Sheets*, couples therapist Marnia Robinson suggests that the journey to orgasm renders us prisoners to dopamine, the pleasure neurotransmitter secreted in the brain's reward centers that underlies other addictive behaviors, from gambling to drug abuse. Orgasm, she suggests, may contribute to distance rather than closeness. In Robinson's view, partners should mutually unite in pleasure, without necessarily expecting or having the sexual relationship crowned by orgasm.

But increasingly, people under age thirty-five are also reporting infidelity. David Atkins at the University of Washington and his coauthor speculate the availability of pornography online might have also something to do with it at any age, since participants who said they'd seen an X-rated movie were more likely to report an extramarital affair—and compared to older generations, more young people say they've watched porn.

Curiously, most survey responders said that cheating is wrong. Yet that doesn't appear to have changed their cheating behavior.

Your Hormones May Drive You Apart: A Tough Pill to Swallow

This year 2.25 million Americans will get married—and 1 million will get divorced. Could birth control contribute to some of these breakups?

Research is showing that the contraceptive pill, which prevents women from ovulating by fooling their body into believing it's pregnant, can change the type of man who lights her sexual fires. And if that's different from the man she married, there could be trouble.

It's all about the scent of a man. We choose our mates based partly on our genetic differences from them, and we can detect some of that by the way they smell. Hidden in a man's smell are clues about his major histocompatibility complex (MHC) genes, which play an important role in immune system surveillance.

Studies suggest that women prefer the scent of males whose MHC genes differ from their own, to increase genetic variety in the offspring. (See Chapter Four, "That Old Black Magic.") But we can be fooled by our sense of smell. When a woman is on the pill and her body thinks she is pregnant, her sense of smell undergoes a shift in preference toward men who share similar MHC genes. A study published in the *Proceedings of the Royal Society* had women sniff T-shirts that men had worn for two nights. They found that women were more likely to rate as pleasant and desirable the scents from genetically similar men after they went on the pill as compared with before. Although no one knows why this is so, some scientists believe that pregnancy—or in this case, hormonal changes that mimic pregnancy—draws women toward nurturing relatives, and that would be those with similar MHC genes.

But a study published in *Psychological Science* found that women paired with MHC-similar men are less sexually satisfied and more likely to cheat on their partners than women paired with men who have a different MHC. Women who start or stop taking the pill, then, may be in for some relationship problems.

Let's say a woman meets and marries a man when she is on the pill—an MHC-similar man. He could ultimately leave her less sexually satisfied, especially if she then goes off the pill during the relationship and the hormonal changes draw her toward more MHC-dissimilar men.

So while mated couples struggle with many obvious issues, it could be that a stealth attack from our immune genes may have a "powerful effect in terms of how well relationships are cemented," says University of Liverpool psychologist Craig Roberts, coauthor of the paper.

Making Love Last: I Get a Kick Out of You

Even with the best of intentions, how do you keep love alive? Is it worn down by children, family crises, stress, conflict, tension, and disagreements? Are poverty and infidelity the deal breakers?

Alas, a study shows simple boredom could be the biggest culprit.

Most marital research has tended to focus on problems and issues. But the major (and often overlooked) problem in long-term marriages could be boredom and a lack of excitement, and that builds up over time, according to some studies by Arthur Aron, a professor of social psychology at Stony Brook University, and his associates, Irene Tsapelas and Terri Orbuch.

The title of their study says it all: "Marital Boredom Now Predicts Less Satisfaction Nine Years Later." The researchers had looked at short-term marital happiness in earlier studies. In their new study of boredom and marriage, they followed 123 couples over sixteen years, interviewing them at years 7 and 16 of the marriage. They found that couples who were not bored in the original interview had a small decrease in marital satisfaction nine years later. Although those who reported being bored at year 7 were no more bored by year 16, they were less satisfied with their marriage as the years went by.

Another major conclusion from the study was surprising: being bored reduces closeness, and reduced closeness causes marital dissatisfaction.

"Increasing rewards may matter as much or more than reducing costs," the researchers wrote in the study, published in *Psychological Science*. "It may be important to focus not just on eliminating negatives, but also on enhancing positives." In other words, keeping the flame of love burning depends on fueling it. Excitement—the unexpected and the risky—pumps out dopamine, several studies show, and keeps sexual attraction hot.

A good fictional example is the 2005 shoot-'em-up film *Mr. and Mrs. Smith*, starring Brad Pitt and Angelina Jolie. It begins with a bored Mr. and Mrs. at their therapist, saying the marriage is not so hot. Unknown to each other, the two are competing assassins. By the end of film, which is filled with mayhem, attempted murder of each other, and close calls, they are steaming up the screen. They meet with their therapist in the last scene and say their marriage is doing well. After a pause, Mr. Smith says the last line of the movie: "Ask us about the sex." And perhaps not incidentally, the two movie stars fell in love in real life during the adrenaline-fueled filming and have been together ever since.

Many dysfunctional marriages limp along because of the spectacular sex after violent arguments (or worse). Some have called it an aphrodisiac. It's the rare (or disbarred) therapist who would suggest trying to murder one another as a therapy for a tepid relationship. But lesser means might yield the frisson to spur excitement.

We are not thinking of skydiving or armed robbery (unless that appeals) but rather just something unexpected and novel, such as sex in an unexpected place, a date night at an incongruous spot, or some other break in the routine. In fact, that brings up another recent film, *Date Night* (2010), in which mistaken identity does just that. Doing something new could put a new energy into your aging relationship.

Can Pornography Help Your Love Life?

Pornography, once relegated to books with plain brown wrappers or smutty postcards, is now available to anyone with a computer that can pick up an Internet connection—and perhaps another player.

A survey of college students in 2008 by psychologist Chiara Sabina of Penn State Harrisburg and her colleagues found that more than 90 percent of the men and 60 percent of the women had watched Internet pornography before age eighteen. In a separate study, the rate of use was less than half as frequent among those between the ages of forty and forty-nine, suggesting that Internet porn consumption may decline with age—although that statistic could reflect generational differences in computer use (or perhaps getting on the Net at a later age).

So far, most people who watch porn seem to be dabblers who claim that occasional use of pornography sites and other online sexual activities isn't associated with serious problems.

Back in 1998 Alvin Cooper, then at the Marital and Sexuality Center in San Jose, California, and his associates conducted an online study of more than nine thousand people who used the Internet for sexual purposes. Slightly fewer than half the respondents, most of them men who were married or in a committed relationship, indulged for an hour or less a week. Forty-five percent reported engaging in online sexual activity between one and ten hours a week. Eight percent used the Internet for such purposes for eleven or more hours weekly.

But a percentage of users indulge excessively in online sexual content. A small but distinctive 0.5 percent reported more than seventy hours a week. And that may not be so good for their real sex life.

Some say pornography puts spice into their monogamous relationships, but studies show that intense use may put a spike in the heart of love, especially for women. Researchers have found that female partners of men who are heavy consumers of pornography don't feel very good about their partner's habits. Psychologist Ana Bridges of the

University of Arkansas and her colleagues noted that although most of the women received low overall scores on a measure of distress about their partner's porn use, most of them also endorsed some statements indicative of anguish. For example, 42 percent agreed that their partner's porn consumption made them feel insecure, 39 percent that the partner's porn use had a negative effect on their relationship, and 32 percent that it adversely affected their lovemaking. Even relatively light users admit it may have a negative effect on a partner or spouse.

Some experts contend that Internet porn can be addictive, but as with so-called sex addiction and other compulsive behaviors, scientists debate whether these are true addictions. They are similar to alcohol and drug addiction, in extreme indulgence and continued use despite negative effects on the user. Skeptics counter, however, that people who indulge in excessive sex or pornography rarely develop tolerance or obvious withdrawal symptoms—two hallmarks of addiction.

Some maintain that the label of "addict" adds unnecessary stigma to the problem, while others argue the opposite: that this description lets people off the hook for socially problematic behaviors that are at least partly under their control.

Love Will Keep Us Together: Lasting Romance Is Embossed in the Brain

Love does not fade with time for all couples. For some, it leaves a lasting impression in their brains as well as their hearts. Arthur Aron and associates looked at another group of the long married. They scanned the brains of ten women and seven men who had been married an average of twenty-one years and insisted that they were still madly in love with their spouses.

Their brains showed they told the truth. When the scientists showed the self-professed lovers photos of their partners, the functional magnetic resonance imaging detected intense activity in the ventral tegmental area of their brains, a region that releases the pleasure-giving neurotransmitter dopamine. A previous study of seventeen people still in the early, lustful months of relationships showed similar activity in the same brain area. "It's always been assumed that passionate love inevitably declines over time," study Aron, a social psychologist, told *Newsday*. "But in survey after survey we always have these people who have been together a long time and say they are intensely in love."

That assertion was always chalked up to self-deception or trying to make a good impression. But Aron and his three colleagues found more than just lasting passion in the happy couples. Their scans also showed activity in their ventral pallidum, a brain region associated with feelings of long-term attachment in the famously monogamous prairie voles, and in the raphe nucleus, which makes the chemical serotonin that's associated with calm and less obsession. This, says anthropologist Helen Fisher, a frequent collaborator with Aron, is "the real difference between early-stage and late-stage romantic love: You feel that deep attachment and that you want to be with the person, but you don't have that early, manic obsession of when you first fall in love of if you don't hear from the person you cry."

Other studies find that age plays a role in marital happiness. A longitudinal study by sociologist Debra Umberson of the University of Texas at Austin and her colleagues measured the independent effect of age—as opposed to duration of marriage—and discovered that the older the spouses, the more likely they are to have a good marriage. They suggest it's perhaps because older couples are calmer and less emotionally reactive in marital conflicts than younger people are, or because they better appreciate their partner's positive traits. Umberson's team also found that although parenthood may have a negative effect early in marriage, it had a positive influence in later years after children have left the nest. In addition, childless couples tend to have lower-quality marriages in old age than couples who have children.

Will You Still Need Me When I'm 64?

Apparently yes, and at 74, 84, 94, and beyond, health willing. Age does not wither sexual desire, it seems. Oh, it may tamp it down a bit, but recent studies and surveys show that your grandparents, and maybe great-grandparents, still enjoy getting it on. They also suggest that in old age, men seem to want sex more than women do—and to get more of it. That could be partially explained by the dearth of men to partner aging women.

The American Association for Retired Persons (AARP) commissioned the Sex, Romance, and Relationships: 2009 AARP Survey of Midlife and Older Adults, the third it has prepared in the past decade. The report queried about 1,670 people aged forty-five and older about sexual attitudes and practices and found that even in old age, men continue to think about sex more often than women do, see it as more important to their quality of life, engage in sexual activities more often, are less satisfied if they don't have a partner, and are twice as likely as women (21 percent versus 11 percent) to admit to sexual activity outside their relationship.

And, the report continues, both the frequency and satisfaction of sexual encounters were higher among those unmarried and dating (or engaged) individuals than among the married: 48 percent of those who are single and dating said they have intercourse at least once a week, compared to 36 percent of those who are married. In addition, 60 percent of dating singles are satisfied with their sex lives compared to 52 percent of those who are married.

Another 2009 AARP poll that asked about being in love (as opposed to having sex) compared American responses to those of the French and concluded, as AARP puts it, that "we are the United States of Amour." The poll found that 70 percent of those aged fifty to sixty-four said they were currently in love, and in the group over sixty-five years old, 63 percent of Americans compared with 46 percent of the French said they were currently in love. And—*zut alors!*—55 percent of Americans aged fifty to sixty-four claimed to be "very much" or "passionately" in love, compared with 49 percent of the French.

Sex among the aging was confirmed by another study of sex life in the United States. "Findings from the National Survey of Sexual Health and Behavior" looked at reports from more than eight thousand people in three databases and found that among those aged sixty-five to seventy-four, 67 percent of men and 40 percent of women said they had been sexually active in the past year. Even among the oldest in the report, those in the group who were seventy-five to eighty-five years old, 38.9 percent of men and 16.8 percent of women were sexually active.

And apparently they were still acting like crazy, irresponsible kids. One of the truly startling findings shows that older is apparently not wiser. The AARP study found that only one in five sexually active older singles, homosexual and heterosexual, reported using a condom regularly, and only 12 percent of the men and 32 percent of women said they used one every time. Not surprisingly, grandparents and even great-grandparents had sexually transmitted diseases (vaginitis, syphilis, gonorrhea, genital warts), and 1 percent had HIV/AIDS.

However, comparing the survey results with those from the 2004 AARP study, researchers found that both the reported frequency of sexual intercourse and overall sexual satisfaction were down close to ten points, although the frequency of self-stimulation and sexual thoughts and fantasies had not changed. They speculate this could be related to the current economic situation, which is causing anxiety and stress over finances, conditions known to interfere with sexual satisfaction—an example of your brain's intricate involvement with your sex life.

Good health is also equated with good sex, and in the AARP survey, health was among the top concerns voiced about sexual satisfaction. Although women outliving their male partners may account for their getting less sexual activity in later years, men lose more years of sexual activity due to health issues than women do. Frailty or mobility problems can take the bloom off sexual performance. Researchers recently tried testosterone replacement therapy in older men with mobility problems, and it did indeed result in promising improvements in strength and endurance—but it also increased cardiovascular and respiratory event side effects.

Remember, however, that all of these studies depended on self-reporting—what the participants said about their sexual activity—and a slightly cynical person might be a wee bit suspicious at the level of activity the elderly men reported. So we might want to take the claims of men about their later-life sexual activity with a grain of salt. Even so, if nothing else, these study results show that older guys are thinking about sex quite a bit. And these findings also suggest that it could make sense, when saving up for your later years, to put a bit more in the pot to secure a private room if you happen to end up at any nursing home in the future.

CHAPTER SEVEN

You've Lost That Lovin' Feelin'
When Love Dies

Maybe the one you love stopped loving you. Or was stolen away by another. Or died. Perhaps your differences were just too great to overcome, or one of you betrayed the other in a way that can't be forgiven. Perhaps your spouse cheated on you, or your best friend lied to you, or your parents abandoned or neglected you.

Some of the sages say it's better to have loved and lost than never to have loved at all. Really? That is cold comfort in the wee small hours of the morning when the pain of a broken heart is overwhelming. And that's physical pain as well as emotional pain, the experts say. When our feelings are hurt, our body aches along with them. It's like going cold turkey from an addiction, and that is not a mere metaphor. Your brain reads love lost as withdrawal from a source of pleasure. And "broken-hearted" is no metaphor either: you can die of a broken heart,

165

or suffer a severe (if temporary) cardiac event that's even called "broken heart syndrome."

We grieve for love lost, no doubt, whether it is your lover who has left, your best friend who has deserted you, or the death of a parent, a child, a sibling, or a pet. People weep over the loss. Love lost hurts. You can see it in your brain.

Breaking Up Is Hard to Do: How Rejection Affects Your Brain

Your brain doesn't like losing love and it likes being jilted even less. Sometimes it retaliates. Rejection has been followed by stalking, threats of violence, and murder. Love lost has led to suicide. It surely has led to hours or even years of weeping, regret, and anguish about what might have been. Being left in love is serious stuff.

One of the better evolutionary-based descriptions of the human heartbreak experience in romantic love is a 2006 summary by Rutgers University anthropologist Helen Fisher. Drawing largely from work by psychiatrists, Fisher surmises that there are two main stages associated with a dead and dying romantic relationship, which is often preceded by a partner's infidelities and betrayals. During the protest stage that occurs in the immediate aftermath of rejection, Fisher suggests, abandoned lovers are generally dedicated to winning their sweetheart back. They obsessively dissect the relationship, trying to establish what went wrong, and they doggedly strategize about how to rekindle the romance. These disappointed lovers often make dramatic, humiliating, or even dangerous displays, including invasions into a beloved's home, vehicle, or place of work—and then storm out, only to return and plead anew. They visit mutual haunts and shared friends. And they phone, text, e-mail, and write letters, pleading, accusing, and/or trying to seduce their abandoner back.

At the neurobiological level, Fisher writes, the protest stage is characterized by unusually heightened, even frantic, activity of dopamine and norepinephrine receptors in the brain, which has the effect of pronounced alertness similar to that found in young animals abandoned by their mothers. Fisher says this impassioned protest stage—if it proves unsuccessful—slowly disintegrates into the second stage of heartbreak—what she calls "resignation/despair." With time, the spurned one gives up pursuit of the abandoning partner. Then he or she must deal with what remains: intensified feelings of helplessness and hopelessness.

"Drugged by sorrow, most cry, lie in bed, stare into space, drink too much, or hole up and watch TV," Fisher writes. "Feelings of protest and anger resurface intermittently, but rejected lovers mostly just feel profound melancholy. Some people in the despair phase of rejection kill themselves. Some die of a broken heart. Broken-hearted lovers expire from heart attacks or strokes caused by their depression. As the abandoned partner realizes that reunion will never come, dopamine-making cells in the midbrain decrease their activity leading to lethargy, despondency and depression."

The experience of heartbreak really does mirror drug withdrawal. Researchers (and most of the rest of us) note that the sexes experience these raw emotions differently: women worldwide are more likely to suffer a major depressive episode when abandoned in love, while men more often turn to alcohol or reckless activities and are three to four times more likely to commit suicide after a love affair gone wrong.

The Jilted Brain

We know how terrible your brain feels to be in the throes of a breakup. Now, thanks to modern imaging technology, scientists know what it looks like too. And it's not a pretty picture.

A study that scanned the brains of the rejected while looking at their rejecter showed activity that related to love, despair, wondering why this happened, good and bad memories, and some very messy and not so nice feelings.

Fisher and several colleagues used functional magnetic resonance imaging (fMRI) to scan the brains of ten women and five men who were still heartsick over losing a lover. When they asked the volunteers to look at a photograph of their former lover and at a neutral picture, they found that the same areas at play in new love—for example, the nucleus accumbens, which governs reward—were still active when the forlorn looked at their lost love. But new areas were also activated, including those that regulate obsessive-compulsive thoughts and anger, suggesting a torrent of mixed emotions. Stress regions also lit up strongly, and there was activity in areas associated with gains and losses, craving and emotion regulation, including regions involved in cocaine addiction, such as the ventral tegmental area, which may help explain the fanatical behaviors associated with rejection in love.

In the interviews after the scanning, the rejected lovers expressed the same mixed emotions as their brain images showed: lingering romantic love, agitation, anger, and despair. Most recounted both happy and unhappy memories.

In the study, researchers say they found further evidence that the passion of romantic love is a goal-oriented motivation state rather than a specific emotion. These findings are consistent with the hypothesis that romantic rejection is a specific form of addiction withdrawal. They suggest that rejection in love involves reward gain and loss systems in the brain that are critical to our survival, which helps to explain why feelings and behaviors related to romantic rejection are difficult to control. This also lends insight into the high rates of stalking, homicide, suicide, and clinical depression associated with rejection in love that are found in many cultures, the study concludes.

"Being rejected in love is among the most painful experiences a human being can endure," Fisher says. She suspects that such brain reactions become moderate over time, probably by biological design and perhaps to aid self-preservation. And if the broken-hearted are lucky, they'll meet someone new, and the biological (and emotional) processes will start all over again.

After the Love Is Gone—You Ache and Ache

It's no wonder you ache. Terms such as *heartache* and *gut wrenching* are no mere metaphors. They are almost universally used to describe the physical experience of emotional pain. The hurt starts in the brain, but you feel it all through your body.

When we feel heartache, we are experiencing a blend of emotional stress and stress-induced sensations in our chest: muscle tightness, increased heart rate, indigestion, and shortness of breath. In fact, emotional pain involves the same brain regions as physical pain, suggesting the two are inextricably connected. But how do emotions trigger physical sensations? When people have their feelings hurt, what is actually happening to cause physical pain?

A major link between body and brain is the hypothalamus, via the autonomic (or involuntary) nervous system that controls many of our basic functions, including heart rate, digestion, respiration rate, and sexual arousal. These are affected by the vagus nerve—a nerve that starts in the brain stem and connects and relays information from and to the neck, chest, and abdomen.

Research from the University of Arizona and the University of Maryland helps explain how an emotional insult can trigger a biological cascade. During a particularly stressful experience, the anterior cingulate cortex, a brain region that regulates emotional reactions, can respond by increasing the activity of the vagus nerve. When the vagus

I Want to Hold Your Hand: It Eases Pain in My Brain

As it is with mice, so it is with humans: empathy is a powerful antidote to pain. An fMRI study shows that simple acts of social kindness, such as holding hands, can blunt the brain's response to threats of physical and emotional pain.

Psychology professors Robert Emery and Jim Coan at the University of Virginia published an fMRI study in humans that supported the finding from empathic mice. They found several human brain regions involved in both anticipating pain and regulating negative emotions, including the right anterior insula (which helps to regulate motor control and cognitive functioning), the superior frontal gyrus (which is involved in self-awareness and sensory processing), and the hypothalamus (which links the nervous system to the endocrine system). (See Chapter Four, "That Old Black Magic.")

Scientists don't yet understand well how the biological pathways underlying these connections between physical and mental pain work, but studies such as these show how intricate the connection is and how very real the pain of heartache can be.

nerve is overstimulated, it can cause pain, nausea—and our gut feelings and reactions.

Heartache is not the only way emotional and physical pain intersect in the brain. Recent studies show that even feeling emotional pain on behalf of another being—that is, empathy—can influence our own perception of pain. And this empathy effect is not restricted to humans. An earlier paper showed that when a mouse observed its cage mate in agony, its own sensitivity to physical pain increased. And when it came into close contact with a friendly, unharmed mouse, its sensitivity to pain diminished.

Can't Live If Living Is Without You: The Widowhood Effect

The death of a loved one is one of life's great sorrows, causing deep suffering and emotional pain. It could also be very bad for your health. In fact, it could be the death of you, according to a new study that confirms past work on the so-called widowhood effect.

Doctors and researchers have long speculated about a bereavement effect, in which a surviving spouse dies very quickly after the death of a mate. Several studies have suggested this is a fairly common occurrence in many cultures. A recent study from St. Andrews University in Scotland verifies it. After examining data on 58,685 married men and 58,415 married women from the Scottish Longitudinal Study, the researchers found an increased risk of death following the loss of a spouse for both genders: 40 percent of widowers and 26 percent of widows died soon after a spouse, with thirty-seven deaths occurring less than ten days after the death of the spouse and twelve on the same day. The risk of death was highest in the six months following bereavement.

These were not elderly, sick, or poor people. The sample members had an average age in the late forties and were predominantly white. They had no long-term illness and lived as couples in owner-occupied houses. The risk of death rises even after controlling for a range of other possible factors such as socioeconomic characteristics or long-term illness.

Paul Boyle, lead author of the study, says it shows once again the many benefits of being married: the married live longer, suffer fewer chronic diseases, and have better health behaviors than single people. Being widowed removes the protective effects of marriage, the study says, which may include social and financial support, health care, and positive attitudes to healthy behaviors. It also shows how vulnerable love leaves us when it leaves, for whatever reason.

Achy Breaky Heart: Can You Die of a Broken Heart?

The widowhood effect can be even more dramatic in some cases known as "broken heart syndrome," where a cardiac event is brought on in seemingly healthy people by extreme and unexpected emotional trauma, such as the unexpected death of a loved one.

The official name is stress cardiomyopathy, and it's connected with emotional stress. The symptoms are severe—so severe they mimic a massive heart attack and send most people immediately for help. That's a good thing, because although they may not technically be having a heart attack, they are suffering heart failure and need prompt and aggressive medical treatment.

Although the cause is emotional, the results are physical: adrenaline and other stress hormones stun the heart. Not every grieving heart is at risk. Postmenopausal women (average age of sixty) are most likely to have broken heart syndrome, and people with a particular kind of heart muscle weakness are especially vulnerable. A team of Mayo Clinic researchers has found that patients with broken heart syndrome have blood vessels that don't react normally to stress. When they are treated promptly and appropriately, people recover completely and don't seem to have another attack. Still, if the Scottish study is correct, the widowed ones aren't out of danger even if they survive a broken heart syndrome attack. As that study shows, they face an increased risk of dying in general for the first several months after the loss of a mate.

Ain't No Cure for Love—But Acetaminophen Could Help

So if heartache isn't a mere metaphor and rejection hurts physically as well as mentally, can taking a pain reliever meant for the body ease the pains in the brain? Apparently so, an intriguing study shows.

Since social and physical pain overlap with neurological wiring that makes us truly feel emotional pain, the study suggested that a dose of acetaminophen (the main ingredient in Tylenol) could ease the sting of both.

The anterior cingulate cortex serves as one of the brain's control centers for that "Why me?" feeling when you get dumped the day before the senior prom or left at the altar or fired the week before your birthday. It also happens to be the same circuitry that induces the emotional component of pain, that desperate feeling provoked by the ongoing throbbing of a toothache. These two types of pain, physical and social, may rely on some of the same behavioral and neural mechanisms, researchers surmised. Evolution may have piggy-backed brain functions that regulate social interaction on top of a more primal pain system. And the very way we speak of rejection ("I'm crushed") hints at just such a connection.

Research on the overlapping functions of this brain circuitry in rodents shows that opiates tended to quell not only painful stimuli but also the tiny squeaks that signal distress. So C. Nathan DeWall, a social psychologist at the University of Kentucky who has researched the neurobiology of rejection for nearly ten years, wondered whether an extraordinarily simple step to tone down these double-duty pain circuits might work in the human brain. But instead of dosing subjects with a prescription opiate, he and colleagues simply handed out either over-the-counter acetaminophen or a placebo to sixty-two volunteers.

In one part of the study, published in *Psychological Science*, participants reported their feelings of rejection on questionnaires. In another part, they played a rejection-style computer game in which they were progressively dumped from a virtual ball-passing group and excluded as time elapsed.

Functional MRI imaging revealed that those in the group who took the acetaminophen appeared to experience fewer feelings of rejection in brain regions associated with distress caused by social pain and physical pain (the dorsal anterior cingulate cortex, the anterior insula, the dorsal anterior cingulate cortex, and the anterior insula) than those who received a placebo.

One study does not a heartache drug make. But if validated, acetaminophen or its over-the-counter cousins may become an invaluable research tool in seeking the neural underpinnings of not only rejection but other mental processes related to social behavior. In an unpublished study, DeWall and his associates have found that moral judgments change after receiving acetaminophen. Recipients become less wracked by indecision when facing the classic moral dilemma in which one person must be sacrificed to save many: they reject out of hand what they perceive to be a ludicrous choice.

If acetaminophen does help resolve internal emotional conflict and the pain of rejection, it might help socially awkward individuals who become distraught when confronted by more routine moral choices. And it could make heartbreak easier to take.

DeWall says he's being asked if those facing possible rejection should pop a painkiller before facing the music. "That's a question I get a lot," DeWall says. "It's a little too early to make a call for widespread use."

Every Time You Say Good-Bye, I Die a Little: Why It Hurts to Leave Your Lover

It's not just being jilted that hurts; even short-term separation can be painful for those in love. Since researchers compare love to a drug, that could be why it hurts so much to be apart from your beloved, even for a short time.

Research and our own experience have shown that long-term and even short-term separation from a romantic partner can lead to increased anxiety, depression, and sleep disturbances. A broken heart can lead to even worse. Researchers have been busy identifying the neurochemical mechanisms behind these behavioral and physiological effects.

They agree that in many ways, separation resembles drug withdrawal. Studies have shown that in monogamous animals, cohabiting and mating have increased levels of oxytocin and vasopressin—hormones that foster emotional attachments and activate brain areas associated with reward.

The same thing happens in humans. In a recent study in which forty-two human couples were separated four to seven days, social psychologist Lisa Diamond of the University of Utah saw minor withdrawal-like symptoms, such as irritability and sleep disturbances, along with an increase in cortisol (the stress neurochemical). Those who reported high anxiety about their relationships had the biggest spikes in cortisol levels, but even those who said they had low levels of stress and anxiety during the separation had some degree of increased cortisol and physical discomfort. These results, like those from some animal studies, show a specific link between separation and increased cortisol. This suggests that cortisol-blocking drugs may help people struggling to cope with partner separation too.

The pair bond in people (and in many other animals) is universal. Researchers believe it evolved from the parent-child bond—our first love relationship (as we saw in Chapter Two, "Learning to Love")—which may explain why we feel romantic attachments so strongly. The same neurochemicals—oxytocin, vasopressin, and dopamine—have been seen in both relationships, and similar behavioral patterns are associated with both parental and romantic bonds and separation.

"We think about parent-child relationships and adult romantic relationships as being fundamentally different," Diamond says, "but it really boils down to the same functional purpose: creating a psychological drive to be near the other person, to want to take care of them, and being resistant to being separated from them."

These findings were no surprise to those who have been studying one of nature's most bonded and monogamous pairs: the prairie voles.

When prairie voles are separated from their partners even for a short time, they exhibit withdrawal-like symptoms, says Larry Young, a behavioral neuroscientist at Emory University's Yerkes National Primate Research Center.

In a 2008 study, Young and colleagues showed that male prairie voles that had been separated from their female partners for four days—a much shorter amount of separation time than researchers had previously found to affect the voles' physiology—behaved as though they were depressed and had increased levels of corticosterone, the rodent equivalent of the human stress hormone cortisol. Males that had been separated from their male siblings didn't show any of these symptoms, suggesting the response was tied specifically to mate separation, and not just social isolation. When the animals were given a drug that blocked corticosterone release, they no longer acted as if depressed when separated from their partners, confirming that stress hormones were at the root of the response.

Future studies about romantic attachment and the broken bonds of love will focus on using the findings to develop new treatments for the broken-hearted who have grief associated with partner separation or loss. And the research may help for disorders that involve social lacks, such as schizophrenia and autism.

Broken Promises: Can the Brain Predict Betrayal?

What if you could tell ahead of time that your beloved would break the promise of undying love, break a wedding vow—and break your heart?

A brain scan may be able to just that: to predict those who are making false promises before they break their word. But it will be awhile before such a technique is ready for consumer use, let alone available as a handy hand-held truth-o-meter to take on a first date.

Can't Get You Out of My Head: Addicted to Grief

The good news for most people is that time eventually heals the wounds of losing a loved one, no matter the cause. The bad news is that's not so for between 10 to 20 percent of the bereaved. For these mourners, accepting and getting over a loss remains extremely difficult, even years later. And you can see it in their brains.

Researchers have taken a step closer to understanding the neurobiological underpinnings of this condition, called complicated grief (CG). A new fMRI study shows that in CG sufferers, reminders of the lost love activate a brain area associated with reward processing, pleasure, and addiction. In effect, that addiction is not allowed to wither and fade.

A team led by Mary-Frances O'Connor of the University of California, Los Angeles, studied twenty-three women—eleven of whom suffered from CG—who had lost a mother or sister to breast cancer in the past five years. While in the scanner, the women saw pictures and words that reminded them of their loved one. Brain networks associated with social pain became activated in all women, but in the CG patients, reminders of the deceased also excited the nucleus accumbens, a forebrain area most commonly associated with reward, pleasure, and addiction.

O'Connor believes this continued neural reward activity could be interfering with adapting to the loss. When we see a loved one or reminders of a loved one, our brains are cued to enjoy that experience, she says. But when a loved one dies, our brains have to adapt to the idea that these cues no longer predict this rewarding experience, and some people just can't do it easily.

Scientists don't yet know why some of us adapt to loss better than others, but they think the findings will lead to new treatment strategies to help the brains and minds of the bereaved understand that the person is gone for good and then move on.

You'll have to get the one who promises you undying love and affection into an fMRI brain scanner, at least for now.

Breaking a promise is a complex neurobiological event, say scientists at the University of Zurich in Switzerland who devised a study using promises about the second most craved substance: money (love, of course, is the first). They scanned the brains of subjects playing an investment game. Those assigned to be "investors" had to decide whether to pledge to share their money with players who were "trustees." This arrangement boosted the amount of money in the pot, but it also could result in a loss to the investor if the trustee chose not to share.

Nearly all the subjects said they would give to the trustee, but in the end, not everyone kept this promise. Based on the fMRI scans, the researchers were able to predict whether and which players would break their promise before they actually had the chance to do so in the game. It seems that promise breakers had more activity in certain brain regions, including the prefrontal cortex, a suggestion that planning and self-control were involved in suppressing an honest response, and in the amygdala, perhaps a sign of conflicting and aversive emotions such as guilt and fear.

Coping with a Breaking Heart

We have all felt the agony of rejection in life and love. The good news is that the pain of rejection will fade with time: that's a fact. The bad news is that it will take time.

When you are in the throes of the pain of heartbreak, your thinking brain is overrun by your emotional brain and what it wants and needs. Remember that there are many more connections running from your amygdala to your neocortex than the other way around. And the hormones in your brain that are connected with reward and love are depleted or running amok. Your cortisol stress hormones rise, your serotonin levels sink, and your dopamine levels seesaw and then plummet.

This mirrors withdrawal from an addiction, and expert advice on getting over a broken heart is based on this fact (and no doubt the personal experience of the experts). Some even suggest joining (or emulating) a twelve-step program based on the supportive group Alcoholics Anonymous, which urges taking life one day at a time.

Some other methods time-tested for easing addiction withdrawal (and heartache) may help. And it turns out that much of this practical advice has a scientific and neurological basis.

And, of course, there is always (yes, *always*) the possibility of a new lover. Remember those studies that show even the very elderly are finding romance and sex? It may take time, and that time may not be pleasant, but for most of us, a broken heart does heal and a new love does appear.

Five Ways to Ease Heartache

1. *Go cold turkey.* Get rid of or at least pack away tokens, photos, and other items that remind you of your loss, and avoid places the two of you used to frequent. As the research on complicated grief shows, viewing photos and other remembrances of love lost activates parts of your brain that expect the rewarding hormones connected with love. They lead to a surge of dopamine, urging your brain to experience that rewarding feeling again and again, but to no avail. This emphasizes your suffering and may prolong your withdrawal.

2. *Exercise.* Yes, this is the cure for almost everything that ails you. For recovering addicts, it offers a way to keep busy, improve physical health and appearance, and pump out endorphins, the pain-easing neurohormones that make us feel better. Studies have shown that even walking briskly for fifteen minutes can cut cravings. If you can't do this alone, join an exercise class, and get a friend to help push you out your door.

3. *Get social support.* The friend who pushes you out your door to your exercise class, and all your other friends, are the ones who will carry you across that bridge over troubled water, especially if they are happy friends. Research shows that happy people have happy friends. This finding is believed to relate to mirror neurons in our brains that reflect what others near us are doing and even feeling. Also, isolation increases anxiety as well as the risks of illness.

4. *Meditate.* Studies show that addicts of many kinds find meditation helps them over the withdrawal hump and helps keep them clean. Mindfulness meditation, which focuses the mind on the moment, helps train your brain to recognize emotions and thoughts as fleeting and to let them pass by without reacting to them. Yoga and tai chi, which focus your mind and breath on the moment, can also help.

5. *Eat dark chocolate* (in moderation, of course). Cocoa-rich dark chocolate is good for your brain: it helps lower blood pressure, stimulates endorphins, and contains the mood-leveler serotonin, along with the mild stimulants theobromine and caffeine.

CHAPTER EIGHT

For the Love of God

Does God have a place in our brain and our hearts? Are we hard-wired to love and need God?

It would seem so. God may or may not exist, but his or her believers certainly do. Nearly every civilization worships some variety of supernatural power, and the concept of a supreme being (or beings) in just about all religions speaks of our love of God and of God's love for the world.

The spiritual quest is as old as humankind itself, but now there is a new place to look: inside our heads. Using functional magnetic resonance imaging (fMRI) and other tools of modern neuroscience in a new discipline called neurotheology or spiritual neuroscience, researchers are attempting to pin down what happens in the brain when people think of God or when they experience prayer, meditation,

181

mystical awakenings, or spontaneous utterances inspired by religious fervor.

In short, they are looking for a "God spot" in the brain to explain our love and need for a supreme being and our belief that God loves us. Neuroscientists are now tackling these and other thorny questions that until recently were reserved for philosophers. And they are finding some interesting, and sometimes puzzling, results.

Searching for God in Your Brain

The search for a God spot is not far-fetched. In many faiths, a specific place is reserved for the ritual of reaching out to God, be it a church, synagogue, temple, mosque, or some other meaningful venue. So it seems logical that researchers have been examining the brain to see whether certain brain locations are activated when a religious believer communes with his or her deity, similar perhaps to the way our brains act and react when we are in love with another human or animal.

Some researchers believe that religious experience grows out of activity in a specific section of the brain; the temporal lobe has been a leading candidate for the God spot. Others point to a broader network of brain areas as the biological basis of spirituality, and fMRI studies show a wide variety of brain areas responding to different spiritual or religious experiences.

Epilepsy, the Temporal Lobe, and God

It has long been noted that people with epilepsy can have mystical and ecstatic spiritual experiences induced by temporal lobe seizures. Indeed, a number of studies and experts suggest that religious icons such as Saint Teresa of Avila, Saint Paul, and Joan of Arc may

IS GOD JUST A TEMPEST IN A TEMPORAL LOBE?

Michael Persinger of Laurentian University in Ontario thought so. He created the "God helmet," a headgear that generates weak electromagnetic fields and focuses them on particular regions of the brain's surface.

In a series of studies, Persinger and his team trained their device on the temporal lobes of hundreds of people. During three-minute bursts of stimulation, they've induced in most of the subjects the experience of a sensed presence—a feeling that someone (or a spirit) is in the room when in fact no one is—or of a profound state of cosmic bliss that appears to reveal a universal truth. Those wearing the helmet translated this perception of the divine into their own cultural and religious language—terming it God, Buddha, a benevolent presence, or the wonder of the universe.

Instead of seeing this as a sign that the temporal lobes are a God spot, Persinger argued that religious experience and belief in God are merely the results of electrical anomalies in the human brain. In his book, *Neuropsychological Bases of God Beliefs*, Persinger says the feeling that such experiences are good is an outgrowth of psychological conditioning in which religious rituals are paired with enjoyable experiences, such as eating, and that thoughts of God become linked with pleasure. Praying before a meal, for example, links prayer with the pleasures of eating. God, he claims, is nothing more mystical than that.

have had mystical experiences triggered by epilepsy or other brain disorders.

As far back as 1892, textbooks on mental illness noted a link between religious emotionalism and epilepsy. Nearly a century later, in 1975, neurologists described a form of epilepsy in which seizures originate as electrical misfirings within the temporal lobes that are often connected with intense religious experiences.

More recently, neuroscientist Vilayanur S. Ramachandran of the University of California, San Diego, asked several of his patients who have temporal lobe epilepsy to listen to a mixture of religious, sexual, and neutral words while he tested the intensity of their emotional reactions. He used a measure of arousal called the galvanic skin response, a fluctuation in the electrical resistance of the skin. He reported an unusually large emotional response to religious words such as *God*, suggesting that people with temporal lobe epilepsy may indeed have a greater propensity toward religious feeling.

Ramachandran speculated that the epileptic electrical activity may spark religious feelings by strengthening the connection between the temporal lobe and the limbic system, which governs emotion and emotional memory, such as the amygdala and hypothalamus.

Strokes of Insight: Brain Changes and Spiritual Awakening

Does this research mean that religion may be nothing more than a neural storm, an electrical or chemical blip stirring up mystical and spiritual passions? Or could such changes in the brain reflect God's presence there?

Either way, there is a definite connection between religious mysticism, and even ecstasy, and some changes in the brain. Spiritual or religious feelings have been reported by people who have undergone brain surgery, experimented with hallucinogenic drugs, or experienced brain damage, stroke, or epileptic seizures. In some cases, they have described these as profound and life-changing awakenings—almost as if part of the brain had to get out of the way to allow spiritual or religious feelings of transcendence.

That's the way neuroanatomist Jill Bolte Taylor described the effects of her stroke. She was thirty-seven when a blood vessel exploded in the left side of her brain, shutting down her brain's analytical and judging functions, along with its ego center and many of her basic skills. The result, which she describes in her book, *My Stroke of Insight*, was a brain injury that involved years of recovery—and a transcendent experience of euphoria and enlightenment that led to a radical shift in her consciousness. She felt her normal perceptions of reality shift and experienced herself "at one with the universe."

Ellen White, one of the founders of what would become the Seventh Day Adventist Church, credited her spiritual awakening to a serious brain injury at age nine. After that, she became devoutly religious, saw visions, and was believed to have the gift of prophecy.

A recent study of brain tumor patients discovered that removing tumors in specific parts of the brain—the left inferior parietal lobe and the right angular gyrus—led to a feeling of inner peace and an increase in spirituality. These areas at the back of the brain are involved in how we perceive our bodies in spatial relation to the external world. The authors of the study say that their findings support the connection between mystical experiences and feeling detached from the body.

Cosimo Urgesi, a cognitive neuroscientist at the University of Udine, studied eighty-eight people with brain tumors to assess the feeling before and after surgery. Three to seven days after the removal of tumors from the posterior part of the brain, in the parietal cortex, patients reported feeling a greater sense of self-transcendence; patients with tumors removed from the frontal regions of the brain did not have this experience.

Chemistry has also invoked spirituality. Hallucinogenic drugs such as LSD and psilocybin are known to prompt transcendent and spiritual awakening. In recent controlled experiments at Johns Hopkins University, study participants who took psilocybin later reported an increase in overall well-being, and several had mystical experiences. One described it as the most personally meaningful and spiritually significant event of her life.

BELIEVE IT OR NOT: RELIGIOUS PRACTICE IS GOOD FOR YOUR BRAIN

Hundreds of millions of people worldwide find that religious and spiritual beliefs contribute to their feelings of well-being. However, belief in God may not be necessary for religious or spiritual practices to help your brain.

Meditation, with or without spiritual context, can help relieve stress, lower blood pressure, and ease other symptoms that are hard on your brain. Prayer can be a form of meditation, and attending religious services may also lift your spirits. Beside prayer, many spiritual and religious services include music, singing, chanting, or praying aloud together, which activate brain regions that contribute to good feelings.

An ongoing Duke University study of nearly four thousand people aged sixty-five or older found many benefits connected with praying or attending religious services. Those who both attended religious services at least once a week and prayed daily were 40 percent less likely to have hypertension: they had consistently lower blood pressure, a risk factor for stroke. Other research from Duke University has shown that people who attended church were less likely to be hospitalized for illness and that older people who were in the hospital recovered from depression faster.

It's difficult for researchers to tell if the positive results are from prayer or from the social factors and mutual support of being with people who share your values that make the difference. Those involved in a community may be less lonely and find friendships, all of which, studies show, help your brain.

Religious Ecstasy Is Like Romantic Love—in the Brain at Least

When we speak of the love of God and God's love for us, we do not usually mean romantic, sexual love. Yet some parts of the brain connected with romantic love, and even erotic feelings, are also active when brains are involved in spiritual activities. The erotic has often appeared in religious art and literature, from the divine, nearly orgasmic joy in Bernini's sculpture of the ecstasy of Saint Teresa to the erotic language of the Song of Solomon in the Old Testament. Perhaps it is why the Catholic nuns are called "brides of Christ."

Jefferson University neuroscientist Andrew Newberg scanned the brains of praying Catholic nuns and meditating Buddhist monks and found some overlap between their neural activity and that of sexually aroused subjects (as seen in scans from other researchers). The correlation makes sense, according to Newberg. Just as sex involves a rhythmic activity, so do religious practices such as chanting, dancing, and repetition of a mantra. Religious experiences produce sensations of bliss, transcendence beyond one's self, and unity with the loved one that is very like the ecstasy of orgasm. That may be why some mystics, such as Saint Teresa, describe their raptures with romantic or even sexual language.

In another study, by Mario Beauregard and Vincent Paquette of the University of Montreal, fifteen Carmelite nuns volunteered to recall the most intense mystical experience of their lives while being scanned in an MRI machine. It wasn't possible to capture the exact moment of the nuns' spontaneous revelation, which they believe is a product of God's grace. Recalling it was as close as the experimenters could get, but this nevertheless revealed some fascinating brain activity.

As the researcher watched, neurons fired in the right temporal lobe and several other brain domains, including the caudate nucleus, associated with emotions such as falling in love (which may reflect their unconditional love of God) and the superior parietal lobule, responsible for the spatial perception of self.

Newberg and his late colleague, Eugene d'Aquili, found similar results in 2003, when they imaged the brains of Franciscan nuns as they prayed. In this case, the pattern was associated with a different spiritual phenomenon: a sense of closeness and mingling with God, as was similarly described by the nuns whom Beauregard studied. These findings seem to confirm our love for God. But the quantity and diversity of brain regions involved in the nuns' religious experience point to the complexity of spirituality.

Feelings about God and about love not only occupy some of the same areas of the brain. In a survey by Newberg and colleagues, college students described both God and their feelings of love in remarkably similar ways. In the online Survey of Spiritual Experiences (also from Newberg), a large percentage of the more than two thousand responders said God "feels like love."

God on the Brain: What Brain Scans Show

Newberg and d'Aquili have also pointed to the involvement of the neural machinery at work during traditional religious practices. In this case, the scientists studied Buddhist meditation, a set of formalized rituals aimed at achieving compassion, enlightenment, and oneness with the universe.

When the Buddhist subjects reached their self-reported meditation peak, a state in which they lose their sense of existence as separate individuals, the researchers injected them with a radioactive isotope the blood carries to active brain areas. The investigators then photographed the isotope's distribution with a special camera—a technique called single-photon-emission computed tomography.

The height of this meditative trance, as they described in a 2001 paper, was associated with both a large drop in activity in a portion of the parietal lobe and an increase in activity in the right prefrontal cortex. They surmise that abnormal silence in the parietal lobe during meditation underlies the perception that physical boundaries have dissolved and the feeling of being at one with the universe. Activity in the prefrontal cortex at the meditation peak may reflect the fact that such contemplation often requires that a person focus intensely on a thought or object.

Yet another study shows that religious musings occur in a variety of brain areas, confirming previous research showing there is no single God spot in the brain from whence all spiritual thoughts emerge, scientists report in the *Proceedings of the National Academy of Sciences of the United States of America*. Study coauthor Jordan Grafman, a neuroscientist at the National Institute of Neurological Disorders and Stroke at the National Institutes of Health, says that recalling a religious experience activates the same brain areas as more mundane musings, such as remembering, say, what you ate for lunch yesterday. And pondering God? Pretty much the same brain patterns as thinking about people you've never met, such as historical figures or movie stars, but it involves brain areas known to be more advanced in humans than other animals. They found this by scanning the brains of forty subjects (who described themselves as religious) while they were asked if they agreed with certain statements such as whether "God is forgiving" or "God is wrathful." Their findings: the thoughts activated areas such as the prefrontal cortex (involved in planning, social behavior, and personality) and temporoparietal junction (believed to be involved in distinguishing between one's own and others' desires and intentions).

Another study shows that thinking about religion is no different from thinking about secular things. In an imaging study to compare religious and nonreligious thoughts, evaluating the truth of either type of statement was found to involve the same regions of the brain.

Researchers at the University of California, Los Angeles, used fMRI to evaluate brain activity in fifteen devout Christians and fifteen nonbelievers as the volunteers assessed the truth or falsity of a series of statements, some of which were religious ("angels exist") and others nonreligious ("Alexander the Great was a very famous military ruler"). They found that when a subject believed a statement, religious or not, activity appeared.

Could Religion Shrink Your Brain?

Many studies have shown that some religious and spiritual practices, such as meditation and prayer, can have beneficial effects on brain function, anxiety, and depression.

A provocative recent study, however, connected both a strong religious belief and a lack of religion with atrophy in the hippocampus, a part of the brain intimately involved in emotion and memory formation. The surprising study evaluated MRI images of the brains of 268 men and women aged fifty-eight and over who were originally recruited for the NeuroCognitive Outcomes of Depression in the Elderly study, but who also answered several questions regarding their religious beliefs and affiliation.

Amy Owen and colleagues at Duke University focused specifically on religious compared to nonreligious individuals. When they measured brain volume, they found significantly greater hippocampal atrophy in those reporting a life-changing religious experience, those who identified as born-again Protestants or Catholics, and those with no religious affiliation, when compared with Protestants not identifying as born-again.

The authors hypothesized that since stress is known to shrink parts of the brain, the atrophy might be related to long-time stress among those in a religious minority or those who struggle with their beliefs or have had a life-changing experience. While that could be true, Andrew Newberg, who reviewed the study, says that it's difficult to connect cause and effect with religious activity. For one thing, changes in a brain reflect everything that happens to a person, so we can't definitively conclude that intense religious or life-changing experiences were in fact the cause of brain atrophy. Participants may have had smaller hippocampi to begin with or maybe that's why they were drawn to religion.

Newberg, who has authored several studies on the effects of religion on the brain, called the new study "intriguing and important."

"It makes us think more about the complexity of the relationship between religion and the brain," he says. "For now, we can be certain that religion affects the brain. We just are not certain how."

The Evolutionary Roots of God Thought

So if not originating from a special brain part created (presumably) by and for God, where did the concept of God arise? Some propose the belief in God (or the supernatural) may have emerged from the most basic components of human thinking.

But why? Evolutionarily speaking, how could the survival of early *Homo sapiens* been aided by belief in something that has no physical evidence of its existence?

Evolutionary biologists Richard Lewontin and the late Stephen Jay Gould of Harvard University proposed that religious thinking is a side effect of tendencies that help humans to thrive. It may relate to our most primitive "agency detector," the ability to infer the presence of others. If the grass rustles in the distance, our first instinct is that someone or something may be lurking. This propensity has obvious evolutionary advantages: if we are right, we have just alerted ourselves to a nearby predator. (And if we are wrong, no harm done, and we can get back to picking berries and making love.)

We humans are also known for instinctually constructing narratives to make sense of what may be a disconnected jumble of events. Nassim Nicholas Taleb, author of *The Black Swan* and a professor of risk engineering, calls this the "narrative fallacy"—we invent cause-and-effect stories to explain the world around us even if chance has dictated our circumstances. God (or gods), empowered with omnipotence and beyond any inquiry, can be used to explain any mysterious event.

Also, humans can imagine the thoughts and intentions of others, including love, and we can imagine that they are different from our own, a trait known as theory of mind. This condition is fundamental to what it is to be human, and it's a small step from imagining the mind of another person to imagining the mind of a deity.

Here's another theory. Religion may have originated as what Gould and Lewontin call a "spandrel." *Spandrel* is an architectural term for the space between an arch and its surrounding structure. The spandrel does not, at least initially, serve any function; it is just a by-product of the arch. Gould and Lewontin borrowed the term to refer to accidental by-products of evolution. Perhaps religion is a spandrel piggybacking on adaptations such as orgasm or theory of mind, both of which serve obvious biological purposes. They speculate that the evolutionary adaptations that made the garden of human society flourish also provided fertile ground for belief in God.

God Neurons May Be Everywhere

Neuroscientists, being human, continue to look for God in the brain. Today spiritual neuroscientists are digging deeper as they attempt to answer some sensitive questions: What is the neural difference between a feeling of connecting with God and connecting with the universe? Can we induce a religious-like feeling in an atheist? Or here's the big one: Does finding a neuronal source for divinity prove God's existence?

If the last one is necessary, we may be out of luck. So far, no one has been able to pin down a God spot in the brain. The brain areas involved are varied not only with different spiritual practices but perhaps with each individual's experience.

"There is no single God spot, localized uniquely in the temporal lobe of the human brain," Beauregard concludes. "These states are mediated by a neural network that is well distributed throughout the brain."

God neurons, it seems, are everywhere.

And no matter what neural correlates scientists may find, the results won't prove or disprove the actual existence of God outside of your brain. Nonetheless, your brain knows what's good for it. As many studies show, loving God and believing in the love of God for the world may help your mental and physical health.

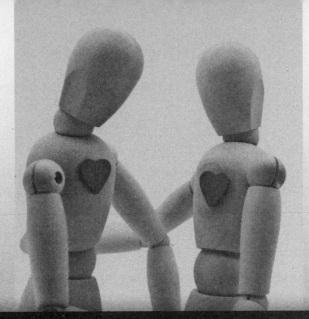

CHAPTER NINE

Technology, Science, and the Future of Sex

In less than a century, our ideas and actions regarding sex and love have undergone radical changes.

Much of that is for the better. We've come a long way from a world where the main purpose of sex was procreation and when sex could be very risky, especially for women. Indeed, sex for women carried the chance of an early death: from childbirth, from the debilitation of multiple pregnancies year after year, from infections or botched abortions. Men and women alike faced and died from venereal diseases with no effective treatments.

Today we can treat and even cure most sexually transmitted diseases, and we've managed to separate sex from reproduction. Reliable contraceptives, a morning-after pill, and safe and legalized abortion put decisions about childbearing within the reach of most women and men.

In fact, thanks to technology, we don't even have to have sex to reproduce. Since the first test-tube baby was born a bit more than thirty years ago, procreation options have multiplied and abound. In vitro fertilization is routine, and egg and sperm donors and surrogate mothers are as close as the want ads. Any woman with the money can buy sperm; any man can buy an egg and rent a womb. In some of the more extreme situations, an unmarried mom living on public assistance produced fourteen children by artificial insemination, including octuplets, and a well-to-do married couple involved four people (the biological father, an egg donor, and two surrogate mothers) to produce two baby boys.

For those who do want to participate in hands-on physical sexual activity (for reproduction or otherwise), we've got pills to give men erections, and apparently we'll soon have medication to stimulate desire in women.

The Wonderful World of Cybersex

If you should prefer sex without physical contact with others, that option is here. With typical human inventiveness, we have created more and more ways to connect without connecting. Forget phone sex and Facebook. We have Skype, where we can see each other and converse (or more) in real time and for free from our computers, sexting (X-rated texting with a mobile phone), and avatars who can perform Internet virtual sex for us.

In fact, enlisting a virtual self for cyberactivity is burgeoning. By some estimates, about 100 million users worldwide populate online virtual communities such as SecondLife.com. This Web site (and others with similar platforms) provides its active user base of 1 million with a real-time experience on their personal computer. They can

create and use digital characters called avatars—online fictional cre-
ations rather like cartoon puppets but more detailed—to wander
around castles, deserted islands, and other fantastic three-dimensional
environments. Through their avatars, people can meet, talk, cuddle,
have simulated sex, and interact in limitless ways.

There's more—and it does involve real humans, if not real touch
(more or less). Using your computer and a special program from sites
such as Sinulate.com and HighJoy.com, you can control and manipulate the sex toys of distant partners, and they can do the same for you.
These sex toys that can be operated by computer are called teledildon-
ics (or cyberdildonics), and some say they are a boon for long-distance
relationships, connecting lovers who are far away in space but right
beside each other in cyberspace (or their dildos are).

Virtual sex may soon be not so virtual. Robots to satisfy desire
are not too far into the future. We can now control artificial limbs with
thought, or, more accurately, electrical impulses. In the near future, we
will be able to send thought to operate distant apparatuses. Some
researchers say we will eventually be able to send such impulses back
in the other direction, allowing a prosthetic hand (or other body part)
thousands of miles away to "feel" what it is touching with lifelike verac-
ity, as those faraway impulses reach and activate parts of the receiving
brain.

Eventually we may separate sexual activity from any actual
human contact at all, even with our own selves. Researchers are discovering more about how our brains are wired for sexual reward and
pleasure and opening possibilities of tweaking these pathways. We
may be able to have sex without bodily experience through direct
conduits to the pleasure parts of the brain. After all, it all takes place
in the brain, doesn't it?

With the correct brain implant you can do it to yourself anytime
you want. That's if you are willing to undergo brain surgery and can
find a doctor who will perform it. We have the technology—and have
had it for some decades, in fact. Research has shown that deep brain

Turn It Up, Dear, and Turn Me On

In his 1973 film *Sleeper*, Woody Allen predicted that people of the future won't bother to get all sweaty and personal for sex: they'll just step into an Orgasmatron where (presumably) a pleasure center in the brain will be stimulated by signals that zap just the right spot.

It's not so far-fetched, since we know stimulation from electrodes implanted in the brain can produce orgasms. In the future, maybe we won't have to resort to brain surgery as wireless stimulation like that suggested by Allen's fictional Orgasmatron will do the trick. Meanwhile, a pain control doctor is advertising spinal implants to help women experience orgasm. The doctor, Stuart Meloy, a North Carolina physician who specializes in implanting spinal electrodes to alleviate pain, found by chance that a slightly off-kilter placement caused one woman to exclaim: "You're going to have to teach my husband to do that."

Meloy ran a small pilot trial, approved by the Food and Drug Administration, and in 2006, he reported that ten of eleven women who had stopped having or never had orgasms experienced sexual arousal with the temporary implant. Of that group, four experienced orgasm. On his patent filing, Meloy calls it "spinal cord stimulation to treat orgasmic dysfunction."

Such surgical aids are not inexpensive and may never become a practical means of adding the buzz back in your love life. Still, it's nice to see someone providing an orgasmic aid for women.

stimulation of implanted electrodes can relieve chronic depression, stop epileptic seizures, and set off orgasms with the push of a remote-control button. In experiments, a monkey with such implants was shown that pressing a button would provoke orgasms, and reportedly obsessively pushed the button nonstop for repeated orgasms, except for sleep breaks.

Sex in Bits and Bytes: The Future of Virtual Sex Is Here

It's not possible to have sex with a computer. Well, not exactly—or at least not directly. But the ways people are using their computers to engage in a variety of online sexual activities foreshadow the future. If Internet porn and virtual sex are prevalent now, what does the increasingly digitalized future hold for sex? Given a logical progression from today's observed effects, nothing very good. Summarizing some of the many studies, it appears that watching (and perhaps participating virtually in) Internet porn is detrimental to face-to-face relationships and may contribute to violence.

Some of this is not new, such as the use of the Internet to hook up with partners (both virtually and in the flesh) and finding fodder for kinky obsessions, including violent sex, illegal child pornography, and whatever else an individual might desire. Online porn of every imaginable (and unimaginable) kind is accessible, affordable, and often anonymous, and viewing it has become a popular pastime.

A small percentage of users indulge excessively in online sexual content: 0.5 percent reported watching online sex more than seventy hours a week in ways that uncomfortably bring to mind those monkeys who could not stop pushing a button that gave them orgasms. That's more than the average workweek—almost double, in fact. And that figure is more than a decade old now. Recently it was estimated that the average (not the obsessed) online community player spends twenty hours a week in virtual environments, which often includes virtual sex. Evidence suggests that such heavy consumption of porn and virtual sex may contribute to sexually aggressive attitudes and behaviors toward women (remember mirror neurons?).

Numerous studies have found associations between the amount of exposure to pornography and sexually belligerent attitudes, such as endorsing coercive sex and sexually aggressive behaviors—say, forcibly holding a woman down. Other findings tie frequent porn use to attitudes such as assigning blame to victims of sexual assault, justifying the actions of sexual perpetrators, and discounting the violence of rape.

These associations are strongest for men who watch violent pornography and for those who already tend to be sexually aggressive. Enthusiasm for porn often accompanies callousness toward women, dissatisfaction with a partner's sexual performance and appearance, and doubts about the value of marriage. True, most of these studies merely show a statistical association between pornography use and such misogynistic beliefs and actions. They don't reveal whether watching pornography is the direct cause of these issues.

These attitudes are obviously bad for relationships with women and could conceivably be linked to crimes against them. More than one case of avatar activity in an online community has involved virtual rape. In another case, a woman who was divorced by her online husband logged into his accounts and "killed" his avatar. Such immersive virtual experiences have also led to several reports of online activities triggering real-world conflicts. One woman filed papers for divorce on the grounds that she caught her husband's avatar being overly affectionate with someone else's. He countered that his wife drove him to virtual infidelity because of her addiction to the online multiplayer role-playing game, World of Warcraft. It would be humorous if it weren't so very sad.

So what does this mean for the future of love? We can expect enormous changes in our modes and means of expressing love—but perhaps not so many changes in its core.

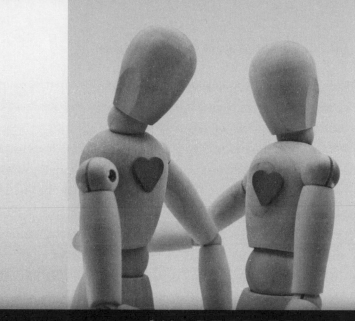

CHAPTER TEN

How Can Love Survive?

One of the triumphs of the human species is our extraordinary ability to adapt and thus survive. But could that very adaptation lead to the end of us, or to the end of love as we know it?

Humans are first-class evolvers. *Homo sapiens* has been doing some major genetic reshuffling since our species formed some 195,000 years ago, and the rate of human evolution may even have increased in recent (relatively) years. Some DNA studies show that over the past 10,000 years, humans have evolved one hundred times faster than at any other period in our history. Looking at some specific areas, researchers found that at least 7 percent of human genes underwent evolution as recently as 5,000 years ago.

Much of the change involved adaptations to particular environments, both natural and human created. We underwent the most dramatic changes to our body shape when our species first appeared, but we continue to show changes to our physiology and surely to our brains—and perhaps to our behavior as well.

We know that the brain adapts to injury or loss, compensating for missing parts or functions. And in fact, it is changing almost minute by minute (albeit subtly) in response to changes in the environment, including what we think, feel, and experience.

As technology invades and infuses every part of just about every life on most of this planet, humans have become increasingly connected with and dependent on machines. Many scientists have predicted that we might link our bodies with robots or upload our minds into computers. This is not mere science fiction. These environmental changes most certainly must be changing something in our brains, though we don't know exactly what yet.

Some changes we might welcome, such as being able to erase painful memories, including those of love lost or betrayed or a broken relationship, as in the film, *The Eternal Sunshine of the Spotless Mind.* When a two-year love affair ends badly in this movie, the lovers each decide separately to have their memories of each other erased by a business conveniently providing such a service.

While this is indeed science fiction, many of us are yearning to forget a love gone wrong. Why else do we drink, smoke pot, seek the bliss of heroin and tranquilizing drugs? We want to muddle up and perhaps block out some of the stuff in our brains, suggests noted neuroscientist and psychobiologist Michael S. Gazzaniga.

Researchers are working even now on many different approaches to changing how we make and keep memories, and that's bound to have some effect on how, or who, we love. Most involve manipulation of the brain's chemistry—not surprising, since there are known to be more than one hundred molecules involved in some way in making memory.

WHY NOT ROBOT LOVE?

Sometimes all that interacting may become just too much, but we will still want to connect. Or maybe the right human lover never turns up. Enter David Levy, who proposes, seriously, that some of us may find love and happiness by marrying robots in the not-too-distant future.

The Internet has already made it possible to fall in love and agree to marry without ever having met face-to-face, he says. And since research shows that those with strong social networks and relationships live longer and happier, "If the alternative is that you are lonely and sad and miserable, is it not better to find a robot that claims to love you and acts like it loves you?" he asks.

Science-fiction fans have witnessed plenty of action between humans and artificial life-forms in books, TV, and films. And the interactions between humans and robots have become increasingly personal as they have moved into homes as computerized interactive games and in the form of digital pets such as Tamagotchis and the Sony Aibo.

So why not into your heart and bed? Levy, the author of *Love and Sex with Robots,* has been exploring the way humans interact with computers, a topic for which he earned his doctorate from the University of Maastricht in the Netherlands. Computers with personalities are already here and can be programmed to interact.

For the sake of good taste, we'll avoid discussion of life-size dolls. But Levy does not: "It's just a matter of time before someone takes parts from a vibrator, puts it into a doll, and maybe adds some basic speech electronics, and then you'll have a fairly primitive sex robot," he says. And by the way, Levy is married to a human (who doesn't share all of his beliefs).

But What of Love?

Still, it's hard for us today to imagine that the tender feelings of love will change just because of new (and sometimes startling) means of sexual expression and human connection. Lust may be fired up and exercised by all the tools, toys, and technology that are now available. And we may find different objects for our love: perhaps robots to serve as sex partners, spouses, pets, or even children, as in the science-fiction film *AI Artificial Intelligence* or with those convenient Internet avatars. The lonely, as we've seen, may find solace in watching their favorite TV characters interact just as in the past and present we have been immersed in reading.

Evolution may be inexorable, but for us here and now, its results are unknowable, and it moves so slowly that it's even harder for us to imagine what changes that might bring to our brains, especially in relationship to new technology.

The emotions and drives of love and loving are basic to human survival. They have not, as far as we can tell, changed much throughout recorded history and the many other effects of evolution. Musings about love written thousands of years ago could as easily describe our feelings today. The sweet love of parent and child, portrayed in words and art over centuries, remains one of the most powerful and empowering of emotions. Tenderness turns on our sentimental side, and we continue to see examples of heroism and self-sacrifice that show a human's love of others.

True, that's only the history of the past few thousand years. But in spite of the headlong rush of today's technology, most of us who indulge in the digital and fictional still eschew hard-core pornography and remain engrossed instead in the televised, filmed, or written tales of romance, friendship, and true love. Soap operas as well as real operas still appeal to both genders across many cultures and millions of people. And the majority of our brains still prefer face-to-face warm body relationships. We are still more interested in hooking up socially on social networks than hooking up sexually on Internet networks.

For our foreseeable future, it seems probable that the deeper emotions of love—those that entangle the thinking and the emotional brain—will endure.

GLOSSARY

addiction—an uncontrollable craving for drugs, alcohol, or some behaviors despite adverse health, social, or legal consequences.

adrenaline—*see* epinephrine.

agape (Greek)—widely used to describe unconditional love, divine love, or even sacrificial love.

Alzheimer's disease—a progressive brain disease that leads to neuron death and dementia. The most common cause of dementia.

amygdala—an almond-shaped area deep in the midbrain that coordinates emotions and activates the fight-or-flight syndrome. Part of the limbic system sometimes called the emotional brain.

androstadienone—a chemical compound related to testosterone found in male sweat and semen; may help put women and homosexual men in the mood for sex.

androstenone—a pheromone, found in both male and female sweat and urine, that is a known aphrodisiac for some mammals, and possibly humans.

anterior cingulate cortex—the brain area that regulates emotional states and helps people control their impulses and monitor their behavior for mistakes.

arginine vasopressin—a neurotransmitter important for social recognition, courtship, and pair bonding. Also known as vasopressin.

SOURCE: This information was compiled from several sources, including the National Institutes of Health.

asexual—indifferent to and uninterested in sexual activity.

autism—a complex neurological disorder that typically appears before age three and affects social interaction and communication skills.

avatar—an image or artifact that represents a person. In computer games or programs, it can be manipulated by a user in lifelike ways.

brain stem—the most primitive brain part. It takes care of the automated basics, such as breathing, heartbeat, digestion, reflexive actions, sleeping, and arousal. Also referred to as the hindbrain.

caudate nucleus—located near the center of the brain on the thalamus, with many receptors for dopamine, the neurochemical of pleasure. It's important in love, learning, and memory.

cerebellum—two peach-size mounds of folded tissue located at the top of the brain stem that control skilled, coordinated movement (such as returning a tennis serve) and are involved in some learning pathways.

cerebral cortex—the thin outer layers of the brain consisting of closely packed neurons or gray matter. Most information processing occurs here. The very top layer is called the neocortex.

cerebrum—the "thinking brain." Accounts for about two-thirds of the brain's mass and is positioned over and around most other brain structures. It's divided into two hemispheres (*see* corpus callosum), has four lobes, and is crowned by the cerebral cortex.

corticosterone—a steroid produced naturally in the body that protects against stress; similar to cortisol.

cortisol—a neurohormone that contributes to alertness and is produced in response to stress and helps prevent inflammation.

coup de foudre **(French)**—literally a thunderbolt, but idiomatically, love at first sight.

dendrite—an extension of the neuron that receives information from other brain cells.

diffusion tensor imaging (DTI)—a technique that measures the flow of water molecules along the white matter, or myelin, that makes up 50 percent of the brain and connects many regions. The technology is not yet easily interpreted.

DNA—deoxyribonucleic acid that you inherit from your ancestors, makes up your genome (or genetics), and contains the instructions for making your unique body and brain.

dopamine—a neurotransmitter best known for its key role in pleasure and addiction; vital for voluntary movement and cognition, attentiveness, and motivation.

DRD2—a gene coding for dopamine receptors associated with compulsive behavior, anxiety, substance abuse, obesity, and attention deficit hyperactivity disorder.

DRD4—a gene coding for dopamine receptors associated with thrill seeking, addiction, attention deficit hyperactivity disorder, liberal attitudes, and a range of mental illness such as schizophrenia, Parkinson's disease, and bipolar disease.

electroencephalography (EEG)—a method of detecting and recording brain activity from electrodes placed on the scalp.

endorphins—neuroactive substances released in the brain to reduce pain sensations and increase pleasure. The word is a combination of *end(ogenous)* and *(m)orphine*.

epigenetics—relating to or involving changes in gene function that do not involve changes in DNA. Those changes may be inherited by your offspring.

epigenome—The name—*epi*[over]*genome*[your DNA])—describes chemical attachments to your DNA or the histone proteins that control its shape within chromosomes. This epigenetic information can amplify or mute gene expression and can be affected by your environment, your actions, and even your thoughts and feelings.

erectile dysfunction (ED)—impotency, that is, an inability for a man to get or sustain an erection.

eros—passionate love, with sensual desire and usually (but not always) sexual love. Also, the god of love (Cupid).

estrogen—collectively, a group of steroid hormones that make women female, regulate reproductive cycles and menstruation, and are important for mental health. Men need some estrogen for sperm production and, possibly, desire.

estrus—periodic sexual excitement in female mammals right before ovulation during which they are receptive to mating, or in heat.

frontal lobe—the most recently evolved part of the brain and the last to develop in young adulthood. It is responsible for so-called higher functions, including thinking, planning, and verbal skills.

functional magnetic resonance imaging (fMRI)—a type of brain scan that can produce images of the brain's activity in real time. Used to detect abnormalities and to map brain activity.

gender identity disorder—medical term describing when a person feels that biological sex and gender identity don't match and thereby experiences dysphoria, a persistent negative emotional state. Some object to defining this as a disorder. Also known as transsexuality.

gene—a segment of DNA found on a chromosome that acts as a blueprint for making the proteins that control virtually every biomedical reaction and structure in the body.

genome—the sum of all the genes that code for a particular organism, including the body and brain.

grey matter—neurons.

hippocampus—a structure located deep within the brain that plays a major role in learning and memory and is involved in converting short-term to long-term memory.

homosexual—a person who is sexually attracted to members of the same gender.

hypoactive sexual desire disorder (HSDD)—lack of desire, or interest, in sex.

hypothalamus—the regulator of many body functions, it controls the autonomic (unconscious) nervous system and the release of most hormones (including dopamine and oxytocin), and it boots the body up for fight-or-flight.

insula—part of the cortex active in synthesizing information, self-awareness, cognitive functioning, and interpersonal experience.

limbic system—also called the emotional brain. A brain region that links the brain stem with the higher-reasoning elements of the cerebral cortex; controls emotions, instinctive behavior, and the sense of smell.

love map—a detailed and highly individual concept and image of an ideal lover.

magnetic resonance imaging (MRI)—uses magnetic fields to generate a computer image of internal structures in the body and brain.

magnetoencephalography (MEG)—an imaging tool that measures the magnetic fields created by the electric current flowing within the neurons and detects brain activity associated with various functions in real time.

major histocompatibility complex (MHC)—a gene region coding for cell-surface proteins that helps the immune system distinguish a person's own cells from those of others.

masturbation—self-stimulation sexually, usually to orgasm.

medial preoptic area—part of the brain important in regulating parenting and sexual behavior.

mirror neurons—neurons that fire both when an animal acts and when the animal observes the same action performed by another; believed to be the basis of imitation, learning, and empathy.

multiorgasmic—experiencing several orgasms in one sexual session, usually in rapid succession.

myelin—a whitish, fatty insulating layer that helps rapidly transmit electrical messages among neurons. Also called white matter, it makes up 50 percent of your brain.

neural—anything related to neurons, which are brain cells.

neurogenesis—the ability of the brain to generate new cells, or neurons, in certain areas.

neurohormone—a hormone produced and released by neurons such as oxytocin or epinephrine; often a neurotransmitter.

neuron—a nerve or brain cell.

neuroplasticity—the brain's ability to change in response to the environment, including thoughts and feelings, and to reassign some of its parts to take over new tasks.

neurotransmitters—the chemical messengers that communicate among neurons to excite or modulate activity in neighboring neurons; often a neurohormone.

norepinephrine—also known as adrenaline, it's produced and released by the adrenal glands in times of stress.

nucleus accumbens—a critical part of the brain's reward system that processes information related to motivation and reward. Intimately involved in sexual arousal and drug addiction.

obsessive-compulsive disorder (OCD)—an anxiety disorder characterized by obsessive thoughts (as about a loved one) and compulsive actions, such as cleaning, checking, counting, or hoarding.

occipital lobe—processes and routes visual data to other parts of the brain for identification and storage.

opioid drugs—any of the psychoactive drugs that originate from the opium poppy or have a similar chemical structure, such as opium, codeine, and morphine.

orbitofrontal cortex—part of the cerebral cortex; involved mainly in making decisions related to emotional behavior. The medial orbitofrontal cortex brain area is involved in the inhibition of motivated behavior.

oxytocin—a neurohormone produced in the brains of newborns, nursing mothers, and at orgasm. It's the hormone of love, trust, and attachment and is involved in bonding.

parasocial relationships—one-sided pseudo-relationships directed at people or characters we might see on TV, in the movies, or on social networks.

parietal lobe—one of the four subdivisions of the cerebral cortex, it receives and processes sensory information from the body, including language, and is involved in attention.

periaqueductal (central) gray matter (PAG)—an area in the midbrain that contains a high density of receptors for neurohormones that are important in bonding. It plays a role in consciousness, modulation of pain, and defensive behavior.

philia (Greek)—brotherly love, generous love, affection, philanthropy, unselfish concern, and efforts of goodwill to better or benefit others.

plasticity—the ability of the brain to change through the formation or strengthening of connections between neurons in the brain.

platonic love—named after the dialogues of the philosopher Plato and his descriptions of a chaste and nonsexual but passionate love between two people.

positron emission tomography (PET)—an imaging technique using radio-isotopes that allows researchers to observe and measure activity in the brain.

postpartum depression—moderate to severe depression in a woman after she has given birth.

posttraumatic stress disorder (PTSD)—an anxiety disorder that can occur after experiencing abuse, trauma, or injury or an event that involved the threat of injury or death.

prefrontal cortex—the brain region involved in planning complex cognitive behaviors, personality expression, decision making, and moderating correct social behavior.

progesterone—a hormone that balances estrogen and has such major effects on fertilization and reproduction that it's known as the hormone of pregnancy.

prolactin—hormone responsible for producing breast milk in mothers; also seems to be involved in creating bonding between a father and his newborn offspring.

psychopath—a person who has significant and serious brain defects in areas that affect the ability to relate to others. Psychopaths lack empathy or often any feelings for others.

raphe nuclei (or nucleus)—a cluster of neurons found in the brain stem that release serotonin. Selective serotonin reuptake inhibitor (SSRI) antidepressants are believed to act here.

reward system—also called the pleasure center or reward circuit.

selective serotonin reuptake inhibitors (SSRI)—a class of antidepressants that acts by increasing serotonin levels.

sensory homunculus—an image of the human body with the areas of richest sensory receptors (in the lips, for example) exaggerated.

serotonin—a neurotransmitter that helps regulate mood along with body temperature, memory, emotion, sleep, and appetite. Too little serotonin is connected with depression, and too much serotonin withers sexual desire.

single photon emission computed tomography (SPECT)—uses a small amount of radioactive tracer to measure and monitor blood flow in the brain and produce a three-dimensional image.

social network—any kind of network of acquaintances and friends; used today to apply to virtual or Internet services and connections such as Facebook.

somatosensory cortex—a swath of tissue on the surface of the brain that contains receptors and processors for tactile information from the body; sometimes referred to as a mental map of the body and portrayed as a sensory homunculus.

storge (Greek)—affection and family love, especially the love of parents for children and children for parents, but also love for other family members.

straight gyrus (SG)—a subdivision of the ventral prefrontal cortex—an area involved in social cognition and interpersonal judgment—related to social awareness.

striatum—a section of the brain between the cortex and thalamus that contains areas activated by love and sex, including the caudate nucleus.

substantia nigra—a brain area involved in reward, addiction, and movement.

synapse—the tiny gap between neurons across which neurotransmitters pass, allowing brain cells to form networks and communicate with each other.

temporal lobe—brain area that controls memory storage area and hears and interprets music, language, and emotion. When stimulated, may produce feelings of spirituality.

temporoparietal junction—a brain region associated with taking the perspective of another person.

testosterone—the principal male hormone, but also made in females; responsible for aggression and for the sex drive in both males and females.

theobromine—a chemical found in chocolate that has a similar, but lesser, effect to caffeine.

theory of mind—the ability to interpret the thoughts of others and to understand that others have beliefs, desires, and intentions that are different from our own.

transsexual—a mismatch between biological (or anatomical) gender and gender identification in which a person identifies with the opposite gender.

vagus nerve—nerve that brings sensory information to nerve fibers in the throat, lungs, heart, esophagus, and the intestinal tract and relays information back to the brain. Responsible for "gut feelings," and explains effects of some emotions on the body and vice versa.

vassopressin—*see* arginine vasopressin.

ventral pallidum—a brain region associated with feelings of long-term attachment.

ventral striatum—a region of the brain connected to many parts of the brain's emotional system; associated with rewards and activated by dopamine, drugs, and pleasure.

ventral tegmental area (VTA)—located in the midbrain at the top of the brain stem. The VTA, one of the most primitive parts of the brain, governs reward and synthesizes dopamine, the neurotransmitter of pleasure.

white matter—*see* myelin.

widowhood effect—a term to describe the increased probability of dying within a few years or even weeks after the death of a mate or spouse.

Introduction

The Basics of Your Brain in Love and Sex: National Institutes of Neurological Diseases and Stroke, several sources, including "Brain Basics: Know Your Brain," 2010, http://www.ninds.nih.gov/disorders/brain_basics/know_your_brain.htm#fore. Stephanie Ortigue and others, "Neuroimaging of Love: fMRI Meta-Analysis Evidence Toward New Perspectives in Sexual Medicine," *Journal of Sex and Medicine*, 2010, *7*, 3541–3552.

Tools for Looking Inside Your Brain: Judith Horstman, "Tools for Looking Inside the Brain," in *Brave New Brain* (San Francisco: Jossey-Bass, 2010).

Chapter One: Born to Love

Harry Harlow experiments: Harry F. Harlow, "The Nature of Love," *American Psychologist*, 1958, *13*, 673–685, and http://psychclassics.yorku.ca/Harlow/love.htm.

Do You See What I See? Giacomo Rizzolatti, Leonardo Fogassi, and Vittorio Gallese, "Mirrors in the Mind," *Scientific American*, Nov. 2006, and David Dobbs, "A Revealing Reflection," *Scientific American Mind*, 2006. Marco Iacoboni, *Mirroring People: The New Science of How We Connect with Others* (New York: Farrar, Straus & Giroux, 2008). V. S. Ramachandran, "Mirror Neurons and the Brain in the Vat," Jan. 10, 2006, http://www.edge.org/3rd_culture/ramachandran06/ramachandran06_index.html.

All the World Loves a Lover: Nicholas A. Christakis and James H. Fowler, "The Spread of Obesity in a Large Social Network over 32 Years," *New England*

Journal of Medicine, 2007, *357*, 370–379. J. N. Rosenquist, J. Murabito, J. H. Fowler, and N. A. Christakisa, "The Spread of Alcohol Consumption Behavior in a Large Social Network," *Annals of Internal Medicine*, Apr. 6, 2010, pp. 426–433.

The Dangers of Involuntary Mind Merging: Jonah Lehrer, "The Mirror Neuron Revolution: Explaining What Makes Humans Social," scientificamerican.com, July 1, 2008, http://www.scientificamerican.com/article.cfm?id=the-mirror-neuron-revolut. Jascha Hoffman, "The Social Brain," *Scientific American Mind*, Oct. 2008. H. Mourasa and others, "Activation of Mirror-Neuron System by Erotic Video Clips Predicts Degree of Induced Erection: An fMRI Study," *Neuroimage*, Sept. 1, 2008, pp. 1142–1145.

Love Is Everywhere: Stephanie Ortigue and others, "Neuroimaging of Love: fMRI Meta-Analysis Evidence Toward New Perspectives in Sexual Medicine," *Journal of Sex and Medicine*, 2010, *7*, 3541–3552.

A Brain Unable to Love: Kent A. Kiehl and Joshua W. Buckholtz, "Inside the Mind of a Psychopath," *Scientific American Mind*, Sept.–Oct. 2010. Truman Capote, *In Cold Blood* (New York: Vintage Books, 1994). Peer Briken, Andreas Hill, and Wolfgang Berner, "Abnormal Attraction," *Scientific American Mind*, Feb.–Mar. 2007. "Pedophilia May Be the Result of Faulty Brain Wiring," *Science Daily*, Nov. 29, 2007, http://www.sciencedaily.com/releases/2007/11/071128092109.htm.

The Power of Love: Julianne Holt-Lunstad, Timothy B. Smith, and J. Bradley Layton, "Social Relationships and Mortality Risk: A Meta-Analytic Review," *PLoS*, *7*(7), 2919, e1000316, doi:10.1371/journal.pmed.1000316.

Baby Face: "The Power to Persuade," *Scientific American Mind*, Mar.–Apr. 2010.

Chapter Two: Learning to Love

Background: "Genetic Factors in Anxiety," *Nature*, Aug. 12, 2010.

How Your Parents Affect Your Love Life: Emily Anthes, "Baby Stress," *Scientific American Mind*, Feb. 2009. S. Maccari and others, "Adoption Reverses the Long-Term Impairment in Glucocorticoid Feedback Induced by Prenatal Stress," *Journal of Neuroscience*, 1995, pp. 110–116. Nikhil Swaminathan, "Mother's Milk and IQ," *Scientific American*, Jan. 2008.

Young Love Is the Best for Making Baby Brains: Paul Raeburn, "The Father Factor," *Scientific American Mind*, Feb. 2009.

Five Great Things Oxytocin Does for Your Brain: Nikhil Swaminathan, "Hormonal Help for Autism," *Scientific American Mind*, Sept.–Oct. 2010.

J. A. Mechanic and others, "Analgesic Effect of Intranasal Oxytocin in Chronic Daily Headache" (paper presented at the Society for Neuroscience meeting, San Diego, Calif., Nov. 10, 2010). Jamie Talan, "Bonding Hormone," *Scientific American Mind*, Feb.–Mar. 2006.

If You Could Read My Mind: Yoshiaki Kikuchi and Madoka Noriuchi, "Baby's Little Smiles," scientificamerican.com, Sept. 23, 2008, http://www .scientificamerican.com/article.cfm?id=smiles-and-mother-baby-bond. Craig Howard Kinsley and Kelly G. Lambert, "The Maternal Brain," *Scientific American*, Jan. 2006.

A Mother's Everlasting Love: M. Arsalidou, E. J. Barbeau, S. J. Bayless, and M. J. Taylor, "Brain Responses Differ to Faces of Mothers and Fathers," *Brain Cognition*, 2010, *74*(1), 47–51. Ferris Jabr, "All About My Mother," *Scientific American Mind*, Sept.–Oct. 2010.

How Parenting Primes Your Brain for Love: Craig H. Kinsley and R. Adam Franssen, "The Pregnant Brain as a Revving Race Car," scientificamerican. com, Jan. 19, 2010, http://www.scientificamerican.com/article.cfm?id= pregnant-brain-as-racecar. Pilyoung Kim and others, "The Plasticity of Human Maternal Brain: Longitudinal Changes in Brain Anatomy During the Early Postpartum Period," *Behavioral Neuroscience*, 2010, *124*, 695–700.

Parenting Rewires the Daddy Brain as Well: Emily Anthes, "The Daddy Brain," *Scientific American Mind*, May–June 2010. Brian Mossop, "The Brains of Our Fathers: Does Parenting Rewire Dads?" scientificamerican.com, Aug. 17, 2010, http://www.scientificamerican.com/article.cfm?id=the-brains-of-our-fathers.

How Father Love Feeds Both Brains: Brian Mossop, "The Brains of Our Fathers: Does Parenting Rewire Dads?" *Scientific American*, Aug. 17, 2010.

Postpartum Depression: Katja Gaschler, "Misery in Motherhood," *Scientific American Mind*, Feb.–Mar. 2008.

Loving the One Who Hurts You: Erica Westly, "Abuse and Attachment," *Scientific American Mind*, Mar.–Apr. 2010.

What If Things Went Wrong with That First Love? Jamie Talan, "Bonding Hormone," *Scientific American Mind*, Feb.–Mar. 2006. Alison B. Wismer Fries and others, "Early Experience in Humans Is Associated with Changes in Neuropeptides Critical for Regulating Social Behavior," *Proceedings of the National Academy of Sciences*, Nov. 22, 2005, pp. 17237–17240. C. Heim and others, "Lower CSF Oxytocin Concentrations in Women with a History of Childhood Abuse," *Molecular Psychiatry*, 2009, *14*, 954–958.

In the End: "Do Parents Matter?" *Scientific American Mind*, Aug. 2009.

Chapter Three: His Brain, Her Brain, Gay Brain, and Other Brains

How Real Are the Differences? Lise Elliot, "Girl Brain, Boy Brain?" scientific-american.com, Sept. 8, 2009, http://www.scientificamerican.com/article.cfm?id=girl-brain-boy-brain. Lise Elliot, "The Truth About Boys and Girls," *Scientific American Mind*, May–June 2010. Larry Cahill, "His Brain, Her Brain," *Scientific American*, May 2005. Sarah Todd Davidson, "Not Mars or Venus," *Scientific American Mind*, Dec. 2005. Christie Nicholson, "Beware of Brain Differences in the Sexes," scientificamerican.com, Oct. 30, 2010, http://www.scientificamerican.com/podcast/episode.cfm?id=beware of brain-differences-in-the-10–10–30&print=true. Christopher Hitchens, "Why Women Aren't Funny," *Vanity Fair*, Jan. 2007.

The Five Genders of the Brain: Kinsey Institute for Research in Sex, Gender, and Reproduction, http://www.kinseyinstitute.org/about/index.html. "Findings from the National Survey of Sexual Health and Behavior (NSSHB)," *Journal of Sexual Medicine*, 2010, *7*(Supp. 3), 243–373. Katherine Bouton, "Peeling Away Theories on Gender and the Brain," *New York Times*, Aug. 23, 2010. Cordelia Fine, *Delusions of Gender: How Our Minds, Society and Neurosexism Create Difference* (New York: Norton, 2010). Diane F. Halpern and others, "Sex, Math and Scientific Achievement," *Scientific American Mind*, Dec. 2007–Jan. 2008.

So What Does This Have to Do with Love? "Scientists Uncover Neurobiological Basis for Romantic Love, Trust, and Self," Society for Neuroscience press release, Nov. 2003, http://www.sciencentral.com/articles/view.php3?article_id=218392171. Martin Portner, "The Orgasmic Mind," *Scientific American*, Apr.–May 2008. Elliot, "Girl Brain, Boy Brain?" Jessica L. Wood, Dwayne Heitmiller, Nancy C. Andreasen, and Peg Nopoulos, "Morphology of the Ventral Frontal Cortex: Relationship to Femininity and Social Cognition," *Cerebral Cortex*, 2008, *18*, 534–540.

Some Myths About Male and Female Brains: Scott O. Lilienfeld and Hal Arkowitz, "Are Men the More Belligerent Sex?" *Scientific American Mind*, May–June 2010. Charles Q. Choi, "Machismo Mayhem," *Scientific American*, Jan. 2010. Emily Anthes, "She's Hooked," *Scientific American Mind*, May–June 2010. Andrea Anderson, "Men Value Sex, Women Value Love?" *Scientific American Mind*, May–June 2010.

Toujours Gay: Nikhil Swaminathan, "Study Says Brains of Gay Men and Women Are Similar," scientificamerican.com, June 16, 2008, http://www.sciam.com/article.cfm?id=study-says-brains-of-gay. J. R. Garcia and others,

"Intimately Affiliative Gestures in Uncommitted and Romantic Relationships," forthcoming.

Scent of a Gender: J. R. Minkel, "What's Smell Got to Do with It?" *Scientific American*, July 2005.

Can Animals Be Gay? Emily V. Driscoll, "Bisexual Species," *Scientific American*, July 2009.

Are People Really Bisexual? "Bisexuality Is a Distinct Sexual Orientation," scientificamerican.com, podcast, Jan. 17, 2008, http://www.scientificamerican.com/podcast/episode.cfm?id=8902D6F8-F97C-E6FE-74B6D67845F05FEA&print=true.

The Third Gender: Jesse Bering, "The Third Gender," *Scientific American Mind*, May–June 2010.

Are There Asexuals Among Us? Jesse Bering, "Are There Asexuals Among Us?" scientificamerican.com, Oct. 29, 2009, http://www.scientificamerican.com/article.cfm?id=are-there-asexuals-among-us-on-the-2009-10-29.

Chapter Four: That Old Black Magic

Daniel G. Amen, *The Brain in Love* (New York: Three Rivers Press, 2007). Used by permission of the author.

How Love and Sex Are Good for Your Brain: S. A. Hall, R. Shackelton, R. C. Rosen, and A. B. Araujo, "Sexual Activity, Erectile Dysfunction, and Incident Cardiovascular Events," *American Journal of Cardiology*, Jan. 15, 2010, pp. 192–197. B. Leuner, E. R. Glasper, and E. Gould, "Sexual Experience Promotes Adult Neurogenesis in the Hippocampus Despite an Initial Elevation in Stress Hormones," *PLoS ONE*, 2010, 5(7), e11597, doi:10.1371/journal.pone.0011597. Melinda Wenner, "How Fantasies Affect Focus," *Scientific American Mind*, Mar.–Apr. 2010. Jens Förster, Kai Epstude, and Amina Özelsel, "Why Love Has Wings and Sex Has Not: How Reminders of Love and Sex Influence Creative and Analytic Thinking," *Personality and Social Psychology Bulletin*, 2009, 35, 1479–1491. Cynthia Graber, "Love Lessens Pain," scientificamerican.com, Oct. 14, 2010, http://www.scientificamerican.com/podcast/episode.cfm?id=love-lessens-pain-10–10–14. Jarred Younger and others, "Viewing Pictures of a Romantic Partner Reduces Experimental Pain: Involvement of Neural Reward Systems," *PLoS ONE*, 2010, 5(10), e13309, doi:10.1371/journal.pone.0013309.

When Love Occupies Your Brain: Aimee Cunningham, "Hungry for Love," *Scientific American Mind*, Oct. 2005.

Who Do You Love? John Money, *Love Maps* (New York: Prometheus Books, 1990). Helen Fisher, *Why We Love* (New York: Holt, 2004). Nicole Branan, "Marrying Mom," *Scientific American Mind*, Feb.–Mar. 2009. Christie Nicholson, "Busting the Myth That Opposites Attract," scientificamerican. com, July 31, 2010, http://www.scientificamerican.com/podcast/episode.cfm? id=busting-the-myth-that-opposites-att-10–08–31.

Can Meditation Make You a Better Lover? Heleen A. Slagter and others, "Mental Training Affects Distribution of Limited Brain Resources," *PLOS*, 2007, 5(6), e138, doi:10.1371/journal.pbio.0050. J. A. Brefczynski-Lewis and others, "Neural Correlates of Attentional Expertise in Long-Term Meditation Practitioners," *Proceedings of the National Academy of Science*, July 3, 2007, pp. 11483–11488. Sara W. Lazar and others, "Meditation Experience Is Associated with Increased Cortical Thickness," *Neuroreport*, Nov. 28, 2005, pp. 1893–1897. David Biello, "Meditate on This: You Can Learn to Be More Compassionate," scientificamerican.com, Mar. 26, 2008, http://www .scientificamerican.com/article.cfm?id=meditate-on-this-you-can-learn-to-be-more-compassionate.

Can't Take My Eyes Off of You: Kurt Kleiner, "See No Beauty," *Scientific American Mind*, Feb. 2009.

You've Got That Lovin' Feelin': "A Fifth of a Second" research, 2011 interview with Stephanie Ortigue.

You Go to My Nose: Josie Glausiusz, "The Hidden Power of Scent," *Scientific American Mind*, Aug.–Sept. 2008. Jason Castro, "Her Tears Will Control Your Mind," scientificamerican.com, Jan. 11, 2011, http://www.scientificamerican .com/article.cfm?id=her-tears-will-control-yo. Headlines, Scent of Alpha Male, *Scientific American Mind*, Oct.–Nov. 2007. Chip Walter, "Affairs of the Lips," *Scientific American Mind*, Feb.–Mar. 2008. S. L. Miller and J. Maner, "Scent of a Woman: Male Testosterone Responses to Female Olfactory Ovulation Cues," *Psychological Science*, Feb. 1, 2010, pp. 276–283.

Anytime You Call My Name: Katherine Leitzel, "C'mere Big Boy," *Scientific American*, Jan. 31, 2008.

A Kiss Is (More Than) Just a Kiss: Chip Walter, "Affairs of the Lips," *Scientific American Mind*, Feb.–Mar. 2008.

You Light Up My Brain: Judith Horstman, *A Day in the Life of Your Brain* (San Francisco: Jossey-Bass, 2009), based on Martin Portner, "The Orgasmic Mind," *Scientific American Mind*, Apr.–May 2008, and Irwin Goldstein, "Male Sexual Circuitry," *Scientific American*, Aug. 2000.

What's Love Got to Do with It? Melinda Wenner, "Sex Is Better for Women in Love," *Scientific American Mind*, Feb.–Mar. 2008.

Need Some Love Potion? Kate Wong, "Hormone Spray Elicits Trust in Humans," scientificamerican.com, June 2, 2005, http://www.scientificamerican.com/ article.cfm?id=hormone-spray-elicits-tru.

I'll Have What She's Having: Jesse Bering, "Reopening the Case of the Female Orgasm," scientificamerican.com, Dec. 1, 2009, http://www.scientificamerican .com/article.cfm?id=reopening-the-case-of-the-female-or-2009-12-01.

Is Sex Really Necessary? Brendan Borrel, "Is Sex Really Necessary?" *Scientific American*, Aug. 2010.

Does the Penis Have a Brain of Its Own? Horstman, A *Day in the Life of Your Brain*, based on Portner, "The Orgasmic Mind," and Goldstein, "Male Sexual Circuitry."

When Things Go Wrong: Olaf Schmidt, "Talk It Up," and "Not Just Pills," *Scientific American Mind*, June 2005. B. A. Arnow and others, "Women with Hypoactive Sexual Desire Disorder Compared to Normal Females: A Functional Magnetic Resonance Imaging Study," *Neuroscience*, Jan. 23, 2009, pp. 484–502. S. Stoléru and others, "Brain Processing of Visual Sexual Stimuli in Men with Hypoactive Sexual Desire Disorder," *Psychiatry Research*, Oct. 30, 2003, pp. 67–86.

When She Doesn't Have That Loving Feeling: Emily Anthes, "A Female Viagra?" *Scientific American Mind*, Mar.–Apr. 2010. Duff Wilson, "Push to Market Pill Stirs Debate on Sexual Desire," *New York Times*, June 16, 2010. "Background Document for Meeting of Advisory Committee for Reproductive Health Drugs, NDA 22–526," June 18, 2010, Office of New Drugs Center for Drug Evaluation and Research, Food and Drug Administration.

Chapter Five: Friendship, Such a Perfect Blendship

Friendship quote: Traditional African saying, quoted by Alan Cohen, "They're Playing Your Song," http://www.alancohen.com/articles/theyreplayingyour song.html.

Is Friendship Declining? Julianne Holt-Lunstad, Timothy B. Smith, and J. Bradley Layton, "Social Relationships and Mortality Risk: A Meta-Analytic Review," *PLoS*, 2010, *7*(7), e1000316, doi:10.1371/journal.pmed.1000316. Miller McPherson, Lynn Smith-Lovin, and Mathew E. Brashears, "Social Isolation in America," *American Sociological Review*, 2006, *71*, 353–375. David Disalvo, "Are Social Networks Messing with Your Head?" *Scientific American*, Jan.–Feb. 2010. John T. Cacioppo, *Loneliness: Human Nature and the Need for Social Connection* (New York: Norton, 2009).

Five Great Things Friendship Does for Your Brain: Greg J. Norman and others, "Social Interaction Modulates Autonomic, Inflammatory, and Depressive-Like Responses to Cardiac Arrest and Cardiopulmonary Resuscitation," *Proceedings of the National Academy of Sciences*, 2010, *107*, 16342–16347, doi:10.1073/pnas.1007583107. "How Your Social Life Protects Your Brain and Memory," *Focus on Healthy Living*, Harvard University newsletter, Sept. 18, 2010.

Are You Lonesome Tonight? Jascha Hoffman, "The Social Brain," *Scientific American*, Oct.–Nov. 2008. John T. Cacioppo, *Loneliness: Human Nature and the Need for Social Connection* (New York: Norton, 2008). Victoria Stern, "So Lonely It Hurts," *Scientific American Mind*, May–June 2008. John T. Cacioppo and others, "In the Eye of the Beholder: Individual Differences in Perceived Social Isolation Predict Regional Brain Activation to Social Stimuli," *Journal of Cognitive Neuroscience*, 2008, *21*(1), 83–92.

You've Got a Friend: "Social Ties Boost Survival by 50 Percent," scientificamerican.com, July 28, 2010, http://www.scientificamerican.com/article.cfm?id= relationships-boost-survival. Karen A. Ertel, M. Maria Glymour, and Lisa F. Berkman, "Effects of Social Integration on Preserving Memory Function in a Nationally Representative U.S. Elderly Population," *American Journal of Public Health*, 2008, *98*, 1215–1220. Valerie C. Crooks and others, "Social Network, Cognitive Function, and Dementia Incidence Among Elderly Women," *American Journal of Public Health*, 2008, *98*, 1221–1227. Kira Birditt and Toni C. Antonucci, "Life Sustaining Irritations? Relationship Quality and Mortality in the Context of Chronic Illness," *Social Science and Medicine*, 2008, *67*(8), 1291–1299.

The Ideal Circle of Friends: Klaus Manhart, "Circle of Friends," *Scientific American Mind*, Apr.–June 2006.

Widening the Social Circle: Julianne Holt-Lunstad, Timothy B. Smith, and J. Bradley Layton, "Social Relationships and Mortality Risk: A Meta-Analytic Review," *PLoS*, 2010, *7*(7), e1000316, doi:10.1371/journal.pmed.1000316.

Imaginary Friends: Fionnuala Butler and Cynthia Pickett, "Imaginary Friends," scientificamerican.com, July 28, 2009, http://www.scientificamerican.com/article.cfm?id=imaginary-friends. Jaye Derrick, Shira Gabriel, and Kurt Hugenberg, "Social Surrogacy: How Favored Television Programs Provide the Experience of Belonging," *Journal of Experimental Social Psychology*, 2009, *45*, 352–362. Jonathan Cohen, "Parasocial Break-Up from Favorite Television Characters: The Role of Attachment Styles and Relationship Intensity," *Journal of Social and Personal Relationships*, 2004, *21*, 187–202.

Until the Real Thing Comes Along: David Disalvo, "Are Social Networks Messing with Your Head?"

Work, the "Other Love" in Your Life: "Job Satisfaction Associated with Helping Others," scientificamerican.com, podcast, Apr. 23, 2007, http://www.scientificamerican.com/podcast/episode.cfm?id=1E7A4EE3-E7F2–99DF-38DB68956691198B.

Can Animals Love? David Biello, "Genetic Secrets of Man's Best Friend Revealed," scientificamerican.com, Dec. 8, 2005. Katherine Harmon, "Do Chimpanzees Understand Death?" *scientificamerican.com*, Apr. 27, 2010, http://www.scientificamerican.com/article.cfm?id=chimpanzees-understand-death&print=true. Peggy Mason, "Empathy Is a Pain So Why Bother?" *Scientific American Mind*, Dec.–Jan. 2007–2008. Nicole Branan, "Pay It Forward," *Scientific American Mind*, Oct.–Nov. 2007. Lisa Stein, "Dogs' Bark: Not Fair! Study Shows Pups Get Jealous," scientificamerican.com, Dec. 8, 2008, http://www.scientificamerican.com/blog/post.cfm?id=dogs-bark—not-fair-study-shows-pup-2008-12-08. Friederike Range, Lisa Horn, Zsofia Viranyi, and Ludwig Huber, "The Absence of Reward Induces Inequity Aversion in Dogs," *Proceedings of the National Academy of Sciences*, Jan. 6, 2009, pp. 340–345, doi:10.1073/pnas.0810957105.

How to Make Friends: Irene S. Levine, "Five Tips for Making Friends After 50," June 3, 2011, http://www.thefriendshipblog.com/blog/5-tips-making-friends-after-50. Irene S. Levine, *Best Friends Forever: Surviving a Breakup with Your Best Friend* (New York: Overlook Press, 2009). Gretchen Rubin, "Friendship: Seven Tips for Making New Friends," http://www.happiness-project.com/happiness_project/2009/02/friendship-seven-tips-for-making-new-friends.html, and *The Happiness Project* (New York: HarperCollins, 2011).

Chapter Six: Only You Can Make My Dreams Come True

Statistics: Rodger Doyle, "The Honeymoon Is Over," *Scientific American*, Mar. 2006.

Grow Old Along with Me: Jana Staton, "What Is the Relationship of Marriage to Physical Health?" National Healthy Marriage Resource Center, 2008, http://www.healthymarriageinfo.org/docs/phnmarriageefs.pdf. L. A. Lillard and L. J. Waite, "'Til Death Do Us Part: Marital Disruption and Mortality," *American Journal of Sociology*, 1995, *100*, 1131–1156.

You Make Me Feel So Good: D. Maestripieri, N. M. Baran, P. Sapienza, and L. Zingales, "Between- and Within-Sex Variation in Hormonal Responses to

Psychological Stress in a Large Sample of College Students," *Stress*, 2010, *13*, 413–424. D. Saxbe and R. L. Repetti, "For Better or Worse? Coregulation of Couples' Cortisol Levels and Mood States," 2010, *98*(1), 92–103.

Finding that Special Someone: Statistics on how spouses met from Nicholas A. Christakis and James H. Fowler, *Connected: The Surprising Power of Our Social Networks and How They Shape Our Lives* (New York: Little, Brown, 2009). Facebook statistics from http://www.facebook.com/index.php?lh=655 6be6ad4f129d802fcf3c5080fb22e&#!/press/info.php?statistics. Statistics on dating services from Stephanie Rosenbloom, "New Online-Date Detectives Can Unmask Mr. or Ms. Wrong," *New York Times*, Dec. 18, 2010, http://www .nytimes.com/2010/12/19/us/19date.html?src=twrhp&pagewanted=print.

Falling and Staying in Love: Robert Epstein, "How Science Can Help You Fall in Love," *Scientific American Mind*, Jan.–Feb. 2010.

I've Grown Accustomed to Your Face: Robert Epstein and Mansi Thakar, "How Love Emerges in Arranged Marriages: A Qualitative Cross-Cultural Study" (paper presented at the 2009 National Council on Family Relations Annual Conference, San Francisco).

My One and Only Love: Karen Schrock, "Monogamy Is All the Rage These Days," scientificamerican.com, Aug. 7, 2009, http://www.scientificamerican .com/blog/60-second-science/index.cfm?tag=love. Emily Anthes, "'Til Death Do Us Part," *Scientific American Mind*, Feb. 2008.

Granny's Got to Have It: Rachel Mahan, "More Sex for Women?" scientific-american.com, podcast, Nov. 3, 2008, http://www.scientificamerican.com/podcast/episode.cfm?id=more-sex-for-women-08-11-03.

Does Domestic Bliss Depend on Sex? Esther Perel, *Mating in Captivity* (New York: HarperCollins, 2006). Marnia Robinson, *Peace Between the Sheets* (New York: Random House, 2003). Marin Portner, "Domestic Bliss," *Scientific American Mind*, Apr.–May 2008. Robert Epstein, "How Science Can Help You Fall in Love," *Scientific American Mind*, Jan.–Feb. 2010.

Your Hormones May Drive You Apart: Melinda Wenner, "A Tough Pill to Swallow," *Scientific American Mind*, Dec. 2008–Jan. 2009.

Making Love Last: Irene Tsapelas, Arthur Aron, and Terri Orbuch, "Marital Boredom Now Predicts Less Satisfaction Nine Years Later," *Psychological Science*, 2009, *20*, 543.

Can Pornography Help Your Love Life? Hal Arkowitz and Scott O. Lilienfeld, "Sex in Bits and Bytes," *Scientific American Mind*, July–Aug. 2010.

Love Will Keep Us Together: Jordan Lite, "This Is Your Brain on Love: Lasting Romance Makes an Impression—Literally," scientificamerican.com, Jan. 2,

2009, http://www.scientificamerican.com/blog/post.cfm?id=this-is-your-brain -on-love-lasting-2009–01–06. Rodger Doyle, "The Honeymoon Is Over," *Scientific American*, Mar. 2006.

Will You Still Need Me When I'm 64? American Association of Retired Persons, "Sex, Romance, and Relationships: 2009 AARP Survey of Midlife and Older Adults," 2009, http://www.aarp.org/relationships/love-sex/info- 05-2010/srr_09.html. Pepper Schwartz, "Love, American Style," *AARP: The Magazine*, Jan.–Feb. 2010, http://www.aarp.org/relationships/love-sex/info- 12-2009/naked-truth-love-american-style.html. Center for Sexual Health Promotion, Indiana University, "Findings from the National Survey of Sexual Health and Behavior (NSSHB)," *Journal of Sexual Medicine*, 2010, 7(Supp. 5). Stacy Tessler Lindau and Natalia Gavrilova, "Sex, Health, and Years of Sexually Active Life Gained Due to Good Health: Evidence from Two US Population- Based Cross Sectional Surveys of Ageing," *British Medical Journal*, 2010, *340*, c810, http://www.bmj.com/content/340/bmj.c810.full. Shehzad Basaria and others, "Adverse Events Associated with Testosterone Administration," *New England Journal of Medicine*, July 8, 2010, pp. 109–122.

Chapter Seven: You've Lost That Lovin' Feelin'

Breaking Up Is Hard to Do: Jesse Bering, "Polyamory Chic, Gay Love and the Evolution of a Broken Heart," scientificamerican.com, Aug. 25, 2010, http:// www.scientificamerican.com/article.cfm?id=polyamory-chic-gay-jealousy- and-the-2010–08–25. Helen Fisher, *Why We Love* (New York: Holt, 2004).

The Jilted Brain: Jamie Talan, "The Jilted Brain," *Scientific American Mind*, June 2006.

After the Love Is Gone: Robert Emery and Jim Coan, "Physical Pain from Hurt Feelings," *Scientific American Mind*, Mar.–Apr. 2010.

I Want to Hold Your Hand: Robert Emery and Jim Coan, "Ask the Brains," *Scientific American Mind*, Mar.–Apr. 2010.

Can't Live If Living Is Without You: Paul J. Boyle, Zhiqiang Feng, and Gillian M. Raab, "Does Widowhood Increase Mortality Risk? Testing for Selection Effects by Comparing Causes of Spousal Death," *Epidemiology*, 2011, *22*(1), 1–5.

Achy Breaky Heart: Johns Hopkins University Initiative for Stress Cardio- myopathy, 2011, http://www.hopkinsmedicine.org/asc/.

Ain't No Cure for Love: Gary Stix, "Feeling the Pain of Rejection? Try Taking a Tylenol," *Scientific American*, Sept. 2010. C. N. Dewall and others,

"Acetaminophen Reduces Social Pain: Behavioral and Neural Evidence," *Psychological Science*, 2010, *21*(7), 931–937.

Every Time You Say Good-Bye, I Die a Little: Erika Westly, "Separation Anxiety for Adults," *Scientific American Mind*, Feb. 2009.

Broken Promises: Allison Bond, "Broken Promises," *Scientific American*, May–June 2010. Thomas Baumgartner and others, "The Neural Circuitry of a Broken Promise," *Neuron*, Dec. 10, 2009, pp. 756–770.

Can't Get You Out of My Head: Nicole Banan, "Addicted to Grief?" *Scientific American Mind*, Oct. 2008.

Chapter Eight: For the Love of God

Searching for God in Your Brain: David Bielle, "Searching for God in the Brain," *Scientific American Mind*, Oct.–Nov. 2007. Kasper Mossman, "God (Neurons) May Be Everywhere," *Scientific American Mind*, Dec. 2006–Jan. 2007. Andrew Newberg and Mark Robert Waldman, *How God Changes Your Brain* (New York: Ballantine Books, 2009).

Is God Just a Tempest in a Temporal Lobe? Michael Persinger, *Neuropsychological Bases of God Beliefs* (Westport, Conn.: Praeger, 1987).

Strokes of Insight: Jill Bolte Taylor, *My Stroke of Insight* (New York: Viking Press, 2008). "Jill Bolte Taylor's Stroke of Insight," talk on TED, Feb. 2008, http://www.ted.com/talks/jill_bolte_taylor_s_powerful_stroke_of_insight .html. Ellen White, "The Early Years," Aug. 2000, http://www.whiteestate.org/ about/egwbio.asp#early. J. Weaver, "Brain Surgery Boosts Spirituality," adapted by permission from Macmillan Publishers Ltd.: scientificamerican.com, Feb. 10, 2010, http://www.scientificamerican.com/article.cfm?id=brain-surgery- boosts-spiritual, copyright 2010. Cosimo Urgesi, Salvatore M. Aglioti, Miran Skrap, and Franco Fabbro, "The Spiritual Brain: Selective Cortical Lesions Modulate Human Self-Transcendence," *Neuron*, Feb. 11, 2010, pp. 309–319. Roland R. Griffiths and Charles S. Grob, "Hallucinogens as Medicine," *Scientific American*, Dec. 2010.

Believe It or Not: A series of studies from the Duke University Center for Spirituality, Theology and Health: H. G. Koenig, "Religion and Remission of Depression in Medical Inpatients with Heart Failure/Pulmonary Disease," *Journal of Nervous and Mental Disease*, 2007, *195*, 389–395, and "Religion and Depression in Older Medical Inpatients," *American Journal of Geriatric Psychiatry*, 2007, *15*, 282–291; H. G. Koenig, L. K. George, and P. Titus,

"Religion, Spirituality and Health in Medically Ill Hospitalized Older Patients," *Journal of the American Geriatrics Association*, 2004, *52*, 554–562; www.spiritualityandhealth.duke.edu. Allison Bond, "Belief in the Brain," *Scientific American Mind*, Mar.–Apr. 2010.

Religious Ecstasy Is Like Romantic Love: "God in the Brain?" scientificamerican.com, podcast, Oct. 11, 2007, http://www.scientificamerican.com/podcast/episode.cfm?id=8F8D78A7-E7F2-99DF-3A2C341CB563B8C7. Solomon H. Snyder, "Seeking God in the Brain: Efforts to Localize Higher Brain Functions," *New England Journal of Medicine*, Jan. 3, 2008, p. 358.

God on the Brain: Bielle, "Searching for God in the Brain." Katherine Harmon, "God on the Brain? Scientists Map Religious Thoughts with Scans," scientificamerican.com, Mar. 13, 2009, http://www.scientificamerican.com/blog/post.cfm?id=god-on-the-brain-scientists-map-rel-2009-03-13. Dimitrios Kapogiannis and others, "Cognitive and Neural Foundations of Religious Belief," *Proceedings of the National Academy of Sciences*, Mar. 9, 2009. Bond, "Belief in the Brain."

Could Religion Shrink Your Brain? Andrew Newberg, "Religious Experiences Shrink Part of the Brain," scientificamerican.com, May 31, 2011, http://www.scientificamerican.com/article.cfm?id=religious-experiences-shrink-part-of-brain. Amy D. Owen and others, "Religious Factors and Hippocampal Atrophy in Late Life," *PLoS One*, 2010, *6*(3), e17006, doi:10.1371/journal.pone.001700.

The Evolutionary Roots of God Thought: Michael Moyer, "Origins: Religious Thought," *Scientific American*, Sept. 2009. John Horgan, "If Religion Is a Side Effect of Sex, Does That Mean God Doesn't Exist?" scientificamerican.com, June 3, 2010, http://www.scientificamerican.com/blog/post.cfm?id=if-religion-is-a-side-effect-of-sex-2010-06-03.

God Neurons May Be Everywhere: Kasper Mossman, "God (Neurons) May Be Everywhere," *Scientific American Mind*, Dec. 2006–Jan. 2007.

Chapter Nine: Technology, Science, and the Future of Sex

The Wonderful World of Cybersex: John Horgan, "The Forgotten Era of Brain Chips," *Scientific American*, Oct. 2005. Judith Horstman, *Brave New Brain* (San Francisco: Jossey-Bass, 2010). Drew Halley, "The Future of Sex: Androids, VR, and the Orgasm Button," May 20, 2009, http://singularityhub.com/2009/05/20/the-future-of-sex-androids-vr-and-the-orgasm-button/.

Turn It Up, Dear, and Turn Me On: T. Stuart Meloy, "Spinal Stimulation for Orgasm," Jan. 2001, U.S. Patent Filing, U.S. Patent Number 6169924, http://www.google.com/patents?id=UMMCAAAAEBAJ&printsec=drawing&zoom=4#v=onepage&q&f=false. Gary Stix, "Turn It Up, Dear," *Scientific American*, May 2009.

Sex in Bits and Bytes: David DiSalvo, "Are Social Networks Messing with Your Head?" *Scientific American Mind*, Jan.–Feb. 2010. Hal Arkowitz and Scott O. Lilienfeld, "Sex in Bits and Bytes," *Scientific American Mind*, July–Aug. 2010. National Institutes of Neurological Diseases and Stroke, "Brain Basics: Know Your Brain," Aug. 18, 2010, http://www.ninds.nih.gov/disorders/brain_basics/know_your_brain.htm. Steven Morris, "Second Life Affair Leads to Real Life Divorce," *Guardian Online*, guardian.co.uk, Nov. 13, 2008, http://www.guardian.co.uk/technology/2008/nov/13/second-life-divorce. "Divorce Wars: Woman Kills Hubby's Avatar," CBS News/Associated Press, Oct. 23, 2008, http://www.cbsnews.com/stories/2008/10/23/tech/main4540763.shtml.

Chapter Ten: How Can Love Survive?

Peter Ward, "What Will Become of Homo Sapiens?" *Scientific American*, Jan. 2009. Michael S. Gazzaniga, "Smarter on Drugs," *Scientific American Mind*, Oct. 2005, and *The Ethical Brain* (New York: Dana Press, 2005). Charles Q. Choi, "Not Tonight, Dear, I Have to Reboot," *Scientific American*, Mar. 2008. Christie Nicholson, "Wiping Out Bad Memories," scientificamerican.com, Mar. 18, 2009, http://www.scientificamerican.com/podcast/episode.cfm?id=wiping-out-bad-memories-09-03-18. Drew Halley, "The Future of Sex: Androids, VR, and the Orgasm Button," May 20, 2009, http://singularityhub.com/2009/05/20/the-future-of-sex-androids-vr-and-the-orgasm-button/.

ILLUSTRATION CREDITS

Some of Your Brain's Most Important Parts: Courtesy Alzheimer's Disease Education and Referral Center, a service of the National Institute on Aging.

If I Could Read Your Mind: From Marco Iacoboni and Mirella Dapretto, "The Mirror Neuron System and the Consequences of Its Dysfunction." Reprinted by permission from Macmillan Publishers Ltd.: *Nature Reviews Neuroscience* 7, 942–951, Dec. 2006, doi:10:1038/nrn2024.

Epigenetics: Volume Control for Your Genes: From W. Wayt Gibbs, "The Unseen Genome: Beyond DNA," *Scientific American*, Dec. 2003. Artist: Terese Winslow.

Thinking for Two: From Craig Howard Kinsley and Kelly G. Lambert, "The Maternal Brain," *Scientific American,* Jan. 2006. Artist: Tami Tolpa. Reproduced with permission. Copyright © 2006 Scientific American, Inc. All rights reserved.

Oxytocin and the Brain: From Paul J. Zak, "The Neurobiology of Trust," *Scientific American,* June 2008. Artist: Logan Parsons. Reproduced with permission. Copyright © 2008 Scientific American, Inc. All rights reserved.

Kiss and Tell: From Chip Walter, "Affairs of the Lips," *Scientific American Mind*, Feb.–Mar. 2008. Artist: Gehirn & Geist/SIGANIM. Source: Penfield and Rasmussen.

Your Brain in Love: From Mark Fischetti, "Your Brain in Love," *Scientific American*, Feb. 2011. Artists: James W. Lewis and Jen Christiansen. Reproduced with permission. Copyright © 2011 Scientific American, a division of Nature America, Inc. All rights reserved.

Twelve Areas of Love in the Brain: Additional images courtesy of James W. Lewis, West Virginia University, and Stephanie Ortigue, Syracuse University.

Judith Horstman is an award-winning journalist who specializes in writing about health and medicine. Her work has appeared in hundreds of publications worldwide and on the Internet.

A long-time print journalist, she was a Washington correspondent for the Gannett News Service and *USA Today,* the recipient of a Knight Science Journalism Fellowship at MIT, and a journalism professor at Oregon State University and a lecturer at Keene (New Hampshire) State College and Santa Clara (California) University. In addition, she was awarded two Fulbright grants to establish a center to teach fact-based journalism in Budapest, Hungary.

She has edited and written for Web sites on amyotrophic lateral sclerosis (also known as Lou Gehrig's disease) and lupus and for the Stanford University Medical Center, the *Harvard Health Letter,* the Johns Hopkins University White Papers, and Time Inc. Health publications. She was a contributing editor for *Arthritis Today,* the magazine of the Arthritis Foundation for which she wrote *The Arthritis Foundation's Guide Alternative Therapies* and is coauthor (with Paul Lam) of *Overcoming Arthritis.*

This is her third brain book in a series of four: Horstman is the author of *The* Scientific American *Day in the Life of Your Brain* (Jossey-Bass, 2009) and *The* Scientific American *Brave New Brain* (Jossey-Bass, 2010). A *Scientific American* book on the aging brain will be published

by Jossey-Bass in 2012. Visit her Web site at www.judithhorstman
.com.

About *Scientific American*

Scientific American is at the heart of Nature Publishing Group's consumer media division, meeting the needs of the general public.
Founded in 1845, *Scientific American* is the oldest continuously published magazine in the United States and the leading authoritative
publication for science in the general media. Together with scientifi-
camerican.com and fourteen local language editions around the world,
it reaches more than 5 million consumers and scientists. Other titles
include *Scientific American Mind* and *Spektrum der Wissenschaft* in
Germany.

INDEX